KINGS IN THE MAKING

H.R.H. THE PRINCE OF WALES.

KINGS IN THE MAKING

THE PRINCES OF WALES

BY E. THORNTON-COOK

WITH PORTRAITS

Essay Index Reprint Series

 BOOKS FOR LIBRARIES PRESS
FREEPORT, NEW YORK

First Published 1931
Reprinted 1968

LIBRARY OF CONGRESS CATALOG CARD NUMBER:

68-22951

PRINTED IN THE UNITED STATES OF AMERICA

TO

HIS ROYAL HIGHNESS THE PRINCE OF WALES
TWENTIETH HOLDER OF THAT HISTORIC TITLE
THIS STORY OF HIS PREDECESSORS
IS BY HIS GRACIOUS PERMISSION
GRATEFULLY DEDICATED

v

God gives not Kings the style of Gods in veine
For on the throne His sceptre do they show.
Observe the statutes of your Heavenly King
And from His laws make all your laws to spring.
                          JAMES I (TO HIS SON).

" The most profytable thyng in this worlde for the instytution of the humayne lyfe is hystorie."—FROISSART.

PREFACE

THE present Prince of Wales is the twentieth holder of the title. Ten have been born the sons of sovereigns and twelve of the twenty have succeeded to the crown.

One (Edward V) was born in the sanctuary of Westminster at a time when his father, the King, had been driven out of the country and the Queen was dependent upon charity for her daily fare. Another, James Francis Stuart, was carried abroad in babyhood to live and die in exile; at times there have been rival claimants for the title.

Henry of Monmouth (Henry V) was so far distant from the throne that a fee of two pounds was considered sufficient emolument for the " wise woman " who officiated at his birth.

One Prince of Wales was born in Bordeaux, two in Scotland, two in the principality, and two in Hanover; one was naturalised by Act of Parliament.

On two occasions the Princes of Wales have been brothers.

Till the birth of the present Prince of Wales none had been born in England of English-born parents since the days of Henry VII and Elizabeth of York four centuries before. Edward VI (son of Henry VIII and Jane Seymour), although son and heir of the monarch for ten years, never received the title; in this respect he was unique.

No Prince of Wales married twice, unless George IV's abortive attempts at matrimony can be counted, but several have gone through more than one ceremony with their brides. Arthur Tudor espoused Katharine of Aragon on four occasions.

ix

Richard II, Henry V, the twelve-year-old Edward V, Henry VIII, the Charles, and George III, all ascended as bachelor kings. Several were betrothed many times over while in their cradles.

Two Princes of Wales, Edward the Black Prince and George V, married English-born princesses.

Anne of Warwick and Katharine of Aragon were widowed as Princesses of Wales, but both became Queens-Consort by subsequent marriages.

Until the time of Edward VII and Alexandra of Denmark no Princess of Wales had succeeded happily with her husband except Caroline of Anspach.

Much has been given to these Princes and much has been demanded of them from the days of the Black Prince onward; then, at fourteen years of age, princelings must have learnt to "hunt the dere to catch an hardynesse . . . and everie daie his armour would essaie in fete of armes." Many have been seasoned warriors in boyhood; at ten Charles Stuart took his seat in the Upper House. In the fourteenth century and in the twentieth a Prince of Wales did battle near the Somme.

Edward VII as Prince of Wales sought knowledge of men in half the courts of Europe. George V encircled the globe. His son was to see a world in arms, and as the King's liege man has carried his father's messages across the Seven Seas : " Ich Dien ! "

E. T. C.

CONTENTS

CONTENTS

CONTENTS

LIST OF ILLUSTRATIONS

xv

The reproduction of the medallion cast for the Investiture of
Edward Prince of Wales, July 13, 1911, is from a print supplied by
William Gray. By permission of the Deputy Master of the Mint.

CHAPTER I

LORD EDWARD OF CARNARVON
(EDWARD II)

" The strongest man of his realm."

EDWARD (OF CARNARVON) PRINCE OF WALES
(EDWARD II)

Born at Carnarvon Castle	April 25, 1284
Created Prince of Wales in Lincoln Parliament .	1301
Ascended	July 7, 1307
Married Isabella of France . . .	1308
Deposed	1327
Died	September 21, 1327

Descent

Edward I, *m.* Eleanora of Castile

|

Edward
(and others)

Contemporary Sovereigns

Scotland : The " Maid of Norway " ; John Balliol and Robert Bruce.
France : Philip IV, Louis X, Philip V, Charles IV.

CHAPTER I

EDWARD OF CARNARVON

1284-1327

In the brave days of old when a king was on the war-path, his queen followed the camp, and the royal nursery was accustomed to being moved on at short notice if the enemy made a daring raid or the fortune of the day went the wrong way. So it was that a son born to Edward I and his consort Eleanora of Castile saw the light in Carnarvon Castle (April 25, 1284), since his father was attempting to subdue Wales.

The King knighted the messenger who brought him the welcome news, for although he had several daughters, but one of his sons remained alive, and that the fragile Roman-born boy whom, in a weak moment, he had permitted the Queen to christen Alphonso.

Legend has it that the King summoned the turbulent Welsh hillsmen and bound them to peace by promising to give them, as prince, one of unblemished character and so truly Welsh that he could speak no word of English. Each man, thinking that he or his son might be the chosen, hastened to agree, and then the door opened and a smiling Welsh nurse appeared, bearing in her arms the new-born Prince.

" Here is your man ! " cried the King.

Six hundred years later another Prince Edward (son of George V) was to be presented to the Welsh people in the half-ruined stronghold wherein Edward of Carnarvon had been born.

There was a state christening, at which the officiating bishops were munificently rewarded, and it was then decided that the royal baby should be removed to Conway for safe keeping, although on account of his tender age the journey must be made in easy stages. He negotiated sixty miles in fourteen days. At four months the baby became heir-apparent by the death of Alphonso, and on account of his increased importance it was decided that he must now have a separate establishment. One of his many little sisters was left to him as a playmate until the son of a Gascon knight ousted her from her place and became " brother Gaveston " to the Prince.

Before Edward of Carnarvon was a year old, Alexander III of Scotland rode to his death and a Norwegian-born child was declared Queen of Scotland. The King of England was quick to see the advantage of bringing about a union between the two kingdoms and opened negotiations, hoping to arrange a marriage between his son and the Maid of Norway.[1]

The Scots showed lack of eagerness, fearing a too complete merging, but by the time Edward Prince of Wales was six years old an agreement had been reached which sufficiently safeguarded the interests of the northern kingdom; the marriage treaty was signed, and " a great ship with a crew of forty men " sailed to fetch home the Prince's bride.

He may have seemed a trifle blasé about the affair, for, despite his tender years, he had occupied a prominent position at the betrothals and weddings of three of his sisters.

But the union of England and Scotland was not to be brought about so early in the nations' history.

Presently there came bruit from the north that the Maid was dead, and then an appeal to Edward I to travel fast to the rescue and decide which of thirteen competitors was justly entitled to wear the crown of Scotland.

During the stormy years that followed, while the

[1] See *Their Majesties of Scotland*, by E. Thornton Cook.

EDWARD II.
Created First Prince of Wales.
From a print in the National Portrait Gallery of the effigy on his monument in
Gloucester Cathedral.

King fought now in Wales and Scotland and again
in France, Edward of Carnarvon, now motherless,
struggled through childhood, suffering the usual ill-
nesses and being doctored according to the knowledge
of the day.   When he had " a spasm in the stomach "
his weight in the best wax candles was offered at the
nearest shrine; when small-pox attacked him he
was swathed in a scarlet robe and every article he
used was hastily dyed the same brilliant colour.

At thirteen years of age the Prince was appointed
titular Guardian of the Kingdom, since oversea
matters required his father's attention, and there
was a brilliant scene outside Westminster Hall when
the King presented his son to the people in this
capacity before he embarked.

But his hope that the popularity of the Prince
would induce the people to submit to further taxation
was vain; so great was the outcry when a fresh
demand was made that Edward of Carnarvon was
obliged to attend Parliament and sanction the enact-
ment that in future no tax should be levied " by us,
the King or our heirs . . . without the consent of
the archbishops, bishops, and other prelates, the earls,
barons, burgesses, and other freemen of our realms."

The war in France proved a long-drawn-out affair.
Both nations were tired of fighting, but no permanent
peace seemed possible till the Pope intervened and
decreed that King Edward of England should marry
the French Princess Marguerite.   She was young
and fair, so the King agreed, being eager to withdraw
his forces from France in order that he might take
up the war in Scotland, and to make a continuance
of the peace more likely, betrothed his son to
Marguerite's niece Isabella, a damsel of four summers.

In dutiful obedience " Lord Edward the King's
Son " signed the necessary documents and appointed
a proxy to act for him at the espousal ceremony.
What interested him a good deal more than Isabella
was the arrival at court of a youth of his own age,

son of a knight who had done good service to the King in his oversea campaign.

Soon " Brother Gaveston " and the Prince became inseparable companions ; together they went hunting, trained their dogs, amused themselves at a smithy, and occasionally thatched a cottage, while every year Edward grew taller, stronger, and more handsome.

Queen Marguerite was now following the camp, as had done Eleanora, for the King was hunting down Sir William Wallace, but he came as far south as Lincoln before his son's seventeenth birthday, summoned a Parliament there, and officially created him Prince of Wales. A year later the youth took his seat in the House and was called upon to preside at Councils when not campaigning with his father.

But his real interest lay not in camp life but in sporting with his friends, in dicing, in music, in dogs and horses. He was often in disgrace with his father, and more than once was driven to appeal to his stepmother to intercede for him ; Marguerite was barely two years older than Edward.

As it happened, Edward was in favour when he came of age, so received Gascony as an Easter gift. A few weeks later there was high festival at Westminster, where the Prince of Wales was to be knighted together with three hundred young companions preparatory to avenging the murder of Sir John Comyn by Robert the Bruce.[1]

There was turmoil with so many acolytes bathing, praying, and meditating as a prelude to their vigils, and the noise of the trumpets and the shifting of the people was so loud that the monks on one side of the choir could not hear the chanting of those on the other. Worse still, some knights failed to struggle through the crowd, and others fainted in the press when armed men rode into the Abbey to clear the way.

The Prince of Wales had to stand on the altar to belt the new-made knights.

[1] See *Their Majesties of Scotland.*

The Scottish expedition was pursued with such
ruthlessness that the Prince, feeling sure of his
father's favour, asked permission to give his mother's
inheritance of Ponthieu to his favourite, Piers
Gaveston, but this was straining matters too far.

" Thou to give away lands ! " cried the furious
monarch. " *Thou* who never won any ! God alive !
Were it not that the kingdom might fall into anarchy
I would take good care that thou shouldst never
come to thine inheritance ! " and he snatched at
his son's hair, pulling it out by the handful.

The dismayed Prince was forced to swear that he
would never give either lands or titles to his boon
companion, while to make doubly sure Gaveston,
after being bound on oath never to accept such favours
from the Prince, was banished for life and forbidden
to return to England under pain of instant death.

The war with Scotland went on, and at last the
strength of the fiery King failed. He died while
gasping orders to his son to ravage the north and
carry his bones to the ultimate victory he had failed
to achieve in life.

Edward of Carnarvon had been Prince of Wales
for six years ; he was to reign for twenty.

Piers Gaveston was recalled and left Regent of the
Kingdom when Edward went to marry Isabella,[1]
" one of the feyrest ladyes of the worlde."

As King, Edward was to lead his army to defeat
at Bannockburn ; to see his favourites hanged before
his eyes ; and, seeking safety in Wales when fleeing
from his avenging wife, be handed over to his enemies.
Parliament required his abdication, and he found
himself a prisoner.

On a September night (1327) men passing Berkeley
Castle after dark crossed themselves and shuddered
at the sound of agonised shrieks ; the deposed King
was struggling in the hands of murderers.

[1] See *Her Majesty : The Romance of the Queens of England*, by
E. Thornton Cook.

CHAPTER II

EDWARD THE BLACK PRINCE

" The Valiant and Gentle Prince of Wales, the Flower of all the Chivalry in the World at that Time. . . ."

EDWARD PLANTAGENET (THE BLACK PRINCE)

Born at Woodstock . . . . June 15, 1330
Created Prince of Wales . . . May 12, 1343
Married Joan " The Fair Maid " . . October 10/11, 1361
Died at Westminster . . . . June 8, 1376

Descent

Edward I

(1) Eleanora of Castile — *m.* — (2) Marguerite of France

Edward II
m. Isabella of France

Edmund of Woodstock (and others)
(Earl of Kent)

Edward III
m. Philippa of Hainault

Edward " the Black Prince " — *m.* — Joan the " Fair Maid of Kent "
(and others)

CONTEMPORARY SOVEREIGNS

SCOTLAND : David II and Robert II.
FRANCE : Philip VI, John II, and Charles V.

CHAPTER II

EDWARD THE BLACK PRINCE

1330—1376

" At 10 of the clocke in the morning in the Scheme
of Whole Nativity, the young Queen Philip was
brought to bed at Woodstock, the 15th day of June,
of her first sonne, the which, at the font-stone was
named Edward, and in the processe of time came to
great proofe of famous chivalrie as in this book shall
more plainlie appear." So runs an old chronicle
describing the birth of one of the most famous of
our Princes of Wales.

The Queen (Philippa, *not* " Philip " !) was barely
sixteen, but the baby was " fair, lusty, and well-
form'd," and she insisted on nursing him herself, to
the joy of many an artist of the fourteenth century
who found in the youthful Queen and baby Prince
romantic models for the Madonna and Child.

As the little mother played with her son lying in
his magnificent state cradle, which was ornamented
with paintings of the four evangelists, she forgot her
first difficult months in England, the fact that she
had not yet been crowned, and even the drear wet
summer and the corn that lay unripened till
Michaelmas.

The King was delighted at the birth of his first-
born son, and the messenger fortunate enough to
bring him the news was rewarded with a pension, as
were the child's nurses and " rockers."

The event was celebrated " on the Mondaie after
St. Matthew's Day " by " a solemne jouste in Cheap-
side," the King with twelve challengers defying all

entrants. Unfortunately, the festivities were marred
by what might have been a serious accident, since
the staging broke, precipitating the Queen and her
attendant ladies into the street, " yet luckilie they
escaped without harme to the rejoicing of the manie
that saw them in such danger."

The unlucky carpenters would have lost their
heads if Philippa had not begged the King's mercy.[1]

At three years of age the stalwart Prince was
belted Earl of Chester, when five hundred marks a
year from the " profits " of that city were granted
to Philippa for the " sustenance " of the new-made
peer.

Perhaps, because the times were troublesome and
King Edward was waging perpetual war, the upbringing of the children was left in the Queen's hands to
a great degree. It was she who chose as her son's
tutor, Dr. Walter Burleigh, an Oxford scholar, who
had been appointed her almoner when first she came
from Hainault ; and to train him in arms, Sir Walter
de Manny, " a knight who had performed so many
gallant deeds in such various places that they were
not to be counted."

The schooling of a prince began early in the
fourteenth century. " At six," such a one " must
sitte at mete seemly in alle nurture " ; at ten years
of age he was expected " to danse and synge and speke
of gentlenesse " and at fourteen should " go hunt the
dere to catch an hardynesse . . . and everie daie
his armour to essaie in fete of armes."

Long before Prince Edward was old enough to
take an active part in the tournaments that were a
feature of the age, he would attend as his father's
page.

The Queen's nursery was becoming crowded, but
for the moment it was only the eldest born for whom
matrimonial negotiations were begun. The King

---

[1] See *Her Majesty: The Romance of the Queens of England*, by E.
Thornton Cook.

EDWARD THE BLACK PRINCE.
From a print in the British Museum.

12]

offered him as consort for a princess of France in
an effort to break the alliance between France and
Scotland, but no agreement could be reached, and
at one time invasion seemed so probable that the
young heir was hurried off to Nottingham for safer
keeping, while his father meditated on the value of
other possible brides—should a baby daughter-in-
law be secured from the nursery of Alphonso the
Brave of Portugal, or from that of the Duke of
Brabant ?

But in the stars it was written that Prince Edward
was to marry neither; his future bride, a cousin
some two years older than himself, was now sharing
his upbringing. She was Joan, daughter of Edmund
Earl of Kent, and when her father was beheaded on
charge of treason, Queen Philippa opened her arms
to the orphan child.

And now the Prince was nearly seven years old.
In a full Parliament at Westminster the King girded
him with a sword, and as Cornwall had now been
raised into a duchy saluted him as the first English
Duke. His small grace's first act was to dub twenty
new knights and bid them go forth " to do some deed
of chivalrie for love of England."

There was to be no lack of opportunity, for war
between France and England was imminent. In a
vain effort to avert the threatened calamity the
Pope sent across two Cardinals and the new-made,
seven-year-old Duke performed an official duty by
welcoming the papal dignitaries a mile from the city
and riding with them to his father the King, at
Westminster.

Soon afterwards the first blows were struck in
what was later to be known as the Hundred Years
War.

" The Frenchmen, by sea, sore troubled the coasts
of this realme . . . at Hastings they burnt the
fishermen's huts and slew some of the inhabitants ;
also about Devon and Cornwall. In Whitsundaie

weeke they landed at Plymouth and burnt part of the towne. Portsmouth and Southampton too suffered onslaught."

This was insult past endurance, for as Edward III pointed out : " We consider that our progenitors the Kings of England were Lords of the English Sea on every side as also they were its defenders. . . . It would grieve us if our royal honour in such defence should perish or be in ought diminished in our time, which God forbid ! "

So the young Duke of Cornwall was appointed *Locum tenens Regis*, or Warden of the Kingdom, while his father went to punish his enemies overseas ; despite his youth Prince Edward attended all Council Meetings, and when writs summoning Parliament went out they ran in the Prince's name.

There were interludes in his periods of theoretical responsibility, as when the King, eager to show off this son who was " a proper hopeful young gentleman and though only ten might well have been fourteen," summoned him to attend the court temporarily established at Antwerp, where the Prince laid the seeds of a life-long friendship with Sir John Chandos. For the rest he attended conferences, the Archbishop of Canterbury at his right hand ; gathered the fleet to repel further invasions, and saw to it that London was fortified by the laying in of a store of palisades, these to be immediately erected when warning signals were given by church bell and beacon.

The King's letters told of his doing " grate hurt " on the Somme, where, indeed, all expected a fierce battle, and such must have been had not the " french king's councillors advised him to the contrarie by reason of certain signs and tokens which they mis-liked, as the starting of a hare among them and suchlike." The astronomers too were against the venture, " and so these two mightie armies departed in sunder without battell, and the King of England returned into Flanders sore indeed that he had not

half the number that the French King had, yet in
trust of the valiancie of his soldiers."

Making a bold bid for an alliance, King Edward
discovered that the Flemings " were bound by faith
and oath, and in the sum of two million florins in the
Pope's chamber, not to make or move any war against
France on pain of losing that sum, and besides to
run the sentence of cursing.

The solution was obvious. Edward III had always
held that the crown of France was his by right of
his mother Isabella of France, and indeed, had sent
ambassadors to make good his claim, only to find
that they " could never be quietly heard," so now he
lent a ready ear to the suggestion of the powerful
burgher Jacob van Artevelde that he, Edward, should
take upon himself the title and arms of King of
France. In such case it would become the lawful
duty of the Flemings to support and obey him.

An assembly was called at Ghent, the pronouncements were made, and the arms of France were
quartered with those of England—to remain there
until tactfully removed by George III four hundred
years later.

With *Dieu et mon Droit* emblazoned as his motto,
Edward III returned to England and his son.

The respite from war was short, for the French were
smarting under the naval victory of Sluys and made
a retaliatory landing. Portsmouth suffered once more,
whereupon the Prince was again appointed Warden
while the King went to besiege Tournay.

Many a town was burnt and sacked before a truce
was established ; Edward being brought to a mood
of acquiescence by lack of funds. He returned to
England full of wrath, and threatened to send out as
hostages those bishops who in their official capacity
were responsible for the financial stringency. Fortunately for them other matters attracted the King's
attention.

A full Parliament was summoned at Westminster,

and Edward Duke of Cornwall, now thirteen years old and "the Delight of the English Nation," was created Prince of Wales and crowned with a golden coronet.

To commemorate the event there were "jousts held at Smithfield for three days together to the great pleasure of all beholders . . . and the challengers came forth, one apparelled like to the Pope, bringing with him twelve others in garments like to Cardinals," while on the defenders' side fought the newly created Prince of Wales, "with manie erles, barons, knights, and esquires innumerable."

Before the fervour occasioned by these jousts had evaporated, a feast of the Round Table was ordained to perpetuate the memory of King Arthur. Heralds were dispatched to advertise the event all over Europe, and safe-conducts were offered to all desirous of taking part in the great feats of arms it was intended to perform beneath the eyes of the Queen, and three hundred "ladyes and demoisels all of noble lynage and aparelled accordingly."

Those eligible to attend the tournament were "persons of Nobility and Dignity renowned for Virtue and Valour and admirably well-skilled in the knowledge of, and use of arms."

Knights took up the idea with enthusiasm and began to flock towards England from every corner of Christendom till Philip of France became alarmed, forbade the attendance of any Frenchman and set up a rival Round Table of his own, hoping to attract "all the Chivalry of Germany and Italy," but it failed of its effects.

In England the affair gave a great impetus to trade, and "the King's tailors were kept busy making robes, hosen, coverchiefs, with a super-tunic for his majesty at a cost of 14/- on which 8 furriers worked for three days and 2 for one day each, each paid at the rate of 6d. a day for working with great haste upon the furs of the same robe."

The festival was an enormous success except in the view of a few malcontents who, " forgetful of the true spirit of chivalry," pointed out that there was " no duress or homage towards women imposed on the Knights of the Round Table—not so much as obliging them to defend the quarrels of Ladyes ! "

At this time it was intended that the gathering should be an annual affair, so, for the better accommodation of the King's future guests, orders were given for the immediate building of a Round Tower at Windsor at a cost of £500.   It was to be erected within ten months, so " a head carpenter and a bricklayer were engaged and given permission to impress labourers from the five surrounding counties while messengers were sent about to secure skilled craftsmen."

As many as six or seven hundred men were working on the building operations at one period, but owing to the perennial shortage of money the numbers were curtailed later and the pay-roll dropped from one hundred pounds a week to twenty-two pounds, and ultimately to thirty-seven shillings !

But even these interesting developments did not divert the minds of the Kings of England and France from the wrongs each had suffered at the hands of the other.   Patience wore thin and yet more thin.

Philip of Valois still held to the duchies of Ponthieu and Aquitaine, and Edward would give no sign of willingness to relinquish the title of King of France.

When news reached England of the drastic punishment by Philip of certain adherents of Edward, it was felt that the time had come for action.

Parliament was summoned and the Prince of Wales took his seat as a peer of the realm.

Both Houses decided that the present truce was unsatisfactory and that the war between France and England must be brought to a definite end " by battle or an honourable peace."

Preparations began, but first Edward decided on

a bold coup. Taking his eldest son with him, he sailed for Flanders to propose that the country should be made a dukedom and that the people should renounce their Prince Louis of Crécy in favour of the Prince of Wales.

Long since, Jacob van Artevelde had brought about a " treaty of friendship and commerce between the three great Flemish towns of Ghent, Bruges, and Ypres, and Edward believed that these cities would welcome the project. But they wavered, then, led by Ghent, revolted. Artevelde was murdered, and the King judged it expedient to withdraw his son and return to hasten warlike preparations in England.

Every man between the ages of sixteen and sixty was called to arms, and free pardons were offered to all criminals who were prepared to make their way to the rendezvous at Portsmouth for immediate enlistment, " but not otherwise."

Attractive rates of pay did much to popularise the coming war. A spearman could command 2*d*. a day and an archer 3*d*. Knights drew 2*s*., earls 6*s*. 8*d*., and the Prince of Wales no less than 25*s*.

Contracts were made with leading citizens who undertook to bring in a stated number of men and so originated the Free Companies that were to disturb the peace of Europe for many a long year.

The Prince of Wales was to raise 4,000 troops from his principality, and ships were commandeered for purposes of transport.

But the pride of the nation was a battery of five guns " all complete with six gonners."

Unfortunately, " horrible tempests " delayed the sailing of the hosts for many a week and, since all had to be paid, the financial strain was considerable.

Restive creditors were driven to petition the King for the right to seize the movable goods of the Prince of Wales, should he fall, and stipulated that, in such case, they might hold his lands forfeit for ten years in order to pay off the accumulated debts.

At last a favourable wind blew up. The Great Seal was handed over, a younger prince was installed as Guardian of the Kingdom, and Edward and his elder son put to sea with "four-and-twenty of the most renowned commanders in Christendom, 4,000 men-at-arms, 10,000 archers, 12,000 Welsh and 6,000 Irishmen."

A landing was made at La Hogue, where the King knighted the Prince of Wales, now fifteen years old, who was quick to make a "right good beginning" by burning and ravaging in all directions.

Barfleur fell, Cherbourg was overrun, and the triumphant English army marched on some six miles a day, pillaging and burning as it travelled. No serious opposition was encountered until it reached Caen, "a place larger than any town in England except London itself."

Five thousand dead were left high piled, "but of the English the death of only one person of note is recorded," and the accumulated plunder, "sufficient in value to pay the whole cost of the expedition," was sent back to England as an earnest of English victories.

The King and the Prince of Wales marched on till Paris herself was in sight. St. Cloud and St. Germains went up in flames while still the original French army languished a hundred and fifty miles away.

Paris was in a panic of fury and fear, but King Philip had now contrived to organise another army, and so took the field with a hundred thousand men.

Judging discretion the better part of valour, the outnumbered English withdrew, and in a hot August, marched seventy miles in six days. On reaching the Somme it was discovered that, most unexpectedly, the French had destroyed all the bridges! Huge bribes were offered to anyone who would guide the tired army across by the ford of which the commanders had heard, but never a prisoner succumbed to temptation.

Nevertheless, the King was not dismayed. "God

and St. George will find us a passage," he promised
his weary men, but it was only at the eleventh hour,
when the French were in close pursuit, that a peasant
named Gobin Agace came forward :

" Yes, Sir, in the name of God and at the price of
my head I undertake to bring you to a place where
you and your host may cross without danger." It
appeared that in one part of the river not far distant
from Abbeville " twice a-day twelve men might
walk abreast."

" Let those who love me, follow ! " cried Edward,
spurring his horse into the river, and, though the
French forces were massing to oppose the crossing,
the English poured over, and " thus was won the
passage of the Somme on the 24th of August, 1346."

(Did the ghostly warriors from the army of the
Black Prince watch the battles of 1914 ?)

The French army came up behind in time to kill
off English stragglers, but the main body was safe
in Ponthieu, which was, so to speak, English territory,
being the dower of Edward's grandmother, Marguerite of France.[1]   Here it was resolved to stand
and dispute the issue of the day with " Philip of
Valois."   No true Englishman would allow this
upstart the title of " King of France."

Gobin Agace was " enriched for life," being given
100 golden nobles as well as a fine horse, and the
plan of battle was drawn up.

The honour of the day was to belong to the Prince
of Wales, but around him some of the most renowned
leaders took up position, among them the Earls of
Warwick and Oxford, Sir John Chandos, and Sir
Thomas Holland.

All were astir early on the following morning,
heard mass, made confession, and took the sacrament.
The King with his reserve forces withdrew to a

[1] See *Her Majesty : The Romance of the Queens of England*, by E.
Thornton Cook.

nearby hill and the boy-Prince appeared in his sombre black armour, which ever afterwards was to be associated with his name.

" The Englysshmen who were in the batayles lyeng on the ground to rest them, as sone as they saw the frenchmen aproche rose up upon ther fete, fayre and sanely, without any hast . . . but the lordes and knyghtes of France came not to the assembly in good order, for some came before and some after, in such hast that one of them dyd trouble another."

When Philip of Valois saw the " Englysshmen " his " blood was moved, for he hated them."

An instant attack was ordered, although the Genoese bowmen in the vanguard of the French army were tired out with a hot six-mile march, and, as they pointed out, the sun was in their eyes.

The English archers were ready and rained their arrows so thickly that " it was like a snow-storm." The Genoese flinched, and the angry French rode through their failing ranks while the Count of Alençon charged towards the Black Prince, who stood beneath the standard of Wales with his men arranged in the form of a harrow. Each man " fought where he stood," the ramparts of dead piled higher and higher and confusion increased in the ranks of the enemy.

As the fight raged more and more fiercely around the Prince, the Earl of Warwick dispatched a runner to the King aloof on his hillock.

" Is my son killed or wounded beyond help or to the earth felled ? " asked the King.

" Not so, Sir, but he is in rude shock of arms and does much need your aid," answered Sir Thomas of Norwich.

" Go back to those who sent you hyther, Sir Thomas, and say that they send no more to me for any adventure that falleth so long as my sonne is in life," commanded the Spartan father, " and also say to them that they suffer him to win his spurs, for,

God willing, this day shall be his and the honour thereof shall rest with him and those that be about him."

"Then the knyght went back and shewed them the King's words which grately hartened them."

But those in charge of the Prince must have been sore afraid, for once at least the boy was thrown to the ground in the turmoil. Richard de Beaumont threw the banner of the principality over his master's body and bestrode it, driving back assailants in fierce desperation, for still the French came on, "being as eight to one, and still the English met them; indeed this battell was right cruell and fell with manie a fete of armes done."

In another part of the field the King of Bohemia, old and blind, fretted on his horse.

"How is it now?" he asked. "And now?"

But the fortune of the day was going against the French and their allies.

"Thus it is, my lord, . . . and thus," they told him unwillingly as he pressed for details, and he divined that Charles of Luxemburg was routed. The father in him writhed, and for the honour of his name he bade those around him lead him forward that he might strike "one blow of his sword in the cause of France."

He was obeyed, "and to the intent that they should not lose him in the press his knyghts tyd all the raynes of ther horses bridles each to the other, and set the Kyng before to accomplish his desire, and so they went to ther enemyes."

Next day the body of the gallant King was found lying dead on the battlefield with his dead knights around him, their dead horses still linked by their bridles. He had had his desire, for he had struck not "one blow," but three or four, and had fought "right valiantly."

Towards the end of the battle Philip of Valois

" departed, as it were by constraint . . . and on
this Saturdaie when the nyght fell and the Englysshmen heard no more noise of the frenchmen, then they
reputed themselves to have the Victory and the
frenchmen to be discomforted, slaine and fled away.
Then they made great fires and lighted torches and
candles against it was verie dark."

The King came down from his little hill . . .
" and he went with all his battell to his sonne the
prince and embraced him in his armes and kissed him,
saying :

" 'Fair sonne, God give you good perseverance,
ye are my good sonne that ye have acquitted you
nobly ; ye are worthie to keep the realme.' "

The Prince inclined himself to the earth, honouring
the King his father, " and this nyght they thanked
God for their good adventure but made no boast
thereof, for the King would that no man should
make any brags in song but humbly thank God."

Next day when the heralds went over the battlefield to " distinguish the quality of the dead by
their coates-of-armes," it was discovered that eleven
sovereign princes had been slain, as well as " fourscore baronets, 12 hundred nyghts and more than
thirtie thousand of the meaner sort. . . . Of such
price were the Englissh bows on that season that
nothing could withstand them," and though the
" battell " had lasted " from three of the clocke till
nightfall," the English losses were reported as small,
only " three knyghts " being killed. Of the " meaner
sort " no mention is made by the chief chronicler.

A truce was granted that the French might bury
their dead, and Edward and his son carried the body
of the King of Bohemia to the nearest Abbey, where
they officiated as chief mourners at the ceremonial
funeral.

The army was kept in the field " till Mondaie in
the morning," and on Wednesday it marched off to

Calais, then the stronghold of pirates " who preyed upon the Englissh."

As the siege promised to be a long one, the English set to the building of houses for themselves, roofing them with reeds and timber. "There was such a number of them that the encampment soon took the name of 'Newtown' and in it markets were held twice weekly so that a man might buy what he would from England and Flanders."

At home, Scotland attempted a diversion to assist her ally, but Queen Philippa dealt "right hardily" with the situation; so King and Prince remained in France while within the walls of doomed Calais food grew scantier and scantier. The famous guns, safe brought from England and each allowanced with "3-4 ozs. of powder, 100 shot and twelve pieces of lead were duly put into action, and the Prince of Wales harassed and burnt the country for a thirty-mile radius."

Philip came marching to the rescue, but before he arrived word stole out from Calais that "everything is eaten, even the cats and dogs," though when the victuals had begun to fail "all the un-useful persons, such as old men, women, and children, were sent out of the gates." To the relief of the garrison the English had not turned them back, "as might have been done thereby the sooner to consume the stores, but had suffered them to pass thro"; indeed, each had been given "to eat" and also "2d. to all of them."

And now the enemy was so craftily entrenched behind the marshes that the French found attack impossible. Discovering this, Philip suggested that Edward should appoint a suitable place for a battle, but King and Prince decided that Calais, on which much time and money had now been spent must fall soon, and saw no reason to meet the adversary "who has kept me wrongfully from mine inheritance," as Edward insisted. So discomforted, Philip, having

marched his army to the scene of war, marched it
away again.   "Thus   was   the   towne   of Calais
gotten the 3rd of August in the yere 1347, after 11
months siege and remayned in possession of the
English 210 yeres."

The Prince of Wales stood by his father's side when
the doomed burghers came to meet their fate, barefooted and with ropes round their necks,[1] and with
the King arranged details as to the means by which
Calais was to be colonised by England.

To this end the original inhabitants were required
to evacuate.   "Everyone was licensed to depart
and void their houses, leaving their belongings behind
them, only a priest and one or two old people being
permitted to remain."

Calais "for the better and more sure defence
thereof" was in future to be peopled "onlie" with
English, so in due course seven-and-thirty selected
families arrived to take possession of "good houses
and fine privileges."

The victorious army sailed for England, but had
a very stormy voyage ; as the winds blew stronger
the King offered up an expostulatory prayer :

"O Mary, Blessed Lady! What should be the
meaning of this : that always in my passage to
France the wind and seas befriend me, but in my
return to England I meet nothing but adverse seas
and distructive elements ! "

But land was made at last and the fighting men
staggered ashore laden with plunder.   So much did
they bring that for months to come "everyone went
dressed in fur and velvet, and all the English maids
and matrons were decked out and trimmed up in
Frenchwomen's jewels."

Stopping only to make offering at the shrine of
Thomas à Becket, the royal party went on to encounter the rejoicing citizens of London, who came

---

[1] See *Her Majesty: The Romance of the Queens of England*, by
E. Thornton Cook.

thronging to cheer the " Black " Prince, the title
the King's son had won for himself at Crécy, some
said on account of his sombre armour, others that
it had been given to him by the French by reason of
his " dread acts in battell."

From now on he habitually wore ostrich feathers
(sometimes one, but more often three in token of his
speedy execution of all he undertook) and used as
his motto either *Ich Dien* or *Houmont* (I serve, or
magnanimous). The first had been the device of the
blind King of Bohemia, who had perhaps carried it
to signify that in that particular battle he was serving
under the King of France ; in the Prince's case it
was taken to indicate that he was still a subject to
the crown of England though a ruler in his own
country. Others hotly denied that the motto had
been derived from the German source, but was in
fact Old English (Ic Den).

Amid the rejoicings the fourteenth-century edition
of the League of Nations was called into being, and
the " Knights of the Blew-Garter " met in the
Round Tower, superseding that order which had
been founded by King Arthur. There were those
who whispered that King Edward III was no more
original in the founding of this companionship than he
had been on a former occasion, for had not Richard I
once bound a thong about the knees of a chosen number of knights to " signify a union of military qualities "
and inspire the wearers with fresh courage ? But for
the most part the royal decision was well received.

When the King determined upon the creation of
the order, he " assembled together erles, lordes and
knyghtes of the realme and showed them his intecyon,
they entertained the notion with great joy and
applause considering that it would prove a very
great advancement to pietie and nobilitie and virtue,
and likewise be an excellent expedient for the uniting
not only of his natives one with another, but of
foreigners with them in Bonds of Amitye and Peace."

Then was there chosen out "a certayne nombre of the most valyantest men of the realme, and they sware and sayled to mentayne the ordynaunces such as wer descryed."

Chief among these "ordynaunces" was the rule that the knights should aid and defend one another, "and never turn their back or run away out of the field in time of battell where there is present their sovereign lord" or even a King's deputy or his banner!

Four of the Founder Knights of the Confraternity of the Order of St. George, among them the Prince of Wales and Sir Thomas Holland, lover of beautiful Joan of Kent, were under twenty years old.

By the King's command the robes and mantles of every knight were to be exactly similar, "thereby intimating that they should all conserve brotherly love among themselves . . . and lest at any time there should be a falling out of the least breath of amitie was the great collar of the order ordained . . . in witness of the bond of faythe, peace and amitie strictly to be observed between the Companions each of whom upon election was called upon to produce a sum of money according to his quality and degree."

The Sovereign put down £26 13s. 1d., a "stranger king" must produce £20, the Prince of Wales £13 6s. 8d., and mere knights £3 6s. 8d. These contributions went to "the relief of the Canons of Windsor" and poor knights fallen on evil times.

It was expressly stipulated that no record of achievements should be set up until the fees were paid.

Two hundred years after the foundation of the Order of the Garter a legend became current as to the origin of the motto *Honi soit qui mal y pense.* It first appeared "in a vain and idle romance published by a stranger to the affairs of England and by him taken on no better ground than the tradition of the common people—too trifling evidence to so

great a building, common bruit being so infamous
an historian that wise men neither report nor give
credit to any information they receive from it," says
one writer.

The tale ran that a lady had dropped her garter
—some said the careless dame had been the
Queen herself, others that the garter belonged to the
Countess of Salisbury; a few *knew* that the culprit
was the fascinating Joan the Fair Maid of Kent;
but all were agreed that the King had picked up the
article of attire in question, though as to what had
happened afterwards there was more dispute.

The minority parties held to the opinion that the
famous phrase had been uttered by Queen Philippa
in answer to a question from her lord, as " to what
men would conjecture of her upon losing her garter,"
or that it was his retort to her when she showed displeasure at his action.   The majority scoffed at such
feeble tales and told among themselves how, when
the King had picked up the pretty trifle, he had seen
his courtiers smile " as at an amorous act."   Whereupon he had cried out :

" Sirs, the time shall shortlie come when ye shall
attribute much honour unto such a garter ! " and
later had decreed that the " posie " *Honi soit qui mal
y pense* (" Be he disgraced who thinks evil of it ")
should be the motto of his newly created order of
chivalry, " thus checking his lords' sinister suspicions
and signifying that his nobles had judged otherwise
of him than the truth."

A loyalist adds, " some may think that so noble
an order had a meane beginning if this tale be true,"
and in consolatory vein reminds his readers that
" manie honourable degrees of estates have had their
beginnings of more base and meane things than of
love, which, being orderlie used is most noble and
commendable."

Yet another writer who sets out to explain why the
true story was not popularly known for two centuries

after the happening finds the whole affair " a vulgare
opinion," and " the English cronicles (being somewhat
shamefaced and fearing leaste they should disbase
the Kinges Regall Majestie if they shoulde seem to
make minde of ane such obskewer matter) rather
thoughte good to leave it cleane untowched."

The festivities and tournaments resulting from the
great gathering at Windsor were hardly over before
the " black death " swept down from the East,
devastating Europe and ravaging England till the
dead had to be buried in trenches.

Parliament could not meet, the Courts dared not
sit, and whereas once a fat goose could have been
bought for 2*d*. and a " pigge " for 1*d*., the price
for food and labour soared till an attempt was made
to stabilise both by statute.   It was decreed that
no one should demand more for his hire than he
had done two years before and those who would not
work at the old rates were to be severely punished.
Any man who asked or paid more than the legal rate
was liable to a fine.

From such troublesome domestic administrations
King and Prince escaped once more to France, stealing
secretly across the Channel when it was discovered
that the French were plotting to regain possession
of Calais " by treachery."

" They fought as simple knights and so fiercely that
it was right pleasant to see them," after which the
prisoners were banqueted, when the Prince and his
young companion knights served the royal table.

The truce with France was re-established and
extended " till the rising of the sun on August 1
and then for one year," and father and son returned
to England to be welcomed with éclat.

These were great days, for the English court was
the most renowned in Europe for its high standard
of chivalry. More than once the Prince of Wales
was called from Berkhampstead to give judgment

on the prowess of knights from overseas who came to contest their differences in the tilting yard at Westminster, after having taken the usual oath " not to employ secret weapons, charms, or other unlawful meanes " to bring about a victory.

And now it fell to the Prince's lot to win laurels in a new sphere. For some little time marauding Spaniards had been molesting English shipping. Every effort to arrive at a peaceful agreement failed, so when the daring sea-dogs captured some English merchantmen homeward bound from Bordeaux, and hinted at invasion, the fleet was assembled.

King and Prince, each with a separate command, awaited the enemy between Rye and Winchelsea off the coast of Sussex, and the King's ship was so splendid a vessel that she had a crew of a hundred sailors.

There were three days of minstrelsy and song before the keen-eyed sailor keeping the watch gave a warning cry, adding: " And there be so many of them that, God help me, I cannot count them ! "

On came the Spaniards, "so handsome that it was a pleasure to look at them," and they " surmounted our ships like castles to cottages." But the English trumpets sounded, and the knights tossed off their wine as each commander selected his victim.

The Prince of Wales steered his ship straight for the tallest Spaniard in the line ; they grappled, and soon the English vessel was " sorlie pierced." English sailors baled vigorously, while sword in hand the Prince led the attack, but it must have gone hardly with them had not Henry of Lancaster with his cry of " A Derby to the rescue ! "—brought his ship up on the other side of the Spaniard so that the enemy was between two fires. Scarcely had the Prince, with his immediate followers, gained a foothold on the Spanish decks before his own ship sank.

The King too had had his victory, but the naval battle went on until " beset with darkness the English

could not discern the 27 Spanish ships remaining
untaken."

Our men cast anchor "supposing nothing finished
so long as anything remained undone." They dressed
the wounded, "flung the miserable Spaniards into
the Sea, refreshed themselves with victuals, and yet
kept Vigilant watch."

When the night was past "the Englisshmen prepared (but in vain) to a new battell . . . the sun
begane to pour and they, viewing the Seas, could not
perceive any sign of the Spaniards!""

So King and Prince landed at Rye and rode to
tell Queen Philippa of that famous victory, the
"Battell of Espagnols sur mer." Never before had
England triumphed over the redoubtable Spanish
sailors, and cheering citizens hailed Edward III as
"King of the Sea!""

But still there was little peace in the troubled
island.

There was sickness everywhere, and such a drought
that "beeves and muttons waxed dere for want of
grasse," and but for the arrival of relief ships loaded
with rye there were many who must have "utterlie
perished, or at least have pittifullie pined."

Then, too, Scotland was making trouble on the
border, and, since all efforts at converting the truce
with France into a permanent peace had failed, a
renewal of war could not be long avoided.

The Prince of Wales, now twenty-four, was entrusted with an independent command and began
to assemble his troops at Plymouth. All young
nobles rushed to arms in their eagerness to serve
under his banner, and profiteers were quick to take
advantage of the unprecedented demand for armour.

Craftsmen hid their stocks and would only produce
one or two sets at a time, so prices soared till royal
wrath was aroused, and the Lord Mayor and his
magistrates were bidden to make search, commandeer

all the armour available, price it according to weight, add a percentage for labour, and sell it to the first-comer !

When such initial difficulties had been overcome the winds were unpropitious, and for forty days the Prince's three hundred vessels were storm-bound.

At last they sailed, Bordeaux was reached, a solemn service was held in St. Andrew's Cathedral, and the Lords of Gascony assembled to tender their oaths of allegiance to the Prince and promise their aid to the making of " a good war."

With 60,000 men behind him the Black Prince set out to ravage the country after the approved manner. Within three months he took " manie good townes by the grace of God." The French King " never had such loss and bad mischief before." And as he passed on his way along the shores of the Bay of Biscay and towards the Mediterranean, the Prince established " the erles and baronets to abide in certain places and make roades and annoy his enemies."

Messengers laden with plunder carried back to England glowing reports of the gallantry of the nation's hero. Five hundred towns and villages had been despoiled, and the Englishmen's horses could hardly move by reason of the weight of accumulated loot.

" Whereof, by God's assistance, if my lord hath the wherewithal to maintain this warre to the King his father's profit and his own honour, he should greatlie increase the English power and win many fair places, for our enemies are wonderfully astonished," wrote Sir John Wingfield, who might perhaps be described as a war correspondent.

But the news from home was not so gratifying. The Scots had seized the opportunity of entering Berwick " by stealth " and capturing it. Therefore, Edward had been obliged to turn his attention to the north, so leaving France free to concentrate her forces.

A clash between French and English was soon

inevitable, and it came in the fields of Beauvoir and Malperte, two leagues from Poitiers, though Cardinal de Perigord, an emissary of the Pope, strove in vain to bring " peace and quietness " to the foes.

The Prince, knowing himself outnumbered, was persuaded to consent to relinquish the plunder his army had taken and bind himself not to bear arms in France for seven years, provided King John would be equally amenable. The elated Cardinal rode back to the French lines, but John was out for harsher terms. Nothing would content him except that the Prince of Wales and a hundred of his chief knights should make an unconditional surrender.

In a very fury of wrath the English hastened their preparations, and the Cardinal, " though he travelled earnestlie betwixt them all that daie," failed to bridge the gulf.

" Fair sirs," cried the Black Prince to the knights who surrounded him, " though we be so few against the mighty power of our enemies, let us not be dismayed, for strength and victory lie not in multitudes, but to those to whom God gives it. . . . I have the noble lord my father, and, fair brothers, you have each of you many a good friend who will avenge us well should the fortune of the day go against us ! Thus then I pray you—fight well this day, and if it please God and St. George I will also do the part of a good knight." (" These words did the Prince speke which greatlie comforted his people.")

King John too was addressing his army : " When you are at Paris, at Orleans, at Rouen," he told his men, " you threaten the English among yourselves and wish that you were near them. . . . Here they now are—I show them to you—now prove your hatred towards them and avenge all the evils they have done you, for without fail we shall fight them ! "

With " slow and equable march " the French

advanced under the hail of the English arrows. "In
older times men had been able to tell after a third,
fourth, or at outside the sixth pull on the bow with
which side a victory would lie," but at Poitiers "a
single archer had fired a hundred arrows, all without
hurry, and still neither side yielded, for this was not
a battell quicklie dispatched or brought to a con-
clusion ; it was fought with such obstinate earnestness that three times that daie were the Englishmen
driven to renew the fight through the multitudes of
enemies that came still upon them. . . .

"The battell went on from prime to vespers, and
the Black Prince fought like a fell lion and took great
delight that daie in the fight." Now it secmed that
the honour of the battle lay with the English, and
now with the French, so fierce was their onslaught.

"We are undone ! " cried one faint-hearted Briton.

"Bastard, thou liest ! " retorted the Black Prince
fiercely. "We are not undone while I yet live ! . . .
Banners, advance in the name of God and St. George ! "
The worthy Prince then dashed forward into the
thickest of the mêlée, "cutting and hewing the Frenchmen with a sharpe sword," and striving to reach
King John, who was fighting valiantly, with his twelve-
year old son, Philip, following close at his heels.

"Father ! Guard to the right ! . . . Father—
guard to the left ! " sounded his shrill cries, but for
all his warnings King John was overpowered and
captured, as was young Philip.

Seeing this, the Black Prince signalled that the
battle was over, so gradually the fighting ceased.

When the unfortunate John was led to the Prince
of Wales, the latter "spoke many comfortable words "
to the vanquished King as he "bent his knee to him
in the best manner."

"Most noble King ! There is no cause wherefore
your grace should be pensive, though God this day
did not consent to follow your will," he told him.
"You singly have won the prize of valour, for it is

apparent to every Englishman that none bore himself so bravely as you ! ''

At the banquet held as was customary on the evening of the battle, the seats of honour were allotted
to the King of France and his nobles, and the Prince
personally waited on his captive, vowing that as yet
he had not sufficiently distinguished himself to permit
of his sitting at table with so valiant a knight.

In addition to the capture of King John and Prince
Philip, the English haul consisted of " an archbishop,
13 counts, 66 barons, and more than 2,000 knights,"
to say nothing of the baggage of the vanquished
army.

All told, the prisoners outnumbered their captors,
so it was deemed advisable to free them on parole,
that they might collect the amount of ransom each
had himself decided was reasonable. When the
money was obtained, they were to report at Bordeaux
not later than Christmas morning.

There was no attempt at hard bargaining as victors
and vanquished sat over their wine, for " the English
knights had no desire to impoverish men of their
own order so that they could not again ride forth
in arms to advance their name and honour."

Next morning, after a solemn service of thanksgiving held on the field of battle, the Prince of Wales
despatched John's golden coronet to England as sure
proof of his victory. The booty-laden army then
marched back to rejoicing Bordeaux, " and so ended
the famous battell of Poictiers."

Once again a truce was agreed between France and
England, this time to be of two years' duration.
During this period, although " private wars " were
to be permitted on fifteen days' notice, any encounter
without notice was to be regarded as unlawful.

A week's official thanksgiving was ordered in
England, and when word was received that the Prince
of Wales was returning, King Edward came riding

down from Scotland to receive his victorious son and the royal prisoners.

The streets of London were hung with tapestry and crowded with excited citizens. The clergy marched in procession, bells were rung, bonfires blazed, and there were " rejoicings marvellous to behold."

The Black Prince, on a black horse, rode beside the captive King, who was royally mounted on a white charger, to where Edward awaited them at the Palace of Westminster. . . . " These daies there were great joustes holden at Smithfield . . . but it was reported that the French King could not dissemble and cloake his inward thoughts whilst he beheld these warlike pastimes." As for Prince Philip, he was " easily moved to bitter tears " when the Black Prince beat him at chess.

John had a companion in misfortune at some of these entertainments, for David of Scotland was a second royal captive.[1]

Now began long-drawn-out negotiations for the ransoming of John and the establishment of a permanent peace, and then, when John was brought to agree to the English terms, all the work was undone because the Dauphin and the French people refused to ratify the treaty, holding that by its terms France would be dismembered. Rather than this King John must remain a prisoner " till God in his own time should provide a remedie."

This ambiguous phrase caused great indignation in England, so when the period of truce came to an end prayers were offered up and yet once more an English army ravaged France and uttered its battle-cry before the gates of Paris ; in swift retaliation French men-at-arms sacked Winchelsea all on a March morning " before sunne up."

Since the Dauphin ignored a royal challenge to single combat, the English, having eaten the country

[1] See *Their Majesties of Scotland.*

bare, moved on to Chartres, and here the elements leagued to assist the Pope in the efforts he had been making to bring about peace.

On Easter Monday, " which daie was full darke of miste," a terrible storm broke. It wrecked the English camp, killed a thousand men and six times as many horses, and brought the English King to vow that he would make reasonable terms with France if only the heavens would clear. The storm ceased most miraculously, and Edward kept his word.

The Prince of Wales was left to conclude the matter under the Treaty of Bretigni (May to October 1360). By this the King of England renounced his claim to the crown of France and agreed to ransom John for £500,000 (three million crowns).

In her turn France confirmed England in her possession of Calais, waived any right of homage for the disputed duchies, and cancelled her alliance with Scotland.

Preparations for the return of John were now set afoot, while the peasantry groaned under the taxes imposed towards the raising of the ransom—flour, bread, pastry, grain, wine, cattle, alive and dead, fish, leather, iron, steel, woollen goods, parchment, all were laid under tribute, and still the first instalment could not be raised. At the eleventh hour a *nouveau riche* Italian stepped forward with an offer to make good the deficit provided his son might marry a French princess.

This was quickly agreed, and with a sigh of relief the country turned to the consideration of hostages. The " Lords of the Fleur de Lis " (the King's brothers and two of his sons), various nobles, certain leading Parisian citizens, and others from eighteen of the principal towns in France were duly assembled for the sacrifice, and presently John, laden with gifts and escorted by the Black Prince, left England for Calais. Here tournaments and pageants were held, for which Edward III crossed the Channel, and then a mass at which the two Kings exchanged the kiss of peace and undertook to maintain the forty-one articles of the Treaty of Bretigni.

The hostages were approved—" six dukes besides erles, lords, and other honourable personages," and at last John was " licensed " to depart.

He took leave of Edward " in the most loving manner " and rode off with the Prince of Wales to Boulogne. The two entered the city on foot, as pilgrims, and went together to make offerings in the cathedral, after which John and the Duke of Normandy " swore to hold and maintain the afore-said peace without fraud or colourable deceit."

The Black Prince now returned to England to play his part in the Parliament called to ratify the treaty, and to take the sacrament together with the Lords of the Fleur de Lis, after which each subscribed to an oath binding themselves " to keep the peace and concord sworn that day."

Yet, after these elaborate ceremonies, one of the Lords of the Fleur de Lis was to break his parole, and John, the remainder of his ransom all unpaid, returned to die in England.

And now for the first time in his life the Prince of Wales found leisure for a purely personal matter.

Joan, the Fair Maid of Kent, that young cousin who had fascinated him in her girlhood days, was again in England. Behind her was a halo of romance —a father who had died on the scaffold, having waited for death till a volunteer from the Marshalsea per-formed the headsman's duty in exchange for a free pardon and rival claimants for her hand in the persons of William de Montacute Earl of Salisbury and Sir Thomas Holland, the latter having abducted her and petitioned the Pope for an annulment of the Salisbury contract. Small wonder that scandal had been busy with her name !

Now, widowed and an heiress, many a man wooed the disturbing beauty, and among those who approached her was the Black Prince (who had stood godfather to one of her children), though ostensibly at least he came to press the suit of another.

No, Joan would not listen; never would she marry again! "And then she showed her subtilty and wisdom—she wept. He, to give her comfort, kissed her," when she whispered that she had "given herself to the most chivalrous knight under Heaven, and for love of him could never wed another. . . . 'My love for him parts me from all other men!'"

The Prince pressed for the hero's name, and Joan, all blushing, begged that he would leave her! He refused and reiterated his question. Then suddenly Joan yielded:

"My dear and indomitable lord!—it is you—and it is for love of you that I will never have any other knight by my side!" she cried in bold avowal, whereon "the prince, greatlie amazed by the love of the Countess," answered:

"My Lady, I also vow to God that as long as you live, never will I have any other woman save you to wife!"

Royal acquiescence, if not royal approval, was obtained, messengers were dispatched for dispensations, and the wedding took place. As a memorial of his marriage the Prince built Our Lady Undercroft.

A temporary court was set up at Berkhampstead, but a few months later it was decided that the Prince should take over the rule of Aquitaine and Gascony, paying his father an ounce of gold a year in recognition of his sovereign claim on the duchies.

Prince and Princess sailed for Bordeaux, and the lords of Gascony came flocking to the brilliant, extravagant court, "the most wonderful since the birth of Christ . . . never before were there such jousts and tournaments, nor such good entertainment, nor more honourable . . . for every day at table there were more than sixty knights with twice as many esquires." The Princess was as extravagant as the Prince, and their finances became yet more involved.

All too soon war was to claim the Flower of Chivalry once more. A messenger came riding in haste bringing word that Castile had risen against her legitimate King Don Pedro and set his illegitimate brother on the throne. Letters "right pyteous" told of the discarded King's "povertie and miserie" and desired the Black Prince "for Goddesake . . . to give him good counsel."

Such an appeal could hardly have been resisted by any knight, so the Prince welcomed the messenger "right merrilie," and called on Chandos for his approval.

"Chandos, Chandos, I have known the time when you would have given other advice!" cried the Prince reproachfully when Chandos uttered a warning.

To the mind of the Black Prince "it was neither decent nor proper that a bastard should possess a kingdom . . . nor drive out of the realme his own brother, heir to the country by lawful marriage. And no King or King's son ought to tolerate it as being of the greatest prejudice to royaltie."

A Parliament was called at Bordeaux and counsel from England was requested. The replies increased the Prince's determination to act, and a wave of enthusiasm surged up when someone recalled an old prophecy to the effect that one day the "leopards of England should wave in triumph over the battle-fields of Spain."

The question of finance alone remained. This was settled by Don Pedro, who, although he had no money in hand at the moment, was lavish in his promises of repayment; meanwhile he would give his daughters as hostages for the necessary loans, and the Prince of Wales could melt down his plate. In addition, as a mere token of gratitude, he would give the provinces of Biscay and Castro Urdiales to his dear brother-in-arms.

Military preparations began, but for a time Joan's clinging hands held back her husband and lover. He must not leave her till her child was born. So the Black Prince awaited the arrival of his second son, Richard, " at whose birth the people were right joyous," then, " on Sunday after the hour of prime, he departed from Bordeaux with great triumph and all his men of warre."

With him too went the " most famous warriors in the whole world."

Small wonder that Najarra was a victory, though it was a " marvellouslie dangerous battell in which many a knight was laid along the earth." The arrows flew through the air like rain in winter time, and soon the river was running with Spanish blood. " It was fought and won by noone, so on the Saturdaye night the English could repose themselves at their ease."

" Give thanks and praise to God and not to me," said the Prince of Wales, " for from Him and not from me have you received this gallant victory."

Great tidings of the triumph in Spain soon spread "over France, England, Almayne, and other countries as to the Prince of Wales and his puyssance in the battell, and there were tremendous rejoicings in the cytie of London." Still, all was not well, for " in the very hour of his triumph Don Pedro forgot his frienlie dutie and was so far from performing his promise of paiement that he cloaked his ill-meaning with a feigned tale and sent the Prince a message spiced with hypocrisy and unthankfulness ; foul faults in a private man, much more odious in a Prince ! "

Week after week passed, and never a penny could the hard-pressed Black Prince obtain towards the payment of his troops. Messengers sent to Don Pedro returned empty-handed, except for the Spaniard's assurances of distress that he could not keep his engagement :

" Our people excuseth themselves and say that
they can make no money so long as the Free Companies be in the country, for they be repeatedly
robbed of the treasure that should have gone to
the Prince of Wales."

So the Prince melted down the remainder of his
plate, and still his men went short.   Disease attacked
the camp and spared no one in its ravages.   The
Prince himself fell a victim, and could hardly mount
his horse when an urgent message was received
from the Princess of Wales, to say that Aquitaine
was in danger of attack and her lord must hasten
to the rescue.

With infinite difficulty the necessary safe con-
ducts were obtained, and the stricken, decimated
army made its way back.

Joan and her young sons met the Prince en route.
" Right sweetlie did they embrace when they came
together . . . and they held each other by the hand
until on foot they reached their lodging."

Still the army clamoured for its pay and the
exchequer was empty.   The harassed Prince insti-
tuted a hearth tax of ten sous on each fireplace in
the duchy, and this proved intensely unpopular.
Malcontents whispered that since all the provisions
of the Treaty of Bretigni had not been fulfilled, the
Prince was under the sovereignty of the King of
France, to whom appeal might be made.   So presently a messenger appeared with a summons to the
Black Prince to appear at Paris to answer to charges
brought against him by the Gascons.

All the blood of the Plantagenets was aroused :
" Willingly will we attend at Paris on the day
appointed since the King of France sends for us,"
answered the Prince, "but it shall be with our
helmet on our head, and 60,000 men in our company!"

The spirit might be strong, but the body was
weakened by dropsy.

A scullion delivered a taunting declaration of war

at the English court, war broke out in a dozen
directions, and Sir John Chandos, friend of the
Prince's boyhood, led out the army his lord could
not command—and was killed.

Then came word that Limoges had surrendered
to the French.

" By the soul of my father," swore the Prince, " I
will retake that city and mete out punishment to
all traitors ! "

If he could no longer ride he would be carried in
a litter ; and so the siege began. A month later
the English having undermined the walls " quite
reversed them into a ditch." The Prince, still in
his litter, was carried through the breach and the
massacre began :

" It was verie grate pitie to see the women and
children who kneeled down on their knees before
the Prince for mercie, but he was so infirmed with
ire that he took no heed to them."

Then suddenly the spirit of the gallant Prince of
old revived in the tortured body. With their
banners before them and their backs to the wall,
he saw three French commanders fighting in the
market-place with the Earls of Cambridge and
Pembroke and the Duke of Lancaster. While the
Prince watched the combat from his litter all other
battle ceased . . . then suddenly the three began
to fail, and the Prince commanded that the
vanquished be allowed to surrender ; all left alive
were permitted to live, though Limoges was " clean
burnt out."

The Black Prince was now carried to Cognac,
where the Princess awaited him, and here " he gave
leave to all his men of warre to depart and do no
more that season, for he felt himself not well . . .
always the sickness increased."

A return to England was decided upon, the Duke
of Lancaster being appointed as his brother's deputy,
and the Prince of Wales was carried on to a ship,

so ill that he could not remain for the funeral of his eldest son, who had just died.

With Princess Joan, and his surviving son, Richard, the Black Prince took up life at Berkhampstead and the news from across the Channel grew steadily worse.

But English air gave a flicker of life to the returned Prince, and he found strength to buckle on his armour once more when a cry for succour came from an English garrison in France. Five weeks at sea, repeatedly beaten back by gales, delayed the army until it was too late to relieve the besieged, and the tortured body of the Prince was carried back once more to Berkhampstead.

Once or twice there came a flicker of energy. When a Great Council was called at Westminster to answer the Pope, who claimed to be Lord Paramount of England and demanded a subsidy, the Black Prince appeared, representing the King, and defied the Archbishop of Canterbury and the lords spiritual and temporal who were willing to acquiesce in the papal decree.

Again, when Prince Richard's heritage seemed in danger, Edward had himself carried into Parliament.

But the end was in sight, and he knew it. In those last days the dying Prince ordered that his door should stand " open to all, even to the least boy."

Prince Richard, " although but a little one," was summoned and " bayde under payne of his father's curse never to chainge or take away the gyfts that he att hys deathe gave to hys servants ! "

" ' I commend to you my son who is very young and little,' said the Prince to those around his bed ; ' pray you, as you have served me, serve him loyally.' And all the princes and barons standing around swore it, sore grieved at his departing. . . .

" So on Trinitie Sundai there passed out of this world the Flower of the Chivalry of England,

Edward Prince of Wales and of Aquitaine, at the King's Palace of Westminster beside London, and so he was embalmed and put in leade and kept till the Feast of St. Michael to be interred with greater solemnity when Parliament should be there. . . .

" He died in the forty-sixth year of his age even in the same month when he was born, ripe for Heaven and full of Honour happily exempt from the Imperfections and Errors of old Age. . . . The year before his Lamented Expiration he was called for by a bearded Comet of considerable magnitude.

" The loss of him struck a general sorrow into the hartes of all the English nation. . . . He was a Prince so full of virtue that he left no place for any vices, and if he had lived in Heroicke times he might have been numbered among the Nine Worthies. . . . Of lamentation and sighing, of crying aloud and sorrowing there was so great a noise that there was no man living in the world who, if he had beheld that grief but would have had pity at heart."

The body was carried by the Pilgrims' Way to Canterbury, and masses for the repose of the Prince's soul were sung in Paris by order of Charles King of France.

CHAPTER III

RICHARD PLANTAGENET (RICHARD II)

" A fair long man as another Absalom. . . . The goodliest personage of all our Kings that had been since the Conquest."

" And there shall be a King in Albion who shall reign for the space of twenty-and-two years in great honour and in great power, and shall be united with those in Gaul ; which King shall be undone in the parts of the north in a triangular place."—(Merlin prophecy.)

RICHARD PRINCE OF WALES (RICHARD II)

Born at Bordeaux	January 6, 1367
Created Prince of Wales . . .	April 23, 1377
Crowned	July 16, 1377
Married (1) Anne of Bohemia . .	1382
„ (2) Isabella of Valois . .	1392
Deposed and died	1399/1400

Descent

Edward III — *m*. — Philippa
|
Edward the Black Prince (and others)
m. Joan, the Fair Maid of Kent.
|
Richard (and another)

CONTEMPORARY SOVEREIGNS

SCOTLAND : Robert II and Robert III.
FRANCE : Charles V and Charles VI.
GERMANY : Charles IV and Wenceslaus.

CHAPTER III

RICHARD PRINCE OF WALES

1367–1400

RICHARD PLANTAGENET, son of a beautiful mother and " that shining star of military glory the Black Prince," was born at Bordeaux on January 6 (1367), the Festival of the Three Kings of Cologne, which gave rise to a legend that three kings were present at his baptism. Astrologers were quick to cast his horoscope, and foretold that the sturdy baby would one day wear the crown of England, although he was but the younger son of a king's son who would never mount his father's throne.

Men recalled this prophecy a few years later when the Prince and Princess of Wales returned to England, for the Black Prince seemed a stricken man and his elder son remained in France awaiting burial.

All London cheered straight-limbed, yellow-haired little Lord Richard when he rode out with his parents towards Berkhampstead, and a fresh outburst of enthusiasm was engendered when King and Prince summoned the High Court of Parliament to safeguard the child's rights. Lords and Commons were called upon to swear that they and their posterity would always be true to the right line, and " especially to Lord Richard," for many saw a dangerous rival in John of Gaunt Duke of Lancaster. " The peers put their individual seals to this ordinance before they went away, but the Commons only expressed their concurrence by holding up their hands and consenting altogether."

The ceremony completed, King and Prince sailed

away towards France in *Le Grace Dieu* (leaving seven-year-old Richard as official Custodian of the King-dom), but were beaten back after some weeks of battle with contrary winds, when men were quick to note that the life of the Black Prince was drawing to its close.

Richard stood by his father's side during the last days of his difficult dying, swore to obey his com-mands, and watched with childish awe when the bishops sprinkled the passing man with holy water and urged him to make his peace with God.

Three weeks later, " being a Wednesday which was the day after St. John the Baptist, the 25th of June," on petition of the Commons, Richard appeared in Parliament that all might see and honour him as heir to the throne in his father's stead.   He was still under his mother's care, but Sir Guichard de l'Aigle and Sir Simon Burley were responsible for the nature of his upbringing.

Upon Richard's entrance the Archbishop spoke " words of commendation," and the Commons, " with one voice, prayed that the Lords would make the boy Prince of Wales as his father had been before him.   But the Lords (with more discretion) answered that it lay not in them but with the King so to do, to whom, however, they would be mediators for this purpose." This was known as the " Good Parliament " according to one chronicler, " but," he adds, " more on account of the many and useful statutes passed by it than for the Popular Air and Quarrelsome humour which appeared therein."

The mediation failed of immediate effect, but five months later King Edward III decreed that his nine-year-old grandson should succeed to his father's honours, so, on St. George's Day, at Havering-atte-Bower, Richard was created Prince of Wales, Duke of Cornwall, and Earl of Chester.   With the princi-pality went " the profits of her ports, knights' fees, rents, meadow-feedings, and fishings."   The duchy

RICHARD II.
From his picture in Westminster Abbey, probably by
Richard Beauneveu.

included other perquisites, such as "whales and sturgeons and the wrecks of the sea."

At Christmas "great satisfaction was given to all who retained a Grateful Sense of the Merit of the Lamented Black Prince" when it was seen that the young Prince of Wales occupied the place of honour at the King's right hand and took precedence of his uncles.

London celebrated the accession of the Prince by a mummery. Some hundred and fifty of the leading citizens, all in gorgeous disguises and preceded by torch bearers, rode to Kennington, where Richard and his mother had their residence, and crowding into the great hall explained to the Princess of Wales that they wished to dice with "London's prince."

Richard was summoned and dice were flung upon the table; all "so obligingly contrived that he always won, whether he cast at them or they at him"!

Gold, and yet more gold, was paid over, until the laughing citizens vowed that they had no more, but must stake a golden bowl, a golden cup, and a golden ring; all of which the fortunate young player secured at three successive throws.

Princess Joan and her attendants proved almost as lucky as the Prince of Wales when it came to their turn to play. Then all "in a contented mood sat down to a banquet of wines and spices," after which the mummers departed, leaving the sleepy winner to count his gains.

The King had been aging fast, so none were surprised when in the New Year Richard was called upon to open Parliament in his grandfather's name. The first sitting was a short affair, since "divers of the Lords and Commons not being come the House adjourned till Nine of the Clocke the next morning." Then, a larger attendance being reported, Richard

took his seat on the throne, looking very small for
all his royal robes, since he was but ten years old,
and the Chancellor delivered an oration bidding
the members " embrace in their hearts and with
their hands, without rancour," before settling down
to the business of dealing with Supply.

In the spring (1377), Richard was made a Knight
of the Garter, as also was his cousin Henry Earl of
Derby, son of the Duke of Lancaster. Perhaps the
gods laughed sardonically as the young cousins
knelt together keeping their vigil on the eve of the
ceremony, for in the stars it was written that Henry
should depose Richard and claim his throne.

Seven months later it became so obvious that the
King was dying that the citizens of London turned
towards the rising sun and made haste to assure
Richard that their " readiness and good-will should
be his immediately after it might please God to call
to his mercie the King now past hope of recoverie
of health."

When the anticipated event occurred, steps were
taken to stop the ports for fear that news of Edward
III's death should reach France while the affairs of
the kingdom were in disorder.

The boy-King rode to Westminster to receive his
crown with Sir Nicholas Bond leading his horse
and Sir Simon Burley carrying a naked sword before
him. The " noise of trumpets and other instruments sounded marvellous on this day of joy and
mirth."

But all was not as serene as it seemed, for a mighty
struggle was raging behind the scenes in connection
with the services to be rendered at the Coronation.
Two claimants contested their right to the office
of Champion ; the Earl of Lincoln demanded that
he be appointed Carver for the day ; the Earl of
Oxford wished to pour out the water in which
the King must wash, and another peer claimed the
privilege of handing the towel on which his young

master should wipe his fingers " before he went
to meate." Others fought for the right to " serve
him his cup " and make the wafer he should eat,
but most arrogant of all was the knight who claimed
the honour of supporting the monarch's right arm
when he held the royal sceptre.

These problems adjusted, Richard passing through
the city, found it richly adorned in his honour, and
" in the Chepe was reaered a four-towered castle,
each tower inhabited by a beautiful virgin of a
stature and age like unto the King's own." These
showered down golden leaves upon his head while
the citizens drank his health from the wine that
flowed freely from each tower. But " to speak of
all the pageants and shows which the people had
caused to be made and set forth in honour of their
new King was superfluous. . . . So, with the joy
of Lords and noblemen he was conveyed into the
Palace for a night's rest."

On the morrow the child was roused at an early
hour and " fetched to the church that he might
kneel and make his prayers " while the Litany was
sung. After this the Archbishop delivered a sermon
on the whole duty of kings, presented Richard to
the people, and blessed him. Then " the Archbishop
tore off the King's garments and, stripping him to
his shirt, annointed his hands, head, breast, shoulders,
and the joints of his arms before robbing him and
presenting the emblems, sword, bracelets, ring, and
spurs, after which Lord Furnival advanced and gave
the King a red glove for the hand into which the
Archbishop was to put the sceptre."

All duly accomplished, the King kissed the bishops
and the abbots and mass began.

At the offertory Richard was escorted to his seat,
when he offered first his sword (which was redeemed
later) and then " as much gold as he would, but
not less than a mark by reason of the custom."

By some error Sir John Dymoke (the victorious

Champion) now arrived at the Abbey prepared to play his part, and was with difficulty persuaded to go away and return later when the King would be " at dinner," for nature had triumphed and it had become necessary for the exhausted little monarch to be placed in a litter and carried into the palace for a rest, " he being somewhat faint." Some support must have been required, for when King Richard returned and was escorted into Westminster Hall for the coronation banquet, he was required to create four earls before " sitting down to meate. . . . To show what royal service was at this feast it passeth our understanding to describe, but the fare was exceedingly sumptuous and the furniture so princlie in all things that if the same should be rehearsed the reader would perhaps doubt of the truth thereof."

Long afterwards people remembered what had passed unnoticed at the time, and whispered to one another how three evil omens had befallen at this coronation. Richard had dropped one of his shoes as he walked in procession, a spur had fallen off, and, worst of all, as he sat at banquet a gust of wind had shifted the crown from his head !

And now, Prince of Wales no longer, but King Richard the Second, the monarch was returned to his mother's charge to play with his half-brothers, the young Hollands, under the eye of his personal guardian the Earl of Warwick. The responsibility of government was vested in a Council which it was decreed should rule " until the King was of an age to know good from evil."

It was well, for the times were difficult, and despite precautions news of Edward's decease reached other countries all too soon. So the Scots re-took Berwick, while French filibusters swooped down on Rye, Hastings, Portsmouth, Dartmouth, and Plymouth. Retaliation was swift. Twenty-six French ships were burnt to the water's edge as they lay off Boulogne, and a public-spirited Londoner fitted out a "navy" at his own expense and captured a noted Scottish pirate who had been preying on coastal shipping.

Unfortunately for him, the official mind of the fourteenth century objected to interference as keenly as his descendant of the twentieth, so the enterprising merchant was called to account for alleged contempt of authority. He was fortunate enough to obtain an acquittal on the ground that the service done was eminent if unorthodox.

Domestic troubles too were rife. For some time past " females had been meddling in matters impertinent to their degree and inconvenient for their knowledge, debating and scanning in their private conventicles of such things as whereabout if they kept silent it were for their greater condemnation." The Lollards too were to be seen posted at street corners and doing penance in white sheets; Wyclif could no longer be ignored, and one John Ball was preaching democracy :

" We be all come from one father and one mother, Adam and Eve ; whereby can they say or shew that they be greater lords than we, saving by that they cause us to win and labour for that they dispend ! "

High taxation played its part in the general unrest, and presently a spark set fire to the heather.

A tax-collector insulted the young daughter of a tiler ; her mother screamed for help, and the father, rushing in, knocked the official such a blow on his head " that his brains flewe out."

A citizen army collected to demand redress of grievances ; Wat the Tyler, Jack Straw, and John Ball came forward as leaders. Princess Joan met the force as she was returning from a pilgrimage, but escaped on payment of a toll of kisses. She reached the Tower, but not safety, for next day a mob gained entrance to seize and execute the Lord Chancellor and Treasurer.

Son of his father, Richard rode to Smithfield to bid the twenty thousand malcontents lay down their arms, and with him went the Mayor of London and a handful of attendants.

The attitude of the mob was truculent, and Wat the Tiler's manner of speech displeased the Mayor.

"False, stinking knave," cried he. "Shalt thou speak thus in the presence of thy King and natural lord?" He struck as he spoke and the people's leader fell. Those behind him wavered, and Richard seized the crucial moment. Spurring his horse forward into their midst, he bade them not be sad at the death of a rogue and traitor, since he himself would lead them and give them redress for their wrongs.

The quick wit and gallantry of the King's action won the day, so the Mayor lived to be rewarded with a knighthood and an annuity, while the city of London was empowered to add a dagger to its arms.

Richard was now sixteen years old, nearly six feet tall and "amiable of countenance." It was time to seek him a wife, and negotiations were opened for Anne of Bohemia, sister of Good King Wenceslaus. Ultimately these negotiations were successful, and "the said Lady Anne was bought for a great price by our lord the King, for she was much sought in marriage."

The nation forgot its troubles for a time when she was sent to England—

"Guarded well with valiant Men of Might."

Wedding bells rang, and soon King and Queen together gave full rein to extravagance. The royal household increased till it numbered 10,000 persons, and every morning twenty-eight oxen and fully three hundred sheep were roasted to feed the multitude.

Garments embroidered with jewels became the fashion, sleeves touched the floor, even the grooms went clothed in silk, and " daily the wrath of God was provoked by the iniquities of the courtiers."

Then there sat " a memorable Parliament that wrought wonders," and the dismissal of certain high officials was demanded. Richard answered that he would not remove a scullion at the bidding of the nation, but stern talk of deposition sobered him, though only for a time.

At twenty-two he struck again, dismissed the lords of the Council, appointed a new Chancellor, and issued a proclamation to the effect that he had assumed the full rights of government in his own person. To celebrate the occasion he ordered a magnificent tournament at Smithfield ; it lasted three weeks, and knights were led to the lists by ladies holding golden chains.

For a few years there was peace except for financial troubles, and then Anne of Bohemia died :

" No child she had, but issueless
She lies without such care ! "

So sang the court poet. Richard had loved her, and in his misery ordered Anne's favourite palace to be razed to the ground.

A year or so later Richard married [1] again, choosing for his bride the eight-year-old daughter of Charles of France and spending £200,000 on the wedding festivities. People groaned, and the groans grew louder when it was found that the King had yielded up Brest and Cherbourg, ports which, although only held in pawn, Englishmen had learned to look upon as their own ; as a consequence a furious quarrel broke out between Richard and the Duke of Gloucester.

The royal will was more tyrannically imposed. When Parliament met, 4,000 of the King's archers

[1] See *Her Majesty: The Romance of the Queens of England.*

surrounded the House. Richard decreed that the
laws of England were in his mouth, not in a statute
book; judges decided that when the King pro-
pounded articles to be handled in Parliament, it was
treason to oppose them, and an obedient Parliament
consented to repeal all acts passed by a previous
assembly, any possibility of a like act by a subsequent assembly being guarded against by Richard,
who undertook to request the Pope to excommuni-
cate any prince who should attempt annulment of
the acts of this House.

Even Nottingham and Derby grew afraid, and
Richard, discovering their "treasonable" conversation, ordered them to meet each other in single combat and then banished Derby for ten years and
Nottingham for a hundred. A few months later,
when the Duke of Lancaster died, Richard, instead
of recalling his son Lord Derby, seized the ducal
property.

He then sailed to subdue Ireland, taking with him
as hostage Henry of Monmouth, Derby's son.

In the middle of the Irish campaign a messenger
arrived from England bringing word that Derby,
now Duke of Lancaster, had landed in Yorkshire.

There were difficulties in the way of an immediate
return, for the ships that had been impressed to
carry the troops were now on their lawful occasions,
so the Earl of Salisbury was sent in advance,
Richard agreeing to follow when he could.

"Never shall I have comfort or repose as long as
that false traitor is alive!" he vowed. "If I could
but get him in my power, I will cause him to be put
to death in such a manner that it shall be spoken
of even in Turkey!"

Henry of Bolingbroke Duke of Lancaster had
come on invitation with a mere handful of followers
in three borrowed ships, but he was skilful in the
art of propaganda, and by the time Richard returned
to England was at Chester with a large army. His

couriers had ranged the country reading his messages to the people gathered at their market crosses. Warned that Richard intended to raise the taxes and oppress them still farther, while Henry would succour and comfort, since his proximity to the crown made it incumbent upon him to love England, they were quick to raise the cry :

"Let Richard be deposed and Henry be Lord and Governor!"

The canker of disloyalty ate into Richard's army as, the victim of divided Councils, he shifted from castle to castle while sending messages to Henry that it would be eternal disgrace to his name should his rightful King "be undone by him."

Standing on the ramparts at Flint, Richard watched his cousin's approach.

"Good Lord," he prayed, "I commend myself to thy holy keeping since it is thy pleasure that I should be delivered into the hands of my enemies! . . ."

King and Duke rode together towards London, and Richard heard himself greeted with shouts of derision ; the Duke was the nation's hero.

"My God! A wonderful land this and a fickle!" said Richard.

London was ringing with the rumour that he was no king nor son of the Black Prince, but "base-born, one sprung not from a father of royal race, but of a Bordeaux canon and a mother given to slippery ways of life."

Parliament met. "First came the prelates, arch-bishops, and bishops . . . next the dukes, mar-quesses, earls, knights, esquires, varlets, archers, and many sort of folk who were neither noble nor gentle. The prelates were close to the King's seat, and on the other side lords of all conditions (great, middling, and less)."

The Archbishop preached his sermon in Latin, and then a document was read informing the House

that Richard had resigned his throne, since he found
himself " neither capable nor worldly wise, nor
prudent nor gentle enough to bear the crown, so
it was his will to resign it into the hands of one of
noble birth and greater wisdom than himself."

" Foreasmuch as it is thus," said the Archbishop,
" . . . it were right and good to choose another
King," and he began to interrogate the House.
Would it have this man, or that, to be the King ?

" No ! " came the shouts, and again " No ! "
" NO ! " till at last came the name for which all
waited.

" Will you have the Duke of Lancaster ? "

" Yes, we will have him and none other ! "

So the Duke, " seeing the Kingdom of England to
be vacant," gave his consent, since it was ordained
by God and by lawful descent from the body of
King Edward the Third, so he took upon himself
the crown as by his right."

The prelates led him to the royal seat, placed the
espousal ring upon his finger, and swore faith,
loyalty, and assistance to the newly-elected sovereign. " A day for the coronation was named, and
then, as they had stayed late without any question, they declared that whosoever did not rejoice
at this election should be likely to lose his head—
and went home."

Within a short time it was seen that while Richard
was alive there would be no permanent peace :
there were plots to restore him to the throne, rumours
that he had escaped, and counter-rumours that he
was dead.

" Have I no faithful friend that will deliver me
from him whose life breeds destruction to me and
disturbance to the kingdom ! " cried Henry in bitter-
ness of spirit, and the Privy Council advised that
the late King should be secured if alive, or shown
if dead.

The demand of the Privy Council was met :

" Item . . . in the year thirteen hundred fourscore
and nineteen the 12th day of March was brought
to the Church of St. Paul, the Mother Church of
London, in the state of a gentleman, the body of
noble King Richard. And true it is that the car
was quite covered in black cloth . . . and there
were a hundred men, all clothed in black and each
bore a torch. And the Londoners had thirty torches
and thirty men all clad in white who met the corpse
of the noble King Richard when he was brought, so
that all men might believe he was for certain dead,
and pray God have mercy on his soul and on all
departed ! Amen."

For two hours the body lay in the Cheape, and fully
twenty thousand passed by to see, but only the face
was exposed, the yellow hair being hidden and all
the body cased in lead. Some said it was not
Richard but his Chaplain Maudelain, who resembled
him ; others answered that Maudelain had been
beheaded after the rising led by Harry Hotspur.

Henry founded a chantry to celebrate a weekly
mass for the soul of King Richard for ever, and also
gave £20 to be distributed to the poor in pence,
" but only the men of Bordeaux mourned him,"
and still the rumours as to his fate persisted.

Men said that Richard had starved himself to
death voluntarily when his friends failed in their
attempt to restore him ; others believed that he had
died, and by starvation, but that food had been
deliberately withheld from him. Then it was
whispered that Sir Pierce Exton, on hearing Henry's
cry that Richard's life meant his death and Richard's
death his life, had gone to Pontefract Castle with
eight companions and struck out the deposed
King's brains on St. Valentine's Day.

A grimmer and yet more circumstantial tale which
held its own for three centuries was that Richard
had escaped to Scotland and been recognised when
working as a scullion by a jester who had once

travelled to the English court. One King and yet another had held him prisoner, until at length he was done to death in Stirling, " being enforced to flee around a post till his barberous butchers inhumanly deprived him of his life. Upon that post the cruel hackings and fierce blows still remain ! "

CHAPTER IV
HENRY OF MONMOUTH (HENRY V)

" Heir of France."

HENRY (OF MONMOUTH) PRINCE OF WALES
(HENRY V)

Born at Monmouth	August 9, 1387
Created Prince of Wales . . .	October 15, 1399
Coronation	April 9, 1413
Married (at Troyes), Katherine of Valois .	May 30, 1420
Died (in France)	August 31, 1422

Descent

Henry III — *m.* — Eleanor of Provence

Edward I   Edmund Earl of Lancaster
(1) Eleanora — *m.* — (2) Marguerite
of Castile   of France

Edward II   Henry Earl of Lancaster
m. Isabella of France

Edward III   Henry Duke of Lancaster
m. Philippa of Hainault

John of Gaunt (4th son)   — *m.* — (1) Blanche of Lancaster
(3) Katherine Swynford   (2) Constance of Castile

Henry (of Bolingbroke) IV (Earl of Derby
and Duke of Lancaster)

m. Mary de Bohun

Henry (of Monmouth) V

CONTEMPORARY SOVEREIGNS

SCOTLAND : James I
FRANCE : Charles VI

CHAPTER IV

HENRY OF MONMOUTH (HENRY V)

1387–1422

HENRY OF MONMOUTH, fourth Prince of Wales, shares with Edward of Carnarvon the distinction of having been born in the principality, but at his birth no one foresaw that he would be either prince or king, and a fee of two pounds was considered sufficient reward for the " wise woman " who officiated at his arrival.

Henry was the eldest of six children ; his mother, aged twenty-four, died when he was seven years old. Richard II was on the throne and the times were turbulent, so young Lord Henry saw little of his father, Henry of Bolingbroke, except in intervals between pilgrimages and continental wars. A delicate child, he was left with his brothers in the hands of a tutor whose salary was 13s. 4d. a quarter, until when eleven years old tradition has it that he was sent to Queen's College, Oxford, where his father's half-brother, Henry Beaufort, was Chancellor.

Young Lord Henry was developing fast : martial exercises, tilting, and hawking now drew him away from the harp he had been taught to play in babyhood, and he was already giving promise of the extraordinary fleetness of foot that was to distinguish him as a man, when with two companions he would sometimes run down a deer.

When Henry of Bolingbroke was banished under suspicion of treason, though 40,000 people thronged the streets to wish him well, his son was old enough to realise the danger of the position and his own powerlessness in the King's hands when Richard summoned him to court. But Richard took a liking to his young kinsman, and though he carried him to Ireland to " learn the art of war," he knighted him on the field of battle.

" My fair young cousin," said the King as the boy rose, " henceforth be gallant and bold, for unless you conquer you will have little name for valour ! "

News from England was scant and irregular, but suddenly, after an ominous interval of six weeks, a scared messenger brought word that Henry of Bolingbroke had landed in Yorkshire and was making a bold bid for the crown. A second dispatch told Richard that the Archbishop of Canterbury was promising remission of sins, in the Pope's name, to all who fought under Henry's standard, and a sure place in paradise to those who fell.

The furious King summoned Lord Henry and warned him that his father's actions might well cost him his inheritance, but he listened to the boy's protestation of his own innocence before sending him under guard to Trim Castle.

A virtual prisoner, Henry waited while his father's star rose and Richard's set. Parliament met, and Henry of Bolingbroke claimed the throne now pronounced vacant by reason of Richard's abdication—

" I being descended from the right line of the blood coming from good King Henry III., and through that right which Grace of God hath sent me, with help of my kin and of my friends to recover it ; the which realm was in poynt to be undone, for default of government and undoing of the gude laws."

So Henry of Monmouth became the son of a King and was summoned back to England in hot haste that he might play a part at his father's coronation and carry Edward the Confessor's famous sword of Justice, Curtana.

HENRY V.
From his picture in the National Portrait Gallery.

The coronation banquet followed, and the boy watched Sir Thomas Dymoke ride thrice round Westminster Hall uttering his challenge :

" If any man, great or small, shall say that his liege lord here present be not the rightful crowned King of England," the King's Champion was ready to prove the contrary there and then.

" If need be, Sir Thomas," interrupted the new-made monarch, " I will in mine own person ease thee of this office ! "

But no friend of Richard's pressed forward from the crowd ; many believed him already dead.

Two days later there was another splendid scene at Westminster when the King " promoted his eldest son Henry by five symbols, to wit the delivery of a golden rod, by a kiss, by a belt, by a ring, and by letters of creation, to be Prince of Wales." The move was so popular that the Commons presented a petition, praying that they might be entered on the Records at the election of the Prince. A second petition ran :

" For-as-much as the Prince is of tender age that he may not pass forth from this realm ; for we, the Commons, are informed that the Scots are coming with a mighty hand."

Intent on strengthening his position, Henry IV soon made an effort to win France by suggesting a marriage between one of her daughters and his attractive young son, but the offer was contemptuously rejected, for France would recognise no King other than Richard II. Further, she demanded the immediate return of Queen Isabella, Richard's child-bride (who was writing urgent letters home), together with her dowry and her jewels. Henry's argument that the dowry should be regarded as a fair set-off for the unpaid ransom on King John of France, due since the day of the Black Prince, fell on deaf ears. Nor was a later effort to secure Isabella for his son more successful, though it was

many a day before the little Queen was sent on her
homeward journey " clad in mourning weeds and
showing a countenance of lowering and evil aspect
to King Henry, scarce opening her lips as she went
her way."

Training in the art of war, having been begun by
Richard II, was continued for the Prince of Wales
by his father, Henry IV. At thirteen he saw war-
fare on the Scottish front, at fourteen he was on the
Welsh marches where Owen Glendower had raised
his standard.

While still in the hands of a tutor he was left in
nominal command of the army, and its deeds of
valour in Wales redounded to his credit so that
Parliament offered him thanks and urged that he
be stationed at Chester. At the Battle of Shrewsbury (July 1403) he was wounded in the face by
an arrow but refused to be carried to the rear.

" How will others fight if they see me, a prince,
the King's son, leaving the field ? " he asked, and
demanded to be taken forward that he might lead
as was his duty.

The youthful commander was often in dire
straits for money, for the royal exchequer was bare.

" The expenses are insupportable to me," he
wrote to the King, and to the Council : " My soldiers
are asking whether they are like to be paid for the
present quarter. They swear that they will not
remain without being promptly paid their wages
according to agreement. . . . We implore you to
make some ordinance for us in time. We have
nothing from which we can support ourselves here
except that we have pawned our little plate and
jewels and raised money from them and with that
we shall be able to remain only a short time. And
after that, unless you make provision for us, we shall
be compelled to depart with disgrace and mischief
and the country will be utterly destroyed, which
God Forbid ! . . . Indeed, the Council must take

measures to supply us promptly or be prepared to
guard the marches otherwise,   Everyone must know
that without troops we cannot do more than another
man of inferior rank," he concludes reasonably.

There were interludes when the young warrior
laid aside his responsibilities and came to court to
give verbal assent to the wedding of the latest bride
proposed for him, now a Danish Princess and now
a daughter of Burgundy, or of Brittany.   Then
Prince Hal went his way, " living insolently," mixing
with the citizens, winning hearts and leading many
a frolic, till men cried that whenever heads were
broken the King's son was in the mêlée.   Had not
he, when in disguise, set upon and robbed his own
rent-collectors—true that he had pardoned them the
money lost and rewarded those who had struck at
him hardest !   And then there was that affair of
the King's Bench.   Men nodded and whispered
vaguely, for the story in all its glory was not current
property in Prince Hal's day.   Not then, but a
hundred and fifty years later it was told how Henry
had advanced threateningly on a Judge who had
sentenced a companion, and how the majesty of the
law, unmoved, had bidden the Prince " ' remember
yourselfe.   I keep heere the place of the King, your
sovereign, ye lord and father to whome ye owe
double obedience.   Wherefore in his name I charge
you to desist your wilfulnesse and unlawful enterprise and from henceforward give good example to
those which shall hereafter be your proper subjects.
. . . And now, for your contempte and disobedience
goe ye to the prison of the King's Bench, where I
commit you, and remain ye there prisoner untill
the pleasure of the King your father be further
known. . . .' And the Prince laid down his weapon,
doing reverence, as he was commanded.   Whereat
his servants, dismayed, came and shewed to the
King the whole affair. . . . He, after studying
awhile as a man all ravished with gladness, cried in

a loud voice : ' O Merciful God, how much I abound to your infinite goodness, specially for that you have given me a judge who feareth not to administer Justice, and also a son who can suffer seemlie and obey ! ' "

Then, the tale lay in the womb of time and men talked instead of the honours showered upon their favourite. Now he was made Warden of the Cinque Ports and Constable of Dover at a salary of £300 a year—now he was Captain of Calais, and had been given the guardianship of the young Earl of March, held by many to be rightful heir of the realm since he was of an older line than King Henry IV in descent from Edward III.

But the earl's claims were forgotten when a daring Plantagenet adherent placarded London with notices that Richard II was still alive and in captivity in Scotland. There was hue and cry till the culprit was caught and executed, by which time certain rumours were about concerning the Prince of Wales. Some said that he had taken for his own pleasures and desires money sent for the use of the troops in Calais. Others hotly denied the charge, but vowed that the Prince was forcing his father's abdication and claiming his crown.

In proof of disagreement at court they pointed to the undoubted fact that the King's eldest son no longer attended Council as he had done, his place being taken by a younger brother.

When the rumours reached the Prince's ears, he took spectacular steps to improve his position. First, he sent out letters to all parts of the realm reproving those who circulated " slanderous devises," then, garbing himself in " blewe sattin full of small oilet holes, with at every hole a needle hanging by a silk thread," he went to court followed by a band of friends. Bidding these stay at a good distance, he advanced and knelt before his father, explaining that he came as liege man and obedient son. He

added that, having made confession and taken the
sacrament, he was prepared to die to ease his father's
mind of its weight of suspicion, and proffered a
dagger ! Rising to the occasion nobly, the King
waved the weapon aside, kissed the Prince, and
vowed that henceforward he would harbour no
doubt of his loyalty.

So for a time all went well, though it was whispered
that the King's sickness was heavy upon him.

The people were acclaiming Dick Whittington Lord
Mayor of London when they learned that Henry IV's
days were numbered : too ill to bear the burden of
the crown any longer, he lay with it on his pillow.
There came an hour when he opened his eyes to find
the emblem gone. Wrath gave the dying man
strength, and he summoned his son.

" Sire," said the Prince, " to mine and all men's
judgment you seemed dead in this world, wherefore I,
your next heir apparent, took that as my own ; not
as yours."

" Fair sonne," answered the King with a great
sigh, " what right I had to it God knoweth ! "

" If you die," said the Prince, " I will have the
garland and trust to keep it with the sword against
all my enemies as you have done."

" ' Of Englishmen, so long as they have wealth
and acres so long shalt thou have obedience,' said
the King warningly, ' but when they be poor they
be always ready to make insurrections at every
motion ' . . . with that he turned himself in bed and
shortlie departed to God in a chamber of the Abbot
of Westminster commonlie called Jerusalem."

A fortnight later, on an April day, " rugged and
tempestuous with wind, snow, and sleet," Prince
Hal was crowned as Henry V, and men spoke of him
as a youth upright and filled with virtues and
wisdom, such a King as any nation might rejoice in
—" of strong and active body, neither shrinking in
cold nor slothful in heat, going commonly with head

uncovered.   He never shrank at a wound, nor turned
away his nose for ill savour, nor closed his eyes for
smoke or dust."

Even the pessimistic few who remembered that as
a prince Henry had " spared nothing of his wishes
and desires " were soon driven to admit that he had
had " a new heart given him and was become another
man than he was before."

One of Henry's first acts was to have the body of
Richard the Second brought from Langley and laid
in the tomb of his consort, Anne of Bohemia, " and
this not without great expense."   He ordered too
that " four tapers should burn night and day about
the grave while the world endureth, and the chanting
of a weekly dirge as well as a requiem, and that after
mass there should be distributed to the poor a dole
of 11/8, this to be increased to twenty pounds on
anniversaries."

Other benign acts followed.   The Earl of March
was given complete liberty and taken into the King's
counsel, and at the coronation feast a pardon was
offered to all offenders, " even those guilty of treason,
provided they applied immediately for royal letters
. . . whence for those same letters he got a large
sum of money."

Then an edict was sent forth bidding all Welsh and
Irish each to get back to his own country, and this
too proved a source of revenue to the hard-pressed
King, for " he gathered to himself much treasure "
by issuing permits to those who would pay to remain
in England !

But perhaps the most popular move was Henry's
treatment of his old boon companions.   Immediately
after the coronation these were summoned into the
King's presence and " charged not to presume to come
within ten miles of the court until they had given
good proof of their amendment in manners, and lest
any one of them should plead want of maintenance
to be any cause of their taking ill courses he gave

every one of them competent meanes whereby to
subsist."

And now the King turned his attention to foreign
affairs. In his very first Parliament an " elegant
oration " was delivered by 'the Archbishop of Canterbury showing clearly Henry's latent right to the
crown of France, since he was descended in strict
line from Isabella, daughter of Philip IV of France,
she having married his great-great grandfather
Edward II. Nothing hindered his claim but the
Salic Law, which, as it was pointed out, " no law of
God bound him to observe."

Within a very short time a letter was sent across
the Channel :

" To avoid a deluge of human blood restore to us
in a peaceable manner our inheritance which you
so unjustly retain," wrote Henry V to Charles VI,
adding that to save France's pride he would accept
Charles's daughter Katherine of Valois as a bride.

The Duke of Exeter, the Archbishop of Dublin, the
Lord High Admiral, and the Bishop of Norwich, who
carried the message with a train of 500 horse behind
them, reported that the court of France received them
" with as great a show of kindness as might be, till
the letter had been read," then " the copy of their
entertainment was altered and they were sent away
with as little compliment as they were before received
with honour."

French ambassadors travelling under safe-conduct
soon brought a reply. Charles would give his
daughter, together with a dowry greater than any
French princess had yet received, also with certain
towns ; farther than that he could not go.

Henry answered that such offers were trifles.
" Tell this to the usurper, your master," he went on
sternly. " Within three months I will enter France
as into my own true and lawful patrimony, appoint-
ing to acquire the sayme not with bray of words
but with deeds of men and dint of swords, and

by the aid of God in whom is my full trust and confidence."

Preparations had been begun. The Cinque ports were under obligation to furnish, on demand, a complement of fifty ships for fifteen days' service, each manned by twenty-four sailors, but Henry had arranged to hire additional vessels from foreign countries and to build others. He was adjusting internal affairs too; had offered to receive Owen Glendower of Wales into favour on conditions, had pledged his crown to the Duke of Clarence as security for necessary borrowings, and was now entering into military contracts with certain nobles ; it was decreed that all prisoners taken should belong to the captors unless they were kings, kings' sons, or high officials, when they were to be handed to the Crown on payment of reasonable recompense.

A modern note was struck by the organisation of a medical service. Henry appointed a physician and a surgeon to attend on his army, and offered them twelve pence a day as well as a guard of three archers. The surgeon was directed to take with him twelve men of his own craft to rank as assistants, and a chariot and two wagons were granted to him as transport and to carry " the instruments necessary and fitting for your mystery."

At the eleventh hour embarkation was delayed by the discovery of a plot to set the Earl of March on the throne, but having punished the ringleaders, Henry went his way and had reached Winchester when a derisive message arrived from the Dauphin, together with " a tonne of tennis balls," which it was suggested were fitter playthings for him than arms, aroused him to fury.

Swearing that it would not be long before he would roll such iron balls among the French that the best arms in France could not hold a racket to return them, Henry put to sea with 1,300 vessels of from 20 to 300 tons burden.

Harfleur fell; the King walked barefooted through the streets to give thanks to God for the success of his first enterprise, placed his own good Englishmen within the city, and forwarded a personal challenge to the Dauphin:

" Well considering that our wars occasion the death of men, the desolation of countries, the lamentation of women and children, and so many evils in general as every good Christian ought to mourn . . . and that we ought to use all diligence to find every means that one can to avoid the ills and distresses above mentioned, in order to acquire the Grace of God and the praise of mankind . . . it seemeth to us (considering that it hath pleased God to visit with infirmity our said cousin your father) that the remedy rests upon ourself and you. To the end that everyone may know that we upon our part will not withdraw from it, we offer you to decide this our quarrel, with God's grace, by combat between our person and yours."

No answer came, and with 10,000 warriors behind him Henry led the way into the heart of France. Heralds approached him asking his intended route.

" The straightest," answered Henry.

Near Agincourt the French army barred the way, and were as six to one.

" Had we but one ten thousand of those men in England that have no work to do ! " sighed Sir Walter Hungerford, but the King cried out fiercely that he would not one man more than he had:

" Few are we in comparison with our enemies, but if God of his clemency do favour us and our just cause (as I trust he will) we shall speed well enough. If, however, for our offenses' sake, we shall be delivered into the hands of our enemy, the less number we be the less damage shall the realm of England sustain."

The night before the battle the French " made great cheer and were verie merrie and pleasant and

full of games as they diced for the prisoners they
meant to take on the morrow. The English too were
of good comfort and nothing abashed, yet they were
hungrie and wearie, and sore travelled and beset
with many cold diseases. So many wished to make
confession that there seemed to be not enough
chaplains."

Henry had selected his ground carefully, and in
addition to preparing an ambush of two hundred
archers he had sharp pointed stakes driven into the
ground to break the attack of the cavalry on his
archers, " who wore jackets long and easy to shoot
in so that they might draw bows of great strength
and shoot arrows a yard long ; their limbs were
at liberty, their hose being only fastened with one
point."

In the morning the French rested themselves,
" waiting for the bloudie blast of the terrible troumpet
till the hour between nine and ten of the clocke,"
but a herald approached the English line asking what
ransom Henry would offer when he was taken.

The taunt did its work. Henry cried out that
England should never be charged with his ransom
nor any Frenchman triumph over him, for " either
by famous death or glorious victory would he (by
God's grace) win honour that day. Do you not
think that God, with this scarcity of strength, can
vanquish the pride of the French, who are glorying
in their numbers and power ? " he asked.

Each army now maligned the other "till passions
were aroused and every man cried ' Forward ! '

" ' Now, in good time, for all England prayeth for
us. . . . Forward in the name of God and St.
George ! ' " came the battle-cry of the King.

The English army was " of a single line, their front
equal to the French, but the French were pressed for
room, and soon confusion ensued, yet sundrie of the
Frenchmen stronglie withstood the fierceness of the
English when they came to hard strokes, so that the

fight was sometimes doubtful and perilous. It lasted
three long hours, till the French, seeing the King's
intent to surround them, were suddenly amazed and
ran away like sheep without order or array."

Immediately the English victory was assured the
army was bidden to fall on its knees and sing the
Psalm of David " and other holy hymns, after which
all marched to the enemies' camp, where the soldiers
had liberty given them to take the spoil."

France had lost heavily. The lowest estimate was
10,000, the highest, " dukes, countless barons, ninety
lords, fourteen thousand gentlemen, and seven
thousand of the common sort. Of English there
lay dead some said twenty-six in all, others not
six hundred. A Miracle rather than a victory in
truth ! "

> " Now all ye toiling English rest and pray,
> Fair fell the victory on St. Crispin's Day,
> When France's envious power sank prone to earth.
> France who derided England's worth ! "

News of the battle " blew " into England four
days later, and there were " great praisings of Almighty
God, and bonfires and joyful triumphs for the fortunate luck sent to the King and his army." When
Henry reached England, he endeavoured to make
his enemies " better contented with their overthrow "
by giving " straight orders that no ballad or song
should be made or sung other than of thanksgiving
to God for the Happy Victory and safe return, all
without words either disgracing the French or extolling
the English." London in her enthusiasm presented
the victor with two gold basins, and Parliament added
a thousand pounds to the gift.

But even yet there was no peace, for France, despite
Agincourt, showed little sign of recognising Henry as
her King.

More ships were built and consecrated by bishops
at the public charge. The Lord Mayor lent money
on security of the crown jewels, the crown was

pawned once more, and after a public leave-taking at
St. Paul's Henry sailed again for France.   Town after
town fell before him, and France wavered when Rouen
was besieged.   The beautiful Princess Katherine was
produced as a bait,[1] and the King " was marvellously
taken with her, yet made no show of it till other things
should be agreed on."

Rouen capitulated, and peace proposals were renewed.   The war went on while terms were hammered
out.   Henry must be appointed Regent ; mentally
incapacitated, Charles VI was to retain his crown
during his lifetime, after which it was to descend to
Henry V and his heirs for ever.   The treaty was
signed at Troyes (May 21, 1420), and on the same day
Henry married Katherine while excitement flamed
high in England and Parliament ordered the making
of a new Great Seal on which the phrase " Regent and
Heir of France " was to appear after Henry's title.

The Dauphin, attainted and denounced, fought on
helped by Scotland, but Henry held Christmas court
in the Louvre before bringing Katherine to England
for her crowning.

Reverses to English arms in France interrupted
the royal progress through England, and Henry
returned to France for the last time.   Katherine
rejoined him a few months later, bringing her boy,
Henry of Windsor (Henry VI), and found the King
stricken.

" How long ? " he asked.

" Sire," answered an attendant, " you must think
on your soul, for unless it be the will of God to decree
otherwise, it is impossible that you should live more
than two hours."

[1] See *Her Majesty: The Romance of the Queens of England.*

CHAPTER V

THREE PRINCES OF WALES

EDWARD OF LANCASTER (SON OF HENRY VI AND MARGARET OF ANJOU).

" A goodlie, feminine, and well-featured young gentleman."

EDWARD OF YORK (EDWARD V), SON OF EDWARD IV AND ELIZABETH WOODVILLE).

" Christened and baptised with small pomp like a poor man's child."

EDWARD EARL OF SALISBURY (SON OF RICHARD III AND ANNE OF WARWICK).

" By the favour of God he will make an honest man."

EDWARD OF LANCASTER

Born at the Palace of Westminster	.	October 13, 1453
Created Prince of Wales	. . .	March 15, 1454
Contracted (at Amboise), Anne of Warwick	August 1470
Killed at Tewkesbury	. . .	May 4, 1471

Descent

Henry (of Monmouth) V — *m.* — Katherine of Valois
|
Henry VI
m. Margaret of Anjou
|
Edward of Lancaster

CONTEMPORARY SOVEREIGNS
IN SCOTLAND : James II and James III.
IN FRANCE : Charles VII and Louis XI.

EDWARD (OF YORK) V

Born in Sanctuary at Westminster	.	November 2/3, 1470
Created Prince of Wales	. . .	July 1471
Contracted to Anne of Brittany .	.	1482
Became King	. . . .	April 9, 1483
Smothered in the Tower of London	.	August (?), 1483

EDWARD EARL OF SALISBURY

Born at Middleham Castle in Yorkshire	1474
Created Prince of Wales	. . .	August 31, 1483
Died	. . . . .	March 31, 1484

Descent

Edward III — *m.* — Philippa of Hainault

Lionel, Duke of Clarence (3rd son)   Edmund of Langley, Duke of York (5th son), and others

Philippa
m. Edmund Mortimer,
Earl of March
|
Roger Mortimer
|
Anne Mortimer — *m.* — Richard, Earl of Cambridge
|
Richard, Duke of York

Edward IV   Richard III
| |
Edward (of York) V   Edward Earl of Salisbury

CONTEMPORARY SOVEREIGNS
SCOTLAND : James III.
FRANCE : Louis XI and Charles VIII

CHAPTER V

THREE PRINCES OF WALES

1453—1484

EDWARD of Lancaster, grandson of Henry V, was born to Margaret of Anjou [1] nearly nine years after her marriage with Henry VI, to the dismay of Richard Duke of York, who, in his nephew's childlessness, had seen the hand of God restoring the throne of England to the older line after fifty years of usurpation.

Rumour, inspired perhaps by Yorkist partisans, was quick to hint that the child was illegitimate, and the young Queen could find no help in the King, for the burden placed upon him in his cradle had proved too heavy.

At three years of age Henry VI had been carried in state to open Parliament, where he had " schriked and cryed." Five years later the crown of England had been set upon his head while he eyed the cheering people " sadlie and wislie," and in his ninth year his custodians took him overseas to be present at the trial of Joan of Arc, after which he was acclaimed King of France in Notre-Dame. Now, outraged nature had had her way ; the seeds of ancestry had come to fruition, Henry VI, " a prince no doubt of excellent parts in their kind, though not of parts kindly for a prince," was mentally unhinged.

When Margaret laid her boy across his knees he turned his head away.

Fiercely the Queen set herself to fight her traducers, and the baby was carried to his gorgeous baptism

---

[1] For her story see *Her Majesty: The Romance of the Queens of England.*

arrayed in a pearl-embroidered robe costing five hundred pounds. Three months later Henry VI was sufficiently recovered to realise the fact of his son's birth.

" And on the Monday afternoon the Queen came to him and brought my Lord Prince with her, and then he asked what the Prince's name was, and the Queen told him Edward, then he held up his hand and thanked God thereof, and he said that he never knew him until that time, nor wist what was said."

Once again Margaret began to rule in the King's name. Richard Duke of York was deposed from his position as Protector, and Somerset, whom he had arrested in the Queen's presence, was released and restored to office.

For a space people murmured, then forgot even the bad news from France, where almost all England's possessions were lost, for the King and Queen were young, and there were brave doings when their son was created Prince of Wales.

But the Duke of York believed that the country was going to ruin under Somerset, and would not rest quiescent. Salisbury and Warwick joined him, and they marched towards London determined to remove the Queen's nominee from power.

The first battle in the Wars of the Roses came at St. Albans (May 23, 1455), where the royal standard was pitched in the main street; it was little more than a scuffle, and lasted barely an hour. But Margaret, waiting at Greenwich with the little Prince, was to hear that disaster had overtaken the Lancastrians. Somerset had been killed and the King wounded—worse, he had yielded himself to the conquerors.

" Let there be no more killing and I'll do what you will ! " said Henry VI to Salisbury and Warwick as they knelt before him ; once again the unhappy King's intellect clouded and his body failed him.

EDWARD OF LANCASTER.
SON OF HENRY VI.
From a print in the British Museum.

Queen Margaret looked on helplessly while the Duke of York was declared Protector of the Kingdom and Defender of the King a second time.

Richard was the representative of the old legitimist claim to the throne on the part of the house of Mortimer which descended through the female line from Lionel Duke of Clarence, the elder brother of John of Gaunt ; he could also claim unbroken male descent from Edward III by Edmund of Langley, younger brother of John of Gaunt.

Queen Margaret, " a ladie of great wit and no less courage," realised the Duke's claim and believed that he was aiming at the crown. Unable to move directly against the league of York, Warwick, and Salisbury, she set herself to court popularity for her little son, carrying him about the country and setting him to distribute badges to his adherents. The King recovered, and once again the Duke of York was set aside. Four years elapsed while enmity smouldered between the rival factions and was fanned into a flame at Blore Heath (September 23, 1459), when Salisbury was forced to retreat.

The trio, York, Salisbury, and Warwick, joined forces speedily and in Worcester Cathedral took solemn oath that they meant nothing against the King or common weal. Henry offered a pardon to them as insurgents, provided they would lay down their arms, but few Yorkists had faith in royal promises. Then came Ludlow and a Lancastrian triumph.

A packed Parliament assembled at Coventry, (it was the first that had been summoned for three years), obediently passed a long bill of attainder against leading Yorkists, and recognised the Prince of Wales as the natural-born heir to the throne.

The Duke of York fled to Ireland, but his son, the Earl of March, took up the leadership in England, where discontent was rife. Northampton was fought (July 10, 1460), and Henry VI fell into Yorkist

hands once more. He was carried back to Westminster to open a Parliament which repealed all acts
and annulled the attainders passed at Coventry.
Having played his part, the King withdrew, and at
the second session the startled lords found themselves
face to face with a crisis, for Richard Duke of York
came demanding the crown as his by right of lineal
descent. If, contrary to all right, the throne had
been usurped by Henry of Bolingbroke and held
from the rightful heirs for half a century, it in no
way invalidated his claim.

After much debate a deputation waited on
Henry VI.

" My father was King, his father also was King.
I have worn the crown since my cradle ; you have
all sworn fealty to me, and your fathers to my
fathers," said the weary King.

The debate went on, and some men were for
Richard and some for Henry. At last a compromise
was reached, and it was agreed that Henry should be
allowed to retain the crown for the remainder of his
lifetime, but that Richard was to be declared Prince
of Wales and heir to the throne on Henry's demise.

King and Duke marched in solemn procession to
St. Paul's :

" In the name of God, I, Richard Duke of York,
promise and swear by the faith that I owe to Almighty
God that I shall never consent, procure, or stir,
directly or indirectly . . . anything that may redound
to the abridgment of the life of King Henry VI."

Henry signed the documents laid before him " to
eschew the shedding of Christian blood," and on the
following Saturday Richard was declared Heir
Apparent.

Men, talking of the new developments, told of two
omens : how a crown had fallen from the top of Dover
Castle, and another in the Parliament just at the
moment Richard was making his claim.

But if Henry had been brought to acquiesce in the

disinheritance of his son, the Queen had not, and there were still men willing to fight for the little Prince who wore the red rose of Lancaster.

After the disaster of Northampton Margaret had fled with her child, seeking safety first in Wales and then in Scotland, where, James II having been killed by the bursting of a cannon ball,[1] his son, a boy of about the same age as the Prince of Wales, was now King. The Queen-Mother, Mary of Gueldres, extended a welcome to the fugitives and gave what help she could.

Six months later Margaret raised the Lancastrian standard once more, and loyalists came flocking. Wakefield (December 30, 1460) brought disaster to the party of the White Rose. Salisbury was taken prisoner and beheaded, while the Duke of York was killed in battle ; his head decked with a paper crown was spiked above York's gate, where it stayed till his victorious son removed it.

Nineteen-year-old Edward Earl of March came marching in hot haste so soon as news of the tragedy reached him, and Warwick returned to the field. Mortimer's Cross gave them hope, but reinforcements joined the Lancastrians, and Margaret went into the second battle of St. Albans, while the seven-year-old Prince watched the trend of the day (February 17, 1461), saw Warwick defeated, and his father rescued from the enemy by his mother.

Young as the child was, he must have caught the spirit of the hour, for when, after the battle, the Queen asked him how the captives should die, he answered that they ought to be beheaded. As Sir Thomas Tyriel was led away to the block with his son he invoked the vengeance of God on those who had taught a child to utter such words ; but neither Queen nor Prince gave heed to curses. The day was won. Henry VI was King again and knighted his son on the battlefield, a gallant little figure in purple

---

[1] See *Their Majesties of Scotland.*

velvet and gold trappings. This done " they went
to the Abbey, where the Abbot and monks received
them with hymns and songs."

The Queen was eager to march on London, but the
troops were already out of hand, declaring that they
had attended her so far voluntarily, and now claimed
in reward the right to ravage the country north of
the Trent.

St. Albans lay at the mercy of the army, and London
feared. When the Earl of March arrived with his
disciplined forces he was hailed as a saviour, and
the people set up " a loud shout " when it was
suggested that, Henry having forfeited the crown
by his behaviour, Edward should be King in the
stead of his father, Richard Duke of York. A song
swept through the country :

> " Comfort al thirsty and drynke with gladnes !
> Rejoyce with myrth though ye have nat to spende.
> The tyme is come to avoyden your distress.
> Edward the Fourth the old wronges to amend
> Is wele disposed in wille and to defend
> His land and people, in dede with Kyngelye myght.
> Goode lyfe long, I pray to God hym sende
> And that Seyent George be with hym in his right ! "

A coronation was arranged in all haste, after which
the new King showered honours on his adherents
and created his young brothers Dukes of Clarence
and Gloucester. This done, Edward pursued the
retreating Queen, and overtaking her in Yorkshire,
fought Towton (March 1461) and left thirty-seven
thousand dead upon the field.

Henry, Margaret, and the Prince of Wales found
themselves fugitives. Scotland offered a temporary
asylum, and Margaret, bidding frantically for support,
agreed to relinquish Berwick, and urged a marriage
between her son and a sister of the King of Scotland.
But a fugitive prince is hardly a good match, and
Margaret of Gueldres hesitated, although she accepted
Berwick in exchange for a pension. All too soon,

Warwick scented danger, and hastened north to drop
the hint that a marriage between the Queen-Mother
of the King of Scots and Edward IV, reigning King
of England, might be more for the public weal than a
union with a landless child-prince.   So, when Edward
urged that " Henry, late usurpant King of our Realm,
Margaret his wife, her son, and other traitors and
rebels " should be yielded up to him, the desperate
Queen invoked the aid of France, pawning Calais to
secure a loan.   Intermittent war went on, ending with
a Lancastrian disaster at Hexham (May 1464), where
the troops melted away and the leaders were captured
and executed.   Afraid to remain together, the King
and Queen separated : Henry rode to Harlech Castle,
and Margaret hid herself and the Prince in Hexham
forest.   Wandering, exhausted and hungry, she encountered a robber outlaw.

" I entrust the King's son to your care," said
Margaret, making a bold appeal to the man's chivalry,
and laid the boy in the man's arms.   He rose to the
occasion nobly, hid mother and son in a cave, fed
them as well as he could, and finally secured them
a safe passage to the Continent.   Scotland was no
longer a safe refuge, for she had signed a permanent
truce with England and bound herself to discard the
Lancastrians.

The next few years were the happiest and most
peaceful Edward Prince of Wales was to know.   A
pension of £80 a year was secured for mother and
child, and despite their poverty a little court formed
about them.   Sir John Fortescue, erstwhile Chief
Justice of the King's Bench and now attainted, came
to help Margaret train her son for the high office
she still hoped he would one day assume.   The young
Prince studied the constitutional laws of his country
and became " a gallant horseman, expert in feats
of arms," while growing towards manhood.   Now
and then hope flickered up, but till news came out of
England of a definite break between Edward IV and

Warwick "the King-Maker" neither Queen nor Prince could see a real chance of success.

Now, when Edward IV had been driven off his throne, surely was the moment to strike! They appealed to France—but already Edward had escaped from his brief imprisonment and had succeeded in raising an army.

Then Warwick came to France, bringing with him a sore and angry heart and great ambition, and when King Louis interceded, Margaret, beating down her pride, agreed to meet him.

The King-Maker asked a high price for his help. He needs must have the Prince of Wales as husband for his second daughter, Anne Neville.[1]

" Never!" cried the Queen, and when Louis tried to persuade her to make the sacrifice she told him that a better match for Edward, and one hardly more bitter to accept, would be Elizabeth, daughter of Edward IV, and towards this there had been a move from England.

But Warwick was at hand, and Louis promised help. After fifteen days of struggle Margaret yielded, but upon terms. Warwick must restore the House of Lancaster to the throne, and till this dowry was assured Anne's marriage should not be consummated. Secure in his own power, Warwick agreed, and the contracting ceremony took place with great pomp, after which shrinking seventeen-year-old Anne, now to be known as the Princess of Wales, was given into the Queen's keeping.

Warwick sailed for England, and ten days after his landing Edward IV was in flight, seeking a refuge at The Hague while his Queen lay in sanctuary awaiting the birth of a child. Henry VI had been freed from the Tower and hailed as King once more. An obedient Parliament obliterated Edward from its memory and confirmed the crown on Henry's heirs for ever!

[1] See *Her Majesty: The Romance of the Queens of England.*

Margaret of Anjou, with the Prince and Princess of Wales in her train, entered Paris amid a whirlwind of enthusiasm scarcely disturbed by news that Edward was already making plans for a return. When he did sail for England it was as Duke of York, and his servants were bidden to shout loudly for Henry. So, till he reached Nottingham and had sounded the pulse of the country, then, finding himself received with enthusiasm, he flung off all disguise, unfurled the White Rose banner, and marched forward.

For fourteen days of storm and contrary winds the Queen with her son and Anne beat about in the Channel. They landed at Weymouth (six months after Warwick's triumphant *coup*) on the evening of the Battle of Barnet (April 14, 1471), and scared messengers brought word that the King-Maker was dead, Henry VI a prisoner in the Tower once more, and Edward IV riding in triumph to St. Paul's.

Lancastrian adherents found the trio at Beaulieu and were stirred to make a fresh effort by the presence of the young Prince, believing that the fact that he was among them would arouse enthusiasm, but fear-stricken Margaret answered that his life was too valuable to be risked at such a juncture, and he must be sent back to France. Almost eighteen, the boy rebelled against his mother and sided with the Lancastrian lords ; he must take his rightful place among them and share their danger.

A council of war was called, and the Lancastrians moved on to Exeter, Bath, and Bristol, hoping to make a junction with additional forces under Jasper Earl of Pembroke and secure a strategic position in Wales. Then : " about foure of the clocke in the afternoon they came to Tewkesbury, having travelled that night past and that day six-and-thirty long miles in a foule country all in lanes and stone walls, betwixt woods, without anie good refreshing, so that as well as the men the horses were right wearic." Too tired to go farther, the Lancastrians determined to abide the adventure God had sent them there, for well they knew that the King followed them very near at hand. And so came Tewkesbury (May 4, 1471).

Prince and Queen rode down the exhausted ranks, but no boyish valour nor woman's courage could avail in such a plight. The Lancastrian forces were routed and the Prince captured.

The Queen, " hiding in a poor house of religion," was told that her son had been killed in battle. Later came more detailed news. The Prince of Wales had been captured and yielded up to King Edward, who asked him how he dared enter the country with an armed force.

" To recover my father's kingdom," came the bold answer, and the furious King struck the boy with his gauntlet.

The Dukes of Clarence and Gloucester with the Marquis of Dorset and Lord Hastings were close at hand, and at a signal swords leapt from their scabbards and the young Prince " was incontinentlie and suddenlie murdered. . . . His bodie was homelie interred with the other simple corpses in the churche of the monasterie of the Black Friars at Tewkesbury."

A fortnight later the Yorkist leaders returned to London, and on the night of their arrival Henry VI died in the Tower, some said " by disconsolate of pure melancholy," but others whispered of murder, and named the Duke of Gloucester as instigator, if not culprit. The general opinion seemed to be that " only by being innocent as a Dove had Henry kept his crown upon his head so long ; but if he had had the wisdom of a Serpent he might have kept it longer."

Margaret of Anjou was taken prisoner and held captive till Louis of France ransomed her, and her spirit was so broken that she consented to sign the papers Edward IV put before her :

" I, Margaret, formerly married in the Kingdom

EDWARD V OF YORK.
From an old print. By permission of the Archbishop of Canterbury.

of England, renounce all I could pretend to in England
by the articles of my marriage."

As for the Princess of Wales, she disappeared.

Two months after Tewkesbury Parliament accepted
and swore fealty to the baby who had been born to
Elizabeth Woodville in sanctuary, at a time when
his father had been driven from the country.

This new Prince of Wales had been ushered into
the world by the humble attendant who officiated on
like occasions for any sanctuary woman needing such
service. He was christened and baptised " with
small pomp, like a poor man's child."

The forlorn Queen and her group of children,
with their few attendants, were dependent upon the
generosity of the outside world for supplies, and
might have gone hungry frequently had it not been
for a butcher of stalwart Yorkist leanings who sent
them a regular weekly supply of " beeves and
muttons " during the winter of Edward IV's absence.

Tewkesbury having been fought, the conqueror dispatched " comfortable messages " to Queen Elizabeth,
and followed these in person, eager to see his first-
born son and remove the whole family from their
ignominious surroundings to Baynard's Castle.

Having secured recognition and status for the baby
Prince, Edward appointed Sir Thomas Vaughan as
the child's chamberlain, and hereafter, wheresoever
the King went, went too trusty Sir Thomas, carrying
the young heir in his arms.

Soon the Prince became the darling of the people.
Caxton, who had just set up his printing press in
the Abbey precincts near the Sanctuary, dedicated
one of his first books to " my redoubted young lord,
my lord Prynce of Wales whom I pray God save and
increase in vertue . . . that he may come unto his
perfect age."

At three years of age the child had his own household, with his maternal uncle, Lord Rivers, as governor,

and the Bishop of Rochester as tutor, but still Sir
Thomas Vaughan remained in watchful attendance.

After careful thought a series of regulations was
drafted by the King " for the virtuous guyding of
the person of our deereste first-begotten sonne."

Edward Prince of Wales was to be aroused every
morning at a convenient hour according to his age,
" and till he be ready to receive no man shall be
suffered to enter his chamber except our ryght trustie
and well-beloved Earl of Rivers, his chamberlayne
and his chaplayne." Matins were to be said, after
which the Prince was to go forthwith to his chapel
or closet to hear mass there " and in no wise in his
chamber without good reason . . . and no man to
interrupt him during mass time." On holydays and
feast days sermons were to be preached before him.

Breakfast came immediately after mass, and
" betweene that and his meate," Edward was to be
occupied with such " virtuous learning as his age
shall suffer him to receive." During dinner, which
must be " honourablie served," improving stories
might be read aloud, and all conversation was to be
such as would incline the Prince to " virtue, honour,
and wisdom ; he must hear nothing that should
move him to vice."

After " his meate, in eschewment of idleness," my
lord Prince was to be kept occupied with his learnings ;
these finished, there might be shown in his presence
such " convenient desports and exercises as it
behooves his state to have experience in." Then
evensong, soon after which Edward was to " be put
to his supper and allowed such disports as could be
devised to make him merry and joyous." Bed by
eight o'clock, and no one in his chamber after nine
except those who were to keep him under sure and
good watch.

Further rules concerned the Prince's household,
which was to be selected with strict attention to
morals. None was to be " a customary swearer,

brawler, backbyter, commonhasorder or adventuror, or to use words of ribaldry . . . a grate officer of the household must be mulcted of 12d. if he uttered a loose word, a gentleman would lose 4d., a yeoman 2d., and a page 1d." As for any who came late for matins, " for such a one his dinner that day shall be bread and water."

It was strictly forbidden "to make debate" in the household, nor must any man " mistreat another, or his wife, daughter, or maidservant under payne of losing service," and at Eastertide " every man must bring writing or witness where he was shriven and when he received the sacrament."

The staff was to include a physician and surgeon "sufficiently cunning to keep the Prince in good health."

The sons of the noblemen and gentlemen of the households were to be the Prince's companions, but in no case were these " to be suffered in idleness or unvirtuous occupations. By the King's orders they were to hear mass daily and be taught in grammar, musick, and other cunning," also " the exercises of humanitie according to their ages and births."

On the administrative side the treasurer and controller were to make a weekly account of the expenses of every department and see to it that accounts were paid monthly. " The dutie of the principal officers of our sonne's household," decreed Edward IV, " is to see to it that their officers be exercised and kept to our sonne's honour. . . . Every man to give his due and sure attendance, no one to be absent without sufficient license, and such as have servants these to be personable, and able to stand in a man's stead and no children."

The wages of the rank and file at least cannot be called excessive. Those of the pantry were to receive as fees " all chippings and broke breads." The cellarer had the " void vessels of wine " and the butlers " worne cups and broken ale," for which they had to send "yeaste to season the bread in the Bake house."

The master-cook had agreed perquisites, and as for "the remnants of the kitchen it need not be rehearsed touching their fees," but "the purveyors of beeves and muttons and calves and lambs" were to have "the beeves' and muttons' heades and the rumps of everie beefe, and the entrails excepte the ox feete."

When five years old the little Prince for whom such thought had been extended was appointed Custodian of the Realm, for his father went to fight in France. At eleven he was betrothed to Anne of Brittany, and a few months later it was decided to set up a court for him at Ludlow, as it was hoped that "the authoritie of his presence there will refrain evil-disposed persons from the boldness of their former outrages."

Lord Rivers was still the Prince's governor, and occupied his leisure in making translations from the philosophers for his young charge, "carefully deleting evil stories and epigrams in disparagement of Ladies."

Before the tranquillising effects of the Prince's presence in Wales had become noticeable, Lord Rivers received a message from the Queen bidding him bring his charge to London under strong escort; the days of princedom were over, Edward IV was dead, and Edward V must needs be crowned King. A later message countermanded the order as to the escort, for Queen Elizabeth's caution had aroused indignant opposition in the Council. Who were the boy-King's enemies? Whom did she suspect of treachery? So asked one and another, and the Queen yielded, but repented before her son reached London.

Jealousy had been aroused long since, in that the Prince of Wales had been left in the hands of his mother's kindred "to the exclusion of others of better quality," and now the Dukes of Gloucester and

Buckingham resolved to remedy the matter, and that right speedily.

Lord Rivers was intercepted and arrested at Northampton, and the young King was met at Stony Stratford with the information that treason was rife among those he counted his friends. His protests of faith were set aside, and presently both Lord Richard Grey, his half-brother, and beloved Sir Thomas Vaughan were sent to join Lord Rivers. Neither tears nor regal rage took effect, and Edward V was forced to ride on in the custody of the Duke of Gloucester.

The child in blue velvet and the man in black entered London, and "the duke bore himself with such reverence before his nephew that it was seen none other could be so meete a Protector ! . . . And now began ambition to boil within the Duke of Gloucester."

Hearing what had happened, Queen Elizabeth fled to sanctuary once more, taking with her her second son, Richard Duke of York, and her five defenceless daughters.[1]

The Archbishop of York found the Queen sitting alone and desolate upon the rushes when he came to comfort her " in the best manner he could," by promising that if any other than her elder son were crowned King, he would himself crown little Richard Duke of York, " but he trusted the matter was nothing so sore as she took it."

Yet the Duke of Gloucester's men were keeping strict watch and ward around the Sanctuary.

Preparations for a coronation were begun, and presently the Archbishop appeared once more, coming as emissary of the Duke of Gloucester, who asked that Richard of York might be sent to be playmate to his brother.

" Can none other be found to play with the King but only his brother, which hath no wish to play because of sickness ? " asked Elizabeth.

[1] See *Royal Elizabeths*, by E. Thornton Cook.

But the Archbishop was in fear that the ruthless Duke might, if denied, violate the Sanctuary, " which had been hallowed by St. Peter in his own person 500 years before (accompanied by a great multitude of angels by night)," and so persisted until the Queen wavered.

" ' Faithful ye be, that I know well,' she answered, ' and I know well ye do be wise . . . but onlie one thing I beseech you for the trust which his father put in you for ever—for the trust I put in you now— that as farre as ye think I feare too much, be you well ware that you feere not farre too little ! ' "

The Council waited in the Star Chamber while the Archbishop did his errand.

" ' For my part I will never give him up,' said the Queen as her tears fell, ' but if you must needs have him, take him, and at your hands I will require him. . . . Fare ye well, my own sweete sonne—God send you good keeping ! ' "

" ' Dear nephew, welcome with all my heart ! ' " said the Duke of Gloucester when the child was put into his arms at the door of the Star Chamber.

And then, for reasons unexplained, the day of Edward V's coronation was postponed while untoward developments occurred.

At a Council meeting the Queen's name was linked with that of Jane Shore (one of the late King's mistresses) on a charge of sorcery, and Lord Hastings was arrested. Then a startling sermon was preached at Paul's Cross from the text " Bastard slips shall not take deep root," and a disturbed and indignant congregation heard that Edward IV's marriage with Elizabeth Woodville had been irregular.

Two days later the Duke of Buckingham delivered an oration at the Guildhall and advanced a claim to the throne on behalf of Richard Duke of York ; when Parliament met, the Yorkists had ready a roll proving the illegitimacy of the late King's children.

The little Princes in the Tower were too young to

realise the full meaning of the move even if Parliamentary news penetrated to their ears, but Queen
Elizabeth and her elder daughters, lurking in
sanctuary, looked at one another with blanched
cheeks.

And now a well-instructed deputation waited on
Richard, who had his answer ready :

" Since I perceive the whole realm is resolved by
no means to admit my dear nephews (being children)
to reign, and feeling that the succession justly belongs
to me as the indisputable heir of Richard Plantagenet,
Duke of York, my illustrious father, we are contended
to condescend to your importunities, and accept the
royal government of the Kingdom."

" Long life to King Richard the Third ! Long life
to Richard the Third ! "

A messenger was dispatched to Yorkshire in haste,
for a queen as well as a king must now be crowned,
and pale Anne of Warwick Duchess of Gloucester
was brought to London.

Twelve years before she had entered Paris to be
cheered as Princess of Wales, but the boy-husband
whose title she had shared had been killed at Tewkesbury, and the world believed that Richard of
Gloucester had been one of his slayers.

In the press of public events that followed Tewkesbury, Anne, a prisoner, had contrived to evade her
captors, helped perhaps by her brother-in-law, the
Duke of Clarence, who had no mind that she should
share his wife's inheritance. But Richard of
Gloucester, who had known her in childhood, sought
her far and wide, and, though she eluded him for
two years, he penetrated her disguise of a kitchen
maid at length and thrust her into the Sanctuary of
St. Martin's-le-Grand while he and his elder brother
argued their respective rights before the King.

Anne, nineteen years old, had been handed over
to become the unwilling wife of Richard, and the

mother of his son Edward, who at four years of age had been created Earl of Salisbury. He and she had lived mostly at Middleham Castle, where the boy had found happiness in riding over the Yorkshire dales. Now, having learnt obedience in a hard school—Anne came to play her part in the coronation pageant.

The little Princes were moved out of the state apartments in the Tower, and Richard and Anne took possession. Side by side, and barefooted, the new King and Queen walked from Westminster Hall to the Abbey, where " both put off their robes for the anointing, standing before the High Altar all naked from the middle up."

Immediately after the coronation the sovereigns started on a royal progress, and Lord Edward was summoned to join them, for he was now the son of a king.

In the Tower two forlorn little Princes languished under the rude care of " Black Will," " lingering on in thought and heaviness till that traitorous death robbed them of their wretchedness."

A second crowning was ordained. It took place at York, where, too, Lord Edward was knighted with great pomp, and letters patent were sent out creating him Prince of Wales, " his singular wit, wherewith (his young age considered) he is remarkably well furnished, do portent that, by the favour of God, he will make an honest man."

Weighted with jewels and wearing his demi-crown, the frail little Prince walked through York holding his mother's hand ; it was almost his only public appearance.

Richard's crown sat uneasily upon his head, and presently the Duke of Buckingham showed signs of discontent ; this increased when the King accepted the offer of a daughter of Spain as a future bride for the Prince of Wales.

When the rebellion came to a head, Richard meted out ruthless punishment, but the leven still worked.

The Elizabeths,[1] mother and daughter, still in the haven of sanctuary, took fresh hope, and before the high altar in Rheims Cathedral Henry Earl of Richmond, sole surviving scion of the House of Lancaster, took solemn oath to marry Princess Elizabeth of York and so unite the lines that the Wars of the Roses, which had cost the lives of 100,000 Englishmen, must end for ever.

The Duke of Buckingham was beheaded and Richmond put under attainder, but Princess Elizabeth worked and hoped, even when King Richard succeeded in inducing the lords to take an oath of fealty to his son and swear to recognise him as their supreme lord " in case anything should happen to his father."

Hardly was this accomplished before the " Ryght hygh and mightie Prince Edward of Wales " fell mysteriously ill and " died an unhappy death " alone at Middleham Castle.

Richard declared a nephew as his heir, and took steps to get the five Princesses of York into his own hands; it was rumoured that Queen Anne was dying, when he would marry Elizabeth himself.

But Henry of Richmond landed at Milford Haven, and, though Richard fulmigated against " the Welsh milksop," men flocked to his standard and he came marching to encounter Richard on Bosworth field.

" When the Earle had obtained victory and slain his mortal enemy, he kneeled down and rendered to the Almightie his hartie thanks, then, ascending to the top of a little mountain, praised and thanked his soldiers. . . . He commanded all the hurt and wounded to be cured and the dead carcases to be delivered to the sepulchere . . . then the people rejoised and clapped their hands, crying to Heaven, ' King Henrie! King Henrie! ' "

There had been three kings within a quarter of a century, and three Princes of Wales in less than fourteen years.

[1] See *Royal Elizabeths*.

CHAPTER VI

ARTHUR TUDOR, PRINCE OF WALES

" 'Tis a fine pastime to have a wife ! "

ARTHUR TUDOR, PRINCE OF WALES

Born at Winchester . . . . . September 19/20, 1486
Created Prince of Wales . . . . October/November, 1489
Married at St. Paul's to Katherine of Aragon November 14, 1501
Died at Ludlow . . . . . April 2, 1502

Descent

Edward III — *m.* — Philippa of Hainault

John of Gaunt (4th son)
m. (thirdly) Katherine Swynford (legitimised 1397)

Katherine of Valois   John Beaufort, Earl of Somerset
(widow of Henry V)
m. Owen Tudor   John Beaufort, Duke of Somerset

Edmund Tudor   — *m.* —   Margaret Beaufort

Henry VII
(Earl of Richmond)

Arthur (and others)

CONTEMPORARY SOVEREIGNS

FRANCE : Charles VIII and Louis XII
SCOTLAND : James IV
ARAGON AND CASTILE : Isabel and Ferdinand II

CHAPTER VI

ARTHUR TUDOR

1486–1502

" Of Arthur, Prince of Wales, by reason of his father's manner of education, which gave no lustre to his children, there is little memory ; only this remaineth, that he was very studious and learned beyond his years and beyond the custom of princes ! " So wrote an historian two hundred years after Arthur's death, but his birth was hailed with even more than the usual enthusiasm, for in his small person he united the rival strains of York and Lancaster.

His father, Henry VII, had held the blood-stained throne a scant four years, and with his Lancastrian blood he had inherited a bar-sinister. True, the line of Beaufort from which he sprang had been legitimised and given royal rank, but a special Act of Parliament had barred them from the crown.

Lancastrian feminists, ignoring the Act, saw Henry's mother, Margaret Beaufort, as true heir ; Yorkists murmured because Elizabeth of York was still uncrowned ; all united in welcoming the puny, prematurely born Prince, the first-begotten son of Henry VII and Elizabeth, daughter of Edward IV.

The child was christened in Winchester Cathedral with great pomp and the train of his baptismal robe was so long that " it had to be supported in the middle by a knight." A new silver font was hallowed for the occasion, and into this he was plunged bodily before being laid on the high altar, then, robed in crimson and gold, he was carried back to his nursery preceded by torch-bearers and trumpeters, " and for three days all the citizens were the King's guests that they might drink the Prince's health without stint." Wise men traced his descent back to the legendary King whose namesake he was—King Arthur of the Round Table, who had once held court in Winchester.

The world was quick to recognise the importance of Henry's son, and, hoping to cement a league between Spain and England, Ferdinand of Aragon and his consort, Isabel of Castile, sent ambassadors to suggest a marriage between their daughter and Prince Arthur before he was a year old.

The Spaniards saw the child first when he lay asleep in his cradle, and then in his royal robes. They were pleased, and negotiations went smoothly till Henry mentioned the dowry that would be required with his son's bride. The amount startled the ambassadors, who hinted that the Prince belonged to an upstart dynasty and for their part they could not understand how their master was willing to promote a marriage with one whose throne was by no means secure, " considering what happens every day to the Kings of England."

But Henry would not abate one jot of his demands. Katherine of Aragon must bring 200,000 golden crowns to fit her to be Prince Arthur's bride. And now, to show the envoys the Prince's full worth, he was displayed " stark naked . . . when they discerned such excellent qualities as seemed scarcely credible and wrote to Spain accordingly."

English ambassadors visited Ferdinand's court and were presented to three-year-old Katherine as she sat on her mother's knee at a bullfight. Finding her promising, a compromise was reached on the dowry question to the extent of agreeing that a quarter of the first instalment might be made in the form of jewels and plate, so the first of the many proxy marriages between Arthur and Katherine was celebrated.

ARTHUR TUDOR.
From a picture by an unknown artist at Windsor. By gracious permission of
His Majesty The King.

Henry VII was eager for the immediate delivery of the little bride and her possessions, but Isabel of Castile refused to yield up her daughter, and Ferdinand made it clear that he would not pay over a penny of the dowry while claimants to the English crown continued to jeopardise it by creating uprisings. Later, when Henry's position was more secure, Katherine should be delivered at the expense of her parents " provided with decent clothing and such ornaments as befitted her rank."

Henry submitted, but sent a request that the future Queen of England should be prepared for an English life—" she must be taught to drink wine, for the water of England is not drinkable, and even if it were, the climate would not allow of the drinking of it."

Meanwhile, there were brave doings in England. A Parliamentary petition and the birth of Arthur brought about the crowning of Elizabeth to the satisfaction of the people, and with almost greater pageantry he was created Prince of Wales. His procession increased in majesty as it travelled through London by the great waterway of the Thames :

First, the King's barge was royally prepared, and at Shene " in the morning after Mass and Breakfast the Lord Prince entered the said barge to be met between Mortlake and Chelsea by the barges of the Lords both ' Espiritual and Temporall,' which lordes in their own persones entered the Prince's barge, with knights and esquires, Kings-of-Arms, Heralds, and pursuivants, trumpeters, and mynsterals. . . . Next came the Lord Mayor in his barge, with all the crafts in their barges with banners and pinnons royally before. . . . At Lambeth the Spanish Ambassador joined the procession, and many merchants of their nation all in rejoycing of the Prince's coming.

" The crafts of London lined the way from the Brigge to the King's Bench in Westminster when the

Prince went to the King's presence in the Bricke Tour. . . .

"When it was night the Prince's bayne was prepared in the King's closet and in the entry between the Parliament Chamber and the Chapelle were the baynes of the erles and lords ; all the remnant were in the Parliament Chamber . . . and the King in his person gave them the Advertisement of the Order of Knyghthood. . . .

"In the Morn, when the Prince had heard his mass, he was . . . princely conveyed through St. Stephen's Chapel to the neither end of the steir where he took his horse. The remnant took their horses and the Erle of Essex bore the Prince's sword and spurs. And so they rode into Westminster Hall, the Prince foremost and the others following in the order of their Baynes, and before the King's Bench they alighted from their horses and so proceeded into Whitt Hall. . . . In tyme the King came. And when the King came the Marquis of Buckley and the Erle of Arundell led the Prince to the Presence . . . then the King gard on his sword and dubbed him knyght . . . and when the Prince had offered the Target and his spurs he went to the King's closet and put upon him his robes of estate. . . . He was led into the King's presence. . . . The Erle of Arundell and the Erle of Derby bore his cape and cornall and the Golden Rod, and the Ring of Gold. And the Erle of Shrewsbury bere the sword, pommell up. And there he was created as accustomed. . . . Then the King departing, the Prince that day kept his state under the Clothe of Estate. . . .

"All the other new-made knyghts sat along the one side of the Chamber and the Prince licensed them to eat their meete.

"After the minstrels had played, the officers of armes cried to the presence of the Prince, and Garter-Kyng-of-Armes gave him Thankings in the name of all for his Largesse, which was XXti pounds."

The new-made-knight and Prince of Wales had yet
to celebrate his fourth birthday.

While Henry VII put down uprisings and hunted
Perkin Warbeck, Queen Elizabeth added to her
nursery. Sisters and a brother joined Arthur, and
under the watchful eyes of Margaret Beaufort the
Princes were well tutored by Linacre, Bernard Andreas,
blind poet and Historiographer Royal, with an annual
pension of ten marks, and Skelton, the Laureate
whose especial pride was Henry. In after years he
was to write :

> " The honour of England I learned to spell,
> I gave him drink of the sugared well."

It was expedient that the boy should acquire
knowledge, for the King had decided that it would
be advantageous to have him trained to be Archbishop
of Canterbury.

For Prince Arthur, Latin was an important study,
since it was his medium of communication with
Katherine of Aragon, to whom, under the surveillance
of his tutors, he wrote dutiful epistles during the seven
years over which the matrimonial negotiations of
Ferdinand and Henry extended :

" Most illustrious and excellent Lady, my dearest
spouse. Truly these letters traced by your own
hand have so delighted me and rendered me so
jocund and cheerful that I fancied I beheld your
Highness and conversed with and embraced my
dearest wife ! "

A second proxy marriage had been accomplished,
since Arthur was now of an age to speak. It was
reported that he had acquitted himself well, " delivering the necessary responses in a loud and clear voice
when asserting his willingness to contract an indis-
soluble marriage with the Princess of Wales not only
in obedience to the Pope and his sovereign majesty

Henry VII, but also from his own deep and sincere love for the said Princess."

Year after year the King had reiterated his demands that Katherine should be sent to England, but always Ferdinand had procrastinated; then the day came when the Spanish Ambassador could write that England was tranquil.

"Now that Perkin Warbeck and the son of the Duke of Clarence have been executed there does not remain one drop of doubtful royal blood," he could assure his master, "the only blood-royal now being that of the King and Queen, and, above all, the Prince!"

Together with this news came a hint that Henry was preparing to break the marriage contract and wed his son elsewhere, so Spain, determined to prevent an alliance between France and England, agreed to dispatch the bride in the following spring, and to make assurance doubly sure Arthur was called upon to celebrate a third proxy marriage.

Katherine started, but took four months travelling from Granada to Corunna. Sailing thence in August (1501), she became lost to the world, for her ship was beaten back into a small port.

England and Spain were in acute anxiety before the Princess landed at Plymouth in October "with a puissant army of ships and accompanied by such a multitude of prelates, high dignitaries, nobles, and knights as heretofore had never been seen in England." She was received "with as much rejoysing as if she had been the Saviour of the World."

Henry outraged Spanish etiquette in his eagerness to see his son's bride, and Arthur, summoned later, discoursed with her through the intermediary of a bishop of linguistic attainments. A fourth espousal ceremony was a prelude to the continuance of the journey to London in separate cavalcades. Here there was tremendous excitement, for never before had a Prince of Wales been married in London, "so there were damsels of goodlie demeanour and lustie young bachelors of amorous countenance lining the streets and citizens standing on scaffolds from Grace Church to St. Paule's."

A raised stage had been erected in the Cathedral, and here, " when all things were set in order upon November the XIV (1501), then being Sundaie, the noble ladie was led to the said mount, and there Prince Arthur openlie espoused hir, both being clad in white, both lustie and amorouse, he being about 15 and she of the age of 18 or thereabouts. . . . After the matrimonie was celebrated the Prince and his wife went up into the choir and here heard a solemn Mass sung by the Archbishop of Canterbury with eighteen Bishops and Prelates all mitred. . . . Then a sumptuous feast and plentiful dancings and disguisings. . . . Howbeit, every day endeth and night ensueth, and so when the night was come the Prince and his beautiful spouse were brought and joined together in one bedd (though some say a grave matron was laid in bedd between them) and when morning came the Prince called for a drink, which heretofore times he was not accustomed to do. One of his chamberlaynes, marvelling, asked him the cause of his drouth, at which the Prince answered merrily :

" I have this night been in the midst of Spain, which is a hot region. . . . To have a wife is a fine pastime ! "

The wedding festivities continued : " there were pageants, prudent speeches, goodlie ballads, and sweet harmony of music on every side, together with martial feats and valiant justes and such fierce fights at the barriers as before that time no man remembered." These things accomplished, it was decided to send the Prince of Wales back to Ludlow, though not before Henry had laid hands on Katherine's dowry and haggling had begun, since the value set on her jewels in Spain and England differed considerably.

Officially, at least, all was going well, and the King wrote to Ferdinand :

" That we might observe the ancient customs of our realm we recently dispatched into Wales the most illustrious Arthur and Katherine, our common children. For although the opinion of many were adverse to this course by reason of the tender age of our son, yet we were unwilling to allow the Prince and Princess to be separated at any distance from each other. Thus do we show unto you, by this our letter, that you may understand our excessive love which we bear towards the most illustrious lady our common daughter even to the danger of our son."

But all too soon a frightened messenger came riding bringing " lamentable news " from Ludlow, and the King's Confessor was bidden break it to his master " in his best manner." Arthur Prince of Wales was dead, and the miniature court in Wales was bereft of its ruler.

Half a dozen years before Henry VII had drawn up instructions for the burying of a prince of the blood royal ; they were ready now for the funeral of his own son :

" If he should be carried he must be laid in a new chest covered over with damask with a cross of red velvet thereon . . . and an image as like the person as can be devised, and put on the image the same robes as he wore when he was crowned as Prince, with the circlet on his head ; and the image must be laid over the chest in a charre."

On the " foulest, coldest wyndyst and wettest " of days the funeral cortège started from Ludlow towards Worcester, and " so verie ill was the way that they were fain take oxen to draw the charre. . . . The herse was the goodlyest and best wrought and garnished that ever was seen."

There were sermons and doles to the poor wherever a stop was made, but at last the procession arrived at Worcester Cathedral, where " with weeping and

sore lamentation it was laid in the grave. The
orisons were said by the Bishop of Lincoln, also sore
weeping. . . . He sett the Cross over the chest and
cast Holy water and earth thereon, and his Officer-of-
Armes, sore weeping, took off their coates-at-armes
and cast them over the chest very lamentably. Then
the Comtroller of the Household, sore weeping and
crying, took the staff of his office by both endes and
over his own head brake it and cast it into the grave ;
in likeness did the Steward of the household and the
Gentlemen-Ushers. This was a piteous sight to those
who beheld it."

There was more " sore weeping " when the heir
of the Earl of Kildare came riding into the Cathedral
mounted on the dead Prince's charger to make offer
of the horse and armour, but at last " all things
thus finished, there was ordayned a great dinner, and
in the morning a proclamation was made openly in
that citie that if any man could show any victualles
unpaid that had been taken by any of the Prince's
servants they should come and show it to the late
Steward-Comtroller and they should be contented.
. . . Thus God have mercye on good Prince Arthur's
soule ! "

CHAPTER VII

HENRY TUDOR, PRINCE OF WALES

" Of persone he was Tall and Mightye."

HENRY TUDOR, PRINCE OF WALES (HENRY VIII)

Born at Greenwich Palace . . June 28, 1491
Created Prince of Wales . . February 18, 1503
Ascended the throne . . . April 22, 1509
Married (to Katherine of Aragon) . June 3/24, 1509
Died . . . . . . January 28, 1547

Edward III — *m.* — Philippa of Hainault
|
John of Gaunt (4th son)
m. (thirdly) Katherine Swynford (legitimised 1397)
|

Katherine of Valois   John Beaufort, Earl of Somerset
(widow of Henry V)
m. Owen Tudor   John Beaufort, Duke of Somerset
| |
Edmund Tudor — *m.* —   Margaret Beaufort
|
Henry VII
|
Henry (VIII) and others

CONTEMPORARY SOVEREIGNS

FRANCE : Charles VIII, Louis XII, Francis I.
SCOTLAND : James IV, James V, Mary Queen of Scots.
SPAIN : Ferdinand II and Isabella (Castile and Aragon), Joanna and
Philip I, Charles I (Emperor Charles V).

CHAPTER VII

HENRY TUDOR (HENRY VIII)

1491–1547

THICK and fast were honours heaped upon the unconscious head of Henry VII's son, Henry Tudor. Before he was out of his cradle he was appointed Warden of the Cinque Ports and Constable of Dover; at two years of age, had he known it, he was an Earl Marshal; at three, having been knighted, he was created Duke of York "with a fee of £40 per annum," and his fifth birthday found him Lord-Lieutenant of Ireland. The bestowal of the duke-dom was carried out with magnificent ceremonial, for the title had been in abeyance for ten years, or more (since Edward V and his younger brother Richard had been smothered in the Tower), and Henry was determined to impress upon the public mind the complete union of the York and Lancaster strains which existed in his children.

Now, having given serious consideration as to the best means of providing for the future of a younger son, the King appointed a group of tutors and bade them ground the babe well in theology, languages, and all such learning as would fit him to become Archbishop of Canterbury.

The intensive course was proceeding according to plan when the Fates intervened. Prince Arthur died at Ludlow, and eleven-year-old Henry became heir to the throne, and only to be displaced from that position in case of the birth of a son to Katherine of Aragon. In view of this possibility Henry was not immediately promoted to his brother's title, and

before the honour became his it was made evident
that the younger brother must inherit the responsibilities of the elder.

When Katherine had come to marry Arthur Tudor
she had brought with her the first instalment of her
wedding portion, for which a receipt had been
required from Henry VII.   In addition she had been
dowered with a third of the revenue from Wales,
Cornwall, and Chester.   Now, special ambassadors
arrived from Spain demanding the return of the
young widow " in the best manner," together with
her dowry ;   it was obvious that so much money
could not be allowed to leave England.   Indeed,
Henry took the view that Spain should have paid
up the full balance ere now.

While the bereaved Princess[1] retraversed her bridal
journey in a black-draped litter, Ferdinand and
Henry opened up a correspondence.   Spain made her
demands plain, but the King of England was tenta-
tively negotiating for another bride than Katherine,
who found herself stranded and held of little account.
Her letters became desperate in tone.   Since coming
to England she had had no money and had been
driven into debt, " and this not for extravagant
things," she added pathetically.   She had applied
to the King, but her tears left him unmoved, and he
asserted that he was under no obligation to give her
anything.   The very food she ate was provided " of
his good-will—and this because your Highness has
not kept promise with him in the money of my
marriage portion," explained Katherine to her father.
" I am in the greatest anguish in the world ! "
She had sold her bracelets to get herself some clothes,
" for I was all but naked."

Ferdinand's reply was to the effect that Katherine
must win the good-will of the King of England and
marry herself to his surviving son.

The struggle went on while Henry, now Prince of

[1] See *Her Majesty : The Romance of the Queens of England.*

HENRY VIII IN HIS LATER ARMOUR.
From an old print.

Wales, pursued his studies, composed " two goodlie masses," sang in the church choir, and practised the art of arms. Other brides were offered, or so the King affirmed, and now an Infanta of Portugal was favoured, and now a Princess of France.

Katherine was driven to sell her plate : " Although I let my servants walk about in rags, and they live in such misery it is shameful to think of, I cannot so much neglect my own person," she wrote to Spain, adding that she was dunned daily by her creditors.

Queen Elizabeth died, and Ferdinand's demands for the return or betrothal of his daughter grew more vehement, but a proposal that the King should marry Katherine himself was not well received, although Ferdinand was willing that he should wed another daughter, the recently widowed Juana of Castile. She was insane, but even if she remained so this would not interfere with her capacity to bear children, and in all probability marriage with such a man as Henry VII would effect a cure. There must needs be a little delay, unfortunately, because at the moment Juana's late husband was still unburied, since she refused to believe him dead. " But," wrote Ferdinand, " I shall endeavour to persuade her by degrees to permit the corpse to be buried " ; then he would advance matters promptly. For the moment, " it might produce an unfavourable impression " were he to press Henry's suit.

But the project came to naught and an amicable settlement was reached regarding Katherine's dowry. Spain agreed to abandon her claim for any repayment provided Katherine and Prince Henry were betrothed without further delay, and the balance of what had been promised to her as Arthur's bride should be handed over within twenty days of her remarriage, this to be solemnised when the Prince was fifteen.

Henry VII's children were well drilled to matrimonial obedience. Arthur had celebrated four proxy ceremonies without protest, Princess Margaret[1] had ridden north to marry unwilling James IV of Scotland, and now it was Henry's turn.

The betrothal was accomplished, but Katherine soon discovered that the new engagement did not better her condition, and although under the same roof the two did not meet for months at a stretch. She felt that her hold on the Prince was precarious, even though she did not know that in further obedience to his father's commands he had registered an official, if secret, protest against his betrothal on the ground that it had been contracted in his minority.

The date when the marriage should have been fulfilled came and passed despite Spain's protests, but as Prince Henry grew older Katherine's very maturity attracted him. As a boy of ten he had led her to her wedding with his brother, seeing her as a woman ; now her six years' seniority seemed less apparent, and he took to writing poetry :

" As the holy groweth grene, never changing hew,
So I am—ever hath bene—unto my lady trew ! "

Henry VII died, and Ferdinand sent a warning message to his daughter. At all costs she must marry the new King ; no other future was before her. If there were difficulties in regard to the accession he would send an army—ships, artillery, engines of war —indeed, he would come himself to assist him !

But no such drastic measures were necessary, for England was rejoicing that " the most learned Prince in Christendom " was now her King, and a stalwart one to boot.

" His Majesty is the handsomest potentate I ever saw," wrote one chronicler. " He is above the usual height, with an extremely fine calf to his leg and a round face so very beautiful that it would become a woman . . . for lacke of cunnying I cannot express the gifts of grace and of nature that God hath endowed

[1] See *Their Majesties of Scotland.*

hym with . . . but it is the prettiest thing in the
world to see him play tennis with his fair skin glowing
through a shirt of fine texture."

Soon there was rejoicing in Spain too, for, either
by reason of her beautiful eyes or on account of the
advice offered by the majority of the eighteen
councillors bequeathed to him by his father, Henry
VIII decided to marry Katherine, and that forthwith :

" When the funeral of the late Kyng was honourablie finished great preparations were made for the
crowning of the new Kyng, during which preparations
the Kyng was moved by some of his counsellors that
it would be honourable and profitable to his realm
to take to wife the Lady Katherine, late wyfe to
Prince Arthur, his brother disseased, least she, having
so great a dowry, might marry out of the kingdom,
which would be unprofitable to hym. . . . By reason
of which the Kyng being young and not understanding
the law of God espoused the said Ladie."

The marriage was a quiet affair in Fleet Street,
but there was no lack of grandeur in the arrangements
made for the coronation. The two rode out from the
Tower and through the city, which was all hung with
tapestry and cloth of gold, and all the " occupations
strod in their liveries, beginning with the leaste and
meane occupations, while last strod the Mayor and the
Aldermen." It was all very fine, for the goldsmiths'
stalls were " replenished with Virgins in white,"
and there were priests and clerks with crosses and
silver censers, and a company of esquires in " skarlet "
and nine beautiful children dressed in blue velvet
representing the nine kingdoms or provinces over
which Henry ruled or considered that he ought to
rule—England, Wales, Cornwall, Ireland, France,
Gascony, Normandy, Anjou, and Aquitaine.

Katherine herself was in white to signify her
virginity, and wore her hair " of a great length "
flowing down her back. After her came " six honourable personages on white palfreys and a chariot full

of ladies all apparelled in white cloth of gold, and then another chariot full of ladies of another sort."

As for the coronation banquet, " it was so plentiful that none of any estate did lacke nor any honourable or worshipful person go away unfeasted."

To increase the general rejoicing an all-embracing pardon had been proclaimed " except for two great extortioners, sometimes barons of the Exchequer " ; the execution of these was a pleasurable anticipation of the future.

There were masks and justs, all of the greatest magnificence. Always the deeds of greatest valour were performed by the King, and as the months and years slipped by Henry's reputation grew. Now he designed a new armour and now invented a plaster that would cure all ills. He was so devout that he would listen to five masses a day, besides vespers and compline in the Queen's chamber, and he was so gallant a dicer that his fame spread abroad, and men travelled from afar to toss a throw with him.

Early in 1510 a son had been born to the young royal couple, but the hastily created Prince of Wales only lived two months, and some shook their heads.

They forgot their forebodings when Henry sailed away to demand the crown of France. His admirals' flags were cloth of gold, and with him went " nobility, gentry, and others to the number of 100,000." The Battle of the Spurs was fought and won, Tournay fell before his onslaught—" a maiden town never before taken." According to the custom of the times the inhabitants ransomed themselves and swore fealty to the King, who, after " many solemn justings," returned to England, rejoicing in the news that a yet greater victory had been won in the north (Flodden, September 9, 1513), to cement a peace with France by marrying his rebellious sister, Mary,[1] to Louis XII when he most conveniently became a widower.

[1] For her romance see *Royal Marys*, by E. Thornton Cook.

Domestic affairs now claimed Henry's attention, for he " having been so much occupied by the need of Christendom, the accustomed good order of his household hath been greatly hindered." Rules and regulations of all kinds were drawn up under the King's vigilant eye :

"*Item.*—It is ordayned that such persons as be appointed to be of the privy chamber shall be loving together and of good unity and accord.

" *Item.*—The King's pleasure is that the said gentlemen shall have a vigilant, reverent respect to his grace, so that by his look and countenance they shall know what lacketh.

" *Item.*—The King's Barber shall be daily by the King's uprising ready and attending in the privy chamber, there having in readiness his water, cloths, knives, combs, sissors, and other stuffs as doth pertain for trimming and dressing the King's head and beard. And the said barber shall take special regard to the pure and clean keeping of his own person and apparell . . . without resorting to the company of vile persons or misguided women to the avoiding of such danger and annoyance as by that meanes he might bring unto the King's most royal person ; failing which to doe he is upon payne of losing his room and further punishment at the King's pleasure.

" *Item.*—For the better avoydance of corruption and all uncleanness of the King's house, which doeth engender infection and is very noisome and displeasant . . . it is ordayned that the three master cooks of the kitchen shall have by way of reward 20 marks yearly to the intent that they provide and sufficiently furnish the said kitchens of such scolyons as shall not go naken of or such vileness as they doe now, and have been accustomed to do, nor lie in the nyghts and dayes in the kitchen on the ground by the fireside, but that they, out of the said monaie, may be found with honest and whole coarse garments without such uncleanness as may be to the annoyance of those

by whome they shall pass, and so to be brought up
in the business as they, being chosen for that purpose,
may learn to be cooks. . . .

"*Item.*—Board wages to be 6d. a day for gentlemen.
Yeomen, grooms, and pages 4d. a day."

The years passed. Other children were born and
died, and the whisperings became murmurs that would
not be stilled :

"If a man shall take his brother's wife he shall
not leave a living child."

It was the beginning of the end so far as Katherine
was concerned. Her princely lover was gone, and
there remained in his place an arrogant King.

Wife succeeded wife, Wolsey rose and fell, England
clashed with Rome; Popes and Parliaments alike
were defied; nobles went to the block, churches were
despoiled, and his effort to unite England and Scotland
by marrying his son Edward to Mary Queen of Scots
deluged the northern kingdom with blood.

Henry died at fifty-five years of age, having
accepted from the Pope the title of Defender of the
Faith. He had been King for nearly thirty-eight
years and Prince of Wales for six. Except for the
brief weeks when his baby son had held this title
there was to be no other Prince of Wales in England
for a hundred years. Preparations had been made
for the creation of Edward VI, but Henry VIII died
before the letters patent were issued.

CHAPTER VIII

HENRY STUART, PRINCE OF WALES

"A Prince most excellent and hopeful."—SIR WALTER RALEIGH.

HENRY STUART, PRINCE OF WALES

Born at Stirling Castle . .	February 19, 1593/4
Created Prince of Wales .	June 4, 1610
Died	November 6, 1612

Descent

Henry VII — *m.* — Elizabeth of York
|
Margaret (and others)
m. James IV of Scotland
|
James V
|
Mary Queen of Scots
|
James VI of Scotland (I of England)
|

Henry	Charles (and others)

CONTEMPORARY SOVEREIGNS

ENGLAND : Elizabeth and James I
FRANCE : Henry IV and Louis XIII
Spain : Philip II and Philip III

CHAPTER VIII

HENRY STUART, PRINCE OF WALES

1594–1612

In the long line of Princes of Wales only two have been Scottish born, and these were brothers. Henry Frederick saw the light at Stirling Castle on a February morning (1593–4), and Charles (later King Charles I) was born in Dunfermline six years later —the last prince or princess of Scottish birth till Margaret, Rose of York, came to Glamis in 1930.

These grandsons of Mary Queen of Scots were the great-great-grandsons of Henry VIII's sister Margaret who had ridden up to Scotland to marry her unwilling bridegroom James IV.

When Prince Henry was born, " to the great joy of the Isle and of all true-hearted foreign princes, especially matchless Elizabeth," his father, James VI, was looking south with eager eyes, for he saw himself as Queen Elizabeth's successor, and she was sixty. It was obvious that the christening of this first-begotten son, a prince who should wear the dual crown of England and Scotland, must be celebrated with magnificence, so the Scottish nobles were summoned to decide the question of invitations and to have it pointed out to them that the Chapel Royal was in ruins and must be entirely rebuilt for the honour of the nation.

A free-will offering of a hundred thousand pounds (Scots) enabled James to convene all the artificers in the country and begin work.

The coping stone was swung into position, the walls were hung with tapestry, red cushions em-

blazoned with the arms of the illustrious guests
were laid in readiness, the ambassadors from Denmark, the States-General, Mecklenburg, and Brunswick arrived to be entertained at the King's expense
and kept in good humour by means of " rare shows
and singular inventions." The baptismal day came,
but, alas ! not the ceremony for which all were waiting.
This had to be postponed not once, but twice, and all
because the eagerly anticipated Earl of Sussex, who
had been appointed to represent England, made no
sign.

Elizabeth had procrastinated for diplomatic reasons,
then, knowing that her representative could not arrive
in Scotland until after the appointed date, had bidden
him wait at Berwick while he ascertained whether
James had permitted the ceremony to take place.
In such case he was to return south immediately,
bringing with him her undelivered gifts.

But the news out of Scotland proved satisfactory,
so the noble earl completed his journey, and the
February baby was prepared for his baptism on the
last day in August.

On the morning of the ceremony the ambassadorial
group was escorted to the Prince's chamber, where
he was discovered lying on a state bed. The " old "
Countess of Mar was in attendance, so " making a
reverence, she mounted the daïs, approached the bed,
lifted the Prince, and delivered him to the Duke of
Lennox, who rendered him to the Ambassador of
England."

Duly wrapped in a pearl-embroidered purple velvet
robe, Sussex carried the princeling to the Chapel Royal,
trumpets sounding melodiously before him, and there
followed a chosen band of nobles, one bearing the
ducal coronet, another a towel, a third a basin, and
a fourth a " laver of water."

And now the royal infant was handed back in order
of precedence from the Earl of Sussex to the Duke of
Lennox, from the Duke of Lennox to the Countess of

HENRY STUART.
From a picture by P. Van Somer in the National Portrait Gallery.

Mar, and she presented him to the Mistress Nurse in order that he might be offered what comfort was necessary during the delivery of two sermons, one in the Scottish tongue and the other in Latin " for the edification of the ambassadors."

These discourses concluded, the still unbaptised Prince made the transit of arms a third time till he reached the haven offered by the embrace of Sussex, when he was at last christened Henry, as by Elizabeth's command.

" Frederick Henry! Henry Frederick! " said the bishop repeating the names after the King.

A fourth passage of arms being successfully effected, the Prince was carried back to his chamber and the ambassadors took their seats, with the exception of Sussex, who " withdrew himself into the aisle while two gentle men of England advanced with basin, towel and ewer that he might wash his hands, which the nobility thought was strange."

All now settled themselves to listen to the Bishop, who gave thanks to God for the benefit of the sacrament just received, and to the ambassadors for their attendance, whereupon they cried : " God save Frederick Henry and Henry Frederick! By the Grace of God Prince of Scotland! "

The concluding ceremony took place in Stirling Castle, where the child was endowed with his hereditary titles, Prince and Great Steward of Scotland, Duke of Rothesay, Earl of Carrick, Lord of the Isles, and Knight of Renfrew, while a coronet was held over his head.

Largesse was flung from the windows to the cheering people, and the ambassadors made their baptismal offerings—jewels and gold from the lesser lights, and a chest of plate from Elizabeth.

To the indignation of the Queen[1] her first-born

[1] For her romantic story see *Her Majesty: The Romance of the Queens of England.*

son was taken out of her hands and handed over to the hereditary guardians of the heir of Scotland. Protest as she might, the King was adamant, and to secure the Earl of Mar in his charge drew up a warrant:

" In case God shall call me at any time, see that neither for the Queen nor Estates, their pleasure, you deliver him till he be 18 years of age and that he command you himself."

Other children came to claim the Queen's attention, but she never lost her sense of grievance; it smouldered while James struggled with his restless kingdom and its scantily filled exchequer. But, sore pressed for money though he might be, he returned a prompt answer to an emissary from the Pope, who offered to secure him sufficient funds to win the crown of England if Prince Henry's education could be directed by a papal appointee; it was impossible for him to hand his son over " to be nourished in that doctrine the truth whereof we ourselves have never been persuaded."

Virtue, or fixity of purpose, had its reward, for shortly afterwards Sir Robert Carey came riding post-haste to Holyrood, having covered the distance from London " in a shorter time than was ever done before on so great a journey." Elizabeth had died on a Thursday, and by supper time on Friday the news was delivered to James by word of mouth!

All Scotland realised that a dangerous duty lay before their King, and James took leave of his wife and children with considerable misgiving. His farewell letter to Prince Henry reminded the boy that " a King's son and heir ye were before and no more are ye now. The augmentation that be likely to fall on you is but of cares and heavy burdens." He enclosed a book which the Prince was to study well.

Nine-year-old Henry, who since his seventh birth-day had been accustomed to send his father a Latin epistle once a year, now copied out the congratulatory letter his preceptors set before him. This assured his

father that while he had "entertained no doubt
that the people of England would call his Majesty
to the throne, yet the unanimity of the decision gave
him incredible satisfaction." The duty performed,
he was set to study his book, and found that it was
a manual on kingship, and had been composed by
James "for the special benefit of my deare sonne
Henry, appointed by God (I hope) to sit upon my
throne."

The preface was in verse :

> " It should be your chief and princelie care
> To follow virtue, vice for to forbeare.
> Your father bids you studie here and redde,
> How to be a perfect King indeed ! "

James enumerated the princely virtues, " Justice,
Clemency, Magnanimity, Liberality, Constancy, and
Humility," and bade his son learn to know and love
God, to whom he owed a double obligation—" First
because he made you a man and next for that he
made you a little God to sit on his throne and rule
over other men. . . . The whole Scripture con-
sisteth of two things," he went on, " a command and
a prohibition—to do such things and to abstain from
the contrarie. Obey in both, nor think it enough to
abstain from evil and do no good. . . . Keep God
sparingly in your mouth but abundantlie in your
heart."

Henry must honour his parents ; " I grant ye we
have our faults which (privately betwixt you and
God) should serve ye for examples to meditate upon
and mend in your own person, but should not be a
matter of discourse to others."

He was to see that the nobility kept the law as
precisely as the meanest ; to guard the poor and
remember that when he sat in judgment he was
sitting on God's throne, and must sway neither to
the right nor the left. " Justice should be blind and
friendless."

The faults of all ranks and estates were discussed and advice offered regarding the making of wars : " First let the justice of your cause be your greatest strength and then omit not to use all lawful means for the backing of the same. . . . Choose old experienced captains and young soldiers . . . be severe in discipline. . . . Be slow in taking on a war and slow too in making peace ; an honourable and just war is more tolerable an evil than a disadvantageous peace."

There were hints on " indifferent things " such as clothes, table manners, the importance of bodily exercises, and mode of speech : " Be not sparing in your courtesies "—and a frank discourse on matrimony—" for marriage is one of the greatest occasions that a man doeth in all his time, especially in taking his first wife.

" Marry then a godlie and virtuous wife, for she must be nearer unto you than any other companion.   Flesh of your flesh, bone of your bone (as God himself said to Adam), and because I know not but God may call me before ye be readie for marriage, I will shortlie set down to you here my advice thereon :

" First of all consider that marriage is the greatest earthly felicity or misery that can come to a man.

" Keep your bodie clean and unpolluted and so give it to your wife to whom onlie it belongeth. . . . Be not ashamed then to keep clean your bodie which is the Temple of the Holy Spirit notwithstanding all allourments to the contrarie, for how can ye justlie crave to be joined to a good and pure virgin if your body be polluted. . . . Why should one be clean and the other defiled ? "   In connection with this Prince Henry was bidden to take warning by the example of his own great-grandfather, who, doubtless in punishment for his sins, had seen his two fair sons die and was compelled to leave his throne to a daughter.

But above all he must marry in his own religion.

This was " strait advice and difficult since the number
of princesses of power and account professing our
religion be very small, yet disagreement in religion
brings with it disagreement in manners . . . neither
pride ye that ye will be able to frame her and make
her as ye please !   That deceiveth Solomon, the wisest
King that ever was ! . . . Choose you a wife as I
advise you to choose your servants, that she be of a
whole, clean race, not subjected to hereditary sickness of the soule or bodie ; for if a man be carefull
to breed horses and dogs of good kinds, how much
more careful should he be for the breed of his own
loins ? "

History must be studied, and also the Scriptures
and the laws of the land.   " Study to know your own
craft, which is to rule your people. . . .
   " Banish idleness, the Mother of all vices."

While the young Prince conned his father's manual
and relaxed occasionally into childish games with
his sister Elizabeth or Baby Charles, a battle was
fought over his head, for, with James safely out of the
country, Anne renewed her demands for her eldest
born, and when denied gave way to such wrath that
she endangered her life, and an appeal was made to
James.   He had measured the mind of the English
and decided that the presence of his Queen and
her children would strengthen his position, so bade
Anne come south with Prince Henry and Princess
Elizabeth [1] ; she obeyed, and spent a leisurely month
travelling to London.

The Prince's first important public appearance was
at his installation as a Knight-of-the-Garter, when
he began to win English hearts ; a few years later
the people had so completely adopted him that few
remembered he was a native of the uncouth northern
kingdom.

For a short space Henry and Elizabeth shared a

[1] For her story see *Royal Elizabeths*, by E. Thornton Cook.

household, and the Princess nearly broke her heart when separate establishments were decreed. But Henry was heir apparent and had duties to perform. Already books were being dedicated to " England's Darling " and " The Hopeful Heir of Britain's Kingdom," and Oxford was requesting royal attention.

The young Prince was required to sit at his father's right hand and listen to " disputes " on such topics as : (1) " Do saints and Angels know the secrets of the heart ?   (2) Would it be lawful to kill a stranger and enemy who had been detained in a hostile port by adverse winds contrary to what had been before stipulated in a truce ? and (3) Do children imbibe the temper with the milk of their nurses ? "

As a reward for intelligent attention Oxford University gave her guest a pair of fringed Oxford gloves and permitted him to matriculate at Magdalen, where he supped " sitting alone in the midst of the upper table with the noblemen and courtiers in the middle of the hall and the Fellows and students on both sides of it."   There was a move to admit Henry as Master of Arts, but the King vetoed the project.

Foreign countries now began to take an interest in the heir to the double thrones of England and Scotland.   The French Ambassador went so far as to advise his master that it was a pity to neglect so promising a Prince, and suggested that France should pension those of his servants who were likely to influence him in the future.   Spain went farther, and presently negotiations began for a marriage between Henry and the Infanta of Spain, but fell through when Spain demanded that the bridegroom elect must be sent to her for upbringing in the Catholic faith. Later, another attempt was made to bridge the gulf, but when it seemed possible that an agreement might be reached it was found that Spain had pledged the elder Infanta in another direction and was now offering the hand of her younger sister. When England pointed out that the younger Infanta was but barely six years old, the sister kingdom answered loftily that " in the matter of great princes there were always inconveniences, and some usually much greater than the disproportion of a few years."

Henry wrote obediently to thank the English Ambassador for his efforts " towards bringing an addition to my fortune," and turned his attention to the enthralling subject of ships.

A vessel, twenty-eight feet long by twelve wide, had been built for him by the royal shipwright, Phineas Pett, and brought to Whitehall Stairs with ensign and pennant flying. Pett was aboard her, having been sworn in as the Prince's servant, and took his young master as far down the river as St. Paul's Wharf, where Henry broke a bowl of wine over his boat, christening her *Disdain*.

But all was not as peaceful as it might seem in England, and though the royal family received an ovation when it rode through London a few days before the opening of James's second session of Parliament, a band of malcontents was at work, and suddenly the country was startled by the discovery of " a plot of treason so damnable and foule that posterity will hardly think it true when they shall hear it."

Leading spirits among the malcontents had secured the lease of a cellar under the Houses of Parliament and had concealed twenty barrels of gunpowder amongst the coal with the object of blowing the place sky-high, when King, Queen, Princes, nobles, and members should have taken their seats.

At the eleventh hour (November 5, 1605) one going by the name of Guy Fawkes was discovered lurking in a dark corner, " and in his pocket was a piece of touchwood, and a tinder to light the touchwood."

Excitement flamed high, and there was a gasp of relief when it was reported that the whole gang had been captured and condemned to death. Some were hanged and quartered, others " merely executed in the Palace Yard at Westminster, to the great joy of the people."

Letters of congratulation poured in from all parts of the world, and one of those directed to Prince Henry came from the ten-year-old Prince Palatine who was later to marry Elizabeth.[1]

Christmas festivities helped to banish the affair from the minds of the royal children ; the three were together again, for Baby Charles had now been brought to England.

When a French bride was suggested for Henry, he discussed the matter with his sister, who promised her approval on condition that a double wedding was arranged so as to make her Queen of France when he became King of England.

The Prince's interest in foreign countries had been stimulated, perhaps by reason of the marriages that had been suggested for him, and he welcomed letters from travelling Englishmen, official or private. When one of his gunners found employment with the Virginia Company and sailed away to land at Chesapeake Bay, "where no Christian had even been before," he was encouraged to keep a journal for Henry's edification, and sent it back to him together with " a draught from James' River and a description of how, since the country seemed fruitful, they had taken possession of it in the name of his Highness's royal father."   Two years later money was raised for the infant settlement by means of a lottery patronised by royalty.

Prince Henry was growing up ; sixteen was old enough for knighthood, and Wales was asking for a prince. Fortunately, custom permitted a special levy for the expenses of the necessary ceremonies, for James's exchequer was bare, and the servants of the royal household had been left so long unpaid that they had forcibly stopped the Lord High Treasurer

[1] See *Royal Elizabeths.*

in his coach and refused to let him proceed until he promised to attend to their grievances. Their success had fired the purveyors of the Prince's household, and these were threatening to cut off supplies unless he would press their demands for arrears upon the Treasury.

Oxford and Cambridge responded to the call, a reasonable amount was raised, and a tilt was decreed at which the Prince was expected to perform such feats of arms as would prove him worthy of the honours to be accorded him. With seven companions he held the barriers from ten o'clock at night till 3 a.m., withstanding " 32 pushes with the pike and upwards of 350 strokes with the broadsword in beating off 56 knights," to the jubilation of the crowds and the admiration of foreign ambassadors ; those of France and Spain outvyed each other in the courtesies they showered upon the young champion.

The letters patent for his creation as Prince of Wales had now been issued, and a wave of loyal enthusiasm swept London, for not the oldest inhabitant could remember the creation of the last prince.

Henry came up the river from Richmond, and spectators crowding the banks watched him as he met the city companies in their fifty stately barges at Chelsea, and received addresses and orations from two beautiful maidens, the one riding a whale and the other poised upon a dolphin.

There were great festivities in Whitehall and Westminster too, for twenty-four knights had been created in honour of the occasion. These had arrived at Durham House in the Strand, there to pray, sup, and bath before the ceremony of investiture. A separate bathing-tub had been provided for every knight, " each lined within and without with white linen and a ticket with every man's name was put upon his tub very orderlie." After the tubbing came a day of prayer and then knightly ceremonies.

Both Houses were assembled, and when the Prince made his appearance, clad in purple velvet and preceded by Garter King-at-Arms bearing the letters patent, he was accompanied by the four-and-twenty new-made knights. There followed a magnificent banquet at Whitehall, when the table, being very long, was served with two dishes of meat, and so much ceremony was shown the Prince that he who sat nearest his royal highness was fully half the distance of the board from him. Next day there was a tilt, and at night naval triumphs on the river with fireworks, " all without the least accident."

The Prince was now formally established in a household of his own with a retinue of 500 persons and an income ; his popularity increased rapidly, and St. James's was soon " gloriously attended with young and sprightly blossoms."

Adam Newton, who had been tutor, now became secretary, despite a warning from Salisbury that such advancement was dangerous, " though judged by his face he is honest if poor, which last could be amended if he but had a fee for every virgin in England who wisheth the Prince of Wales her maidenhood ! "

With a new weight of responsibility upon his young shoulders, Henry decreed that a survey of his resources should be made, and drew up careful rules for the conduct of his household, which he meant to have well ordered.

All " ragged and unsweet persons " were warned to keep away, and the grooms-of-the-chamber were bidden to apparel themselves handsomely, nor approach their Prince with doublets unbuttoned nor hose untied.

Those whose duty it was to lie on the pallets in the privy chamber were to rise early and see to it that the hall was " well strawed, aired, and made clean " before the Prince appeared. The gentlemen ushers were required to prevent any lewdness in the presence of their royal master, nor let anyone press too near him.

Unemployed persons must be ejected from the chamber when the Prince dined, and no attendant was to be permitted to lodge any boys, lackeys, or sick persons, nor such as have not " a shift of linen."

There was to be no bribery nor extortion, and every member of the household was required to take the sacrament four times a year under pain of dismissal, " and if he took it twelve times it would be better."

Bad language was prohibited, and boxes were placed about the palace for the fines collected from utterers of oaths ; the money was to be distributed to the poor.

Other rules affected the stables. Those who purloined hay or girths were to be punished, and any who drew women to haunt the stables were to be dismissed after warning, as were " night walkers, drunkards, quarrellers, disobedient and disorderly persons, upon proof of the quality of their offence, except there be an appearance of amendment."

Above all—" none shall be a busybody to raise dissensions."

Those connected with the commissariat were to know that an ox for the Prince's household should weigh 600 lb. and " cost commonlie £9. 10 or thereabouts." A mutton should be of 44 or 46 lbs. and 2/3 per stone of 8 lb. was the correct price. As for " veals, these go not by weight but by goodness. Price about 27/- and lambs 5/8."

Such matters adjusted, the Prince could give his attention to public affairs. He went with the King to Deptford to witness the launching of a ship for the West Indies, " a great vessel of 1,200 tuns," which James christened *Trade Increase*, leaving Henry to baptise the pinnacle as " Peppercorn."

A red-letter day was that when he was deputed to go to Woolwich and inspect the progress made in shipbuilding and the state of the navy. It was no casual tour, for Henry went armed with a notebook, but the most joyful moment came when, all unsuspecting, the Prince stood on the poop of the largest ship, and the Master Gunner of England discharged the whole volley of thirty brass cannon which had been brought from the Tower for the occasion. So impressed was the Prince that he asked for a repeat volley, but this was considered too great a risk to run a second time, so Phineas Pett persuaded his master to descend into his barge, whence, in greater safety, he could signal with his handkerchief when the cannon should be fired.

Prince and mariner had formed a friendship, and when later Pett was accused of misappropriating naval funds Henry stood by his side during the trial, and, judgment being delivered in his protégé's favour, declared that the accusers deserved hanging.

Other projects to which this young Prince of Wales gave attention were the building of ships in Ireland, " vessels of 100 to 600 tuns to be delivered at a cost of £5 a tun," and the discovery of the north-west passage. Pett was bidden to select suitable ships for this purpose, and the Prince watched them sail victualled for a voyage of eighteen months.

The question of a bride was now becoming urgent. Spain was out of favour, so France seized the opportunity to offer her King's sister.

Prince Henry was sounded on the subject, but showed acquiescence rather than enthusiasm. He felt " no particular affection move him, but desired that the state should be well served." If the marriage was agreed on, he urged that the Princess should be delivered promptly, since there would be the greater likelihood of her conversion.

These ideas were advanced with diffidence, " since it was fitter for his majesty to decide upon the course to be taken by rules of States than for me who am so little acquainted with subjects of this nature. . . .

Besides, my part, which is to be in love with any one of them, is not yet at hand."

Unfortunately, as the negotiators admitted, " the Lady cannot be made riper than her age permits, which is no more than nine years."

The project grew less pleasing in the eyes of Prince Henry when Elizabeth was betrothed to Frederick V, Count Palatine of the Rhine, for brother and sister began to dream of how one might ride with the other upon her wedding journey and choose a bride for himself from Germany.

But hardly had Henry given the first welcome to Frederick when the illness against which he had been struggling for some weeks could no longer be hidden. He fainted at a Guildhall banquet, and a frightened people learned that their favourite had " fallen sick of the popular malignant fever."

Rival doctors differed as to methods. One democrat boldly insisted that the patient's rank must be forgotten, and that, if not accorded such treatment as would be given an ordinary person, the Prince must die ; and as they argued the Prince raved in delirium.

A cock was " cloven on the block " and applied to the soles of the patient's feet, but all without effect.

In desperation, the Queen applied to Sir Walter Raleigh, who, from his prison in the Tower, sent a potion guaranteed to cure " unless the patient hath been unfairly dealt with."

Henry died, and as usual people cried that he had been poisoned. Some whispered of the King's jealousy of the Prince's popularity ; others hinted that Somerset had feared him as a rival in love. Had he been done to death by means of poisoned grapes or deadly perfumed gloves ? But the wise shook their heads and told how they had foreseen disaster since King James had removed his mother's remains from Peterborough, so dooming to an untimely death some younger member of the royal family—Prince

Henry had fallen victim because he had never shed his first teeth.

Two thousand mourners followed the Prince to his grave and listened to the blast of the trumpeters, crying :

" Long life to his next brother, his highness Prince Charles ! "

CHAPTER IX

CHARLES STUART, PRINCE OF WALES
(CHARLES I)

". . . the most Illustrious flowering Bud of many Kingdomes' Royall Blud."

CHARLES STUART, PRINCE OF WALES

Born at Dunfermline . . .	November 19, 1600
Created Prince of Wales at Whitehall .	November 3, 1616
Crowned at Westminster . . .	February 2, 1625
Married at Canterbury (to Henrietta Maria)	June 24, 1625
Crowned at Holyrood . . .	June 15, 1633
Executed in Whitehall . . .	January 30, 1649

NOTE.—For descent, see Henry Stuart, p. 124.

CHAPTER IX

CHARLES STUART, PRINCE OF WALES
(CHARLES I)

1600–1649

CHARLES STUART, son of King James I and Anne of
Denmark, occupied a very small share of public
attention until the death of his elder brother Prince
Henry. Delicate health and retarded physical development had handicapped him, as had the fact
that he had been left behind in Scotland when his
father came to claim the crown of England. It was
not until a twelvemonth later that the younger son
was brought south by a doctor who had been sent
to cure him of some infantile ailment. Advertisement
was as potent in the seventeenth as in the twentieth
century, so, as the result of royal patronage, this
doctor's practice increased " by leaps and bounds,
enabling him to acquire greater wealth than is usual
with physicians."

In his babyhood Charles was no Prince to be displayed with pride. At four years of age he could
not walk and stood alone with difficulty ; his joints
were so loose that his ankles seemed dislocated.

There had been manœuvring and string-pulling
among the ladies of the court who had hoped to be
entrusted with the charge of the Prince, but when
they saw his delicacy " they judged him unlikely to
live," and on his being given into Lady Carey's hands
her enemies rejoiced, thinking that so soon as the
feeble nursling died, she and her husband would be
driven from court in disgrace.

Shocked by the sight of his little son, James was

for taking drastic steps to cure his ills. The child's limbs must be encased in iron to strengthen them and the " spring " beneath his tongue should be cut to hasten his halting speech. But Lady Carey was a woman of character and a seventeenth-century devotee of the nature cure; the King was persuaded to let her have her way, and the Prince began to develop. When he passed out of Lady Carey's hands at eleven years of age he was normal.

But state ceremonies cannot always be delayed, and when soon after the little Prince's arrival at court James decided to follow the precedent created by Henry VII—knight his second son and create him Duke of York—Charles had to play his part in the pageant from the haven of the Earl of Nottingham's arms, and another tongue than his uttered the knightly oath :

" I shall fortify and defend the true Christian religion.

" I shall be loyal and true to my sovereign lord the King's Majesty.

" I shall fortify and defend Justice . . . and that without favour or fear.

" I shall defend my native realm from all aliens and strangers. . . .

" I shall defend the just actions and quarrels of all Ladies of honour and of all true and friendless widows and orphans and of maidens of good fame. . . .

" I shall do diligence whenever I hear there is any murderer, traitor, or any that oppresseth the King's lieges. . . .

" I shall maintain and uphold the Noble Order of Chivalry. . . .

" I shall seek to have knowledge and understanding of all the articles and points enumerated in the Book of Chivalry."

Serious attention was now paid to the education of the small duke, and a tutor was appointed, part of whose stipend was in the form of authority to collect

CHARLES I.
From a picture by D. Mytens in the National Portrait Gallery.

debts due to various attainted and deceased persons,
and presently Charles was able to write attractive
letters :

" SWEET FATHER,
        " I learn to decline substantives and adjectives;
give me your blessing. . . . I am now reading the
Conversations of Erasmus, from which I am sure I
can learn both the purity of the Latin tongue and
elegance of behaviour."

So, gradually he made his way, and was ready
to take his brother's place in the hearts of the people
and to stand by Princess Elizabeth's side when, the
tears for her lost brother hardly dry, she married the
Elector Palatine.

At twelve years of age Prince Charles was appointed
Lord High Admiral of England for life, " with all the
profits arising therefrom except pirates goods," and
this enabled him to set up a household of his own,
whereupon he showed himself a sporting prince by
engaging only such footmen as had secured honours
in running.

" Never was there a braver prince nor one more
fitted to command," said the crowd approvingly as
they watched him at the tilt.

" Charles," said his delighted father, " can manage
a point in theological controversy with the best-
studied divine of you all ! "

And hearing of the many attributes of the King's
son, Wales hinted that she had now been some years
without a sovereign prince, and felt it time that the
deficiency was made good.

The ceremony took place and the citizens had their
water-pageant, but in court circles the affair was not
a success. The Queen was still grieving for lost
Prince Henry, and refused to be present, the Bishop
offered up a prayer for the dead Prince instead of the
living, and the knights new-made in honour of the

event contrived to offend the wives of London's leading citizens at the Guildhall banquet, and it was complained that the forty noble gentlemen of the Inns of Court who had been appointed to exchange blows in honourable combat had acquitted themselves indifferently well at the barriers, though all agreed that they had played the man's part at the subsequent feast.

Simultaneous celebrations in honour of the " joyfull creation " were held at Ludlow and went better. Charles's name as Prince of Wales was inscribed on the gates of the town, in the churches, and on the posts in the market square. Proceedings began at nine in the morning with a parade of the magistrates and burgesses " verie richlie clad " ; all walked in a procession led by the church choir, singing psalms and escorted by two hundred soldiers with corselets and muskets, the lieutenants and sergeants being bravely arrayed. The free scholars gave recitations, and there was a great volley of shot " and such a noyse of drummes and sound of trumpets, flutes and other instruments as the like in these parts hath not been seen," and then " a verie learned sermon an hour-and-a-half long," after which every one joined in song :

> " Thrice blessed by thy heavenly Providence
> That gav'st a Prince of such magnificence,
> Who is the most Illustrious flowering Bud
> Of many famous Kingdomes' Royall Blud
> And our Great Britaine's hopefull ornament."

All Ludlow assembled on the castle green to call down blessings on the head of the eleventh Prince of Wales and wish him long life, royal issue, and happy days for the good welfare of our Church and Commonwealth, whereupon, " all the people with a loud voice prayed and cryed ' Amen ! Amen ! ' " and another volley of shot was let fly, when, being nearly one o'clock, all adjourned to dinner.

An account of the solemnisation which had been held for " the Glory of God, the honour of the King and the Prince of Wales, and to testify to the loyalty and hearty joy of his majesty's loving subjects " then assembled was despatched to London, where it must have seemed as a flicker of sunlight among gathering clouds. Negotiations for a marriage between Prince Charles and a sister of Louis XIII of France had been set afoot some time before, but even while these were in progress James was attracted to the idea of a Spanish match. There were secret messages, difficulties of all kinds, a break with France, and impossible demands made by Spain on behalf of Catholics in England. Catholics and Protestants were at variance on the Continent too, where Princess Elizabeth had been crowned Queen of Bohemia. Her reign was brief—civil war broke out and spread; this danger, together with home difficulties, forced James to summon a Parliament, which met in no easy mood after an interregnum of six years.

In the speech from the throne the King pointed out that his son, Prince Charles, now sat among them, and hoped that " ye, with him, shall have the means to make this the happiest Parliament that ever was in England . . . and when it shall please God to set him in my place," added James, " he will remember that he was once a member of your House and so be bound to maintain all your lawful privileges and like the better of you all the days of his life."

Work was found for the Prince immediately, for when the Chancellor, Francis Bacon, was impeached, Charles was appointed to lead a deputation to his father asking that the seals of office should be sequestered. He returned to report that his majesty had " most willingly yielded."

Commons and Lords were equally busy these days, for there was a scarcity of money in the land, " for want of which men are as it were . . . turned out of the inheritance of their hands " and lay idle. Every member had his remedy, and day after day they argued on the means to be taken to restore prosperity to England. "One cried that it could be done if instead of importing tobacco from Spain we brought it from places which are under the protection of our King . . . for thereby we shall enrich those countries under our dominions and also ourselves. . . . Another rose to bid us take example from France : ' There is an edict at Rochelle that none shall import any Gascoign wine into their town until their own country wines are sold, and yet we permit other countries to import into our Kingdom foreign corn, to the great hindrance of the sale of that which is grown here ! ' " Could they have known it, other members of Parliament were to speak to the same effect three hundred years later.

But Prague fell, the King and Queen of Bohemia were put to flight, and Spain invaded the Palatinate, and an unwary citizen, blind to the trend of feeling, aroused the nation by uttering "false, malicious, and spiteful speeches against the King's daughter," Elizabeth. He was hauled to the bar of the Commons and sentence passed upon him for "scandalising the Princess." The culprit was bidden to ride from Westminster to the Exchange, "sitting upon a horse without a saddle, with his face backwards towards the horse's tail, holding the tail in his hand, there to stand upon the pillory for two hours ! " The performance was to be repeated on the following day in another part of the city, after which the sinner was fined a thousand pounds and consigned to the Fleet.

With the House in such a mood it was not surprising that it showed enthusiasm for a war with Spain when that Catholic power threatened Protestantism in the form of the Elector Palatine, and voiced its disapproval of the Spanish marriage proposal.

From his court held at Newmarket an indignant King indited a letter to the Speaker bidding him " acquaint the House with our pleasure that none

therein shall presume to meddle with anything concerning our government or the mysteries of state,
namely, not to speak of our dearest son's match with
a daughter of Spain."

The letter was read aloud, and a disturbed Parliament decided that its members were " not fit to debate
this thing until we have considered of it and digested
it." This was agreed, but one member pointed out
that the House must not rise " as in discontent, but
rather resort to prayer and then come to the consideration of this great subject."

Resolute in his determination not to be thwarted,
James gave his consent to a romantic project.
Charles should go to Spain, persuade that country
to see reason in her demands, and bring back the
bride. The Prince was eager, for a good report of
the Infanta had been received—" her face," it was
said, " had a contour that showed her to be well-
born—without one ill-feature. Her figure is perfect,
and some say that before she is dressed she is incom-
parably better than after. To sum up, she is straight
and well bodied and as good as she is beautiful, since
she spends three to four hours daily in prayer. . . .
A likely ladie to make a prince happy."

Donning false beards as a disguise, Prince Charles
and the Marquis of Buckingham set off together,
dubbing themselves Thomas and John Smith—and
aroused immediate suspicion by giving a ferryman
too large a tip ! Riding on, they encountered the
French Ambassador travelling up from Dover and
had to take to the fields to avoid recognition. At
Canterbury the authorities threatened to arrest them
as evil-doers, and the situation required all Buckingham's tact. Then came a tempestuous crossing and
the long ride to Paris, where Charles caught a glimpse
of the Queen and saw little Princess Henrietta Maria
practising her dancing steps.

" ' Sweete Boyes,' wrote James, ' News of your
going has already so blown abroad as I am feared

for your safety and post this bearer after you who will give you best advice as to your journey. God bless you both, my sweete babes, and send you a safe return.'"

So with a single postilion the two set off again, and ten days later rode into Madrid, where they went straight to the house of the English Ambassador. "Mr. Thomas Smith" entered with his portmanteau under his arm while "Mr. John Smith" lurked across the way until his identify was explained, when the Ambassador fetched him in in haste.

Presently the two were writing exciting letters home. Madrid was seething with rumours; they had had to discover themselves and had been well received. The Count of Olivares was to escort them to the King, "who longs and dies for a sight of our woer." Indeed, the Spanish monarch was so delighted at the trend of events that it was said he had sent a dispatch to the Pope begging for the necessary dispensations to enable the marriage to take place, since he felt that he could deny King James's son nothing in his kingdom; if the papal decree were not forthcoming and the Infanta was therefore debarred from becoming Charles's wife, "they will give her to him as his wench," wrote Buckingham in triumph.

Charles was asking for a sight of the Infanta, but it was pointed out to him that this was difficult, "since it was Lent," but as he reiterated his entreaties it was arranged that the Spanish royal family should drive down a road whereon he might take up a position in a closed coach, and that the Infanta should wear a blue ribbon on her arm for purposes of identification. The plan was carried through, the Spaniards being better than their word, since the blushing Infanta passed three times, and Charles confessed himself thrilled by her beauty. "All he ever yett saw is nothing to her," reported Buckingham.

Interchanges of visits were arranged despite diffi-

culties of etiquette and questions of precedence. The
King of Spain and the Prince of Wales walked hand
in hand, and the Queen showered presents upon him,
an " embroidered night-gowne " among other things.
There were fireworks at night, bull-fights by day, and
showers of Spanish blessings on Charles's head whenever he appeared ; the King of Spain gave him a
golden latch-key to the Palace, and issued a command
that the Marquis of Buckingham should be served
" with a full and generous diet."

Charles wrote accounts of happenings to his " Dere
Dad," and James replied that he was making ready
ships and looking out jewels as presents to the Infanta
and also for Charles to distribute as gifts, for he must
be " as sparing as you can in your spending there, for
God knows my coffers are already drained." He
implored " my Babie " to " take heed of being hurt
if you run at tilt," and described how the bells of
London had rung merrily and there were bonfires in
the streets when the news of his safe arrival in Spain
had reached England.

The foundation stone of St. James's Chapel was
laid—for the Infanta—the Marquis cf Buckingham
became a Duke, and in Spain, at Easter, there was a
" great baiting of Bulls by men " done before the still
blushing Infanta in honour of the Prince, " but all
though the Bulls overthrew manie there fell out no
great danger at all."

So the weeks slipped into months and the object of
the Prince's visit seemed no nearer, though, in
answer to a request from Charles, James sent a
warrant : " We do hereby promise by the word of a
King that whatsoever our sonne shall promise in our
name we shall punctually perform."

So rare were the opportunities afforded the Prince for
meeting the Infanta that he took to sitting in a closed
coach outside her door for hours at a stretch waiting
for her outgoing, watching " as a cat does for a
mouse," and the Duke of Buckingham wrote home to

the Duchess asking her to send glasses to enable
Charles to obtain a better view of her.

" I send the best I could get," she reported, " and
I am sorry that the Prince is kept at such a distance
that he needs such to see her."

Papal letters reached the Prince, and as a result
he and Buckingham wrote to James urging him to
grant indulgences to his Catholic subjects, and they
asked so much that the King took fright. If the
Spaniards held to such terms Charles must come
" right speedilie away. Alas ! I now repent me sore
that ever I suffered you to go. I care for match nor
nothing, so I may once more have you in my arms
again ! God grant it ! God grant it ! "

But Charles had learnt that the Infanta often took
the air in a shady orchard. Determined to advance
his cause, he scaled a wall and jumped down at her
feet, so scaring the well-trained Spanish maiden that
she fled screaming, while her terrified duenna implored
the lover to return by the way he had come before his
rash action cost her her head.

Despite this contretemps the Duke of Buckingham
could write that matters were advancing and that
they hoped to bring the Infanta with them upon
their return. The Prince had been promoted to
sitting beside her in public, he had even conversed
with her in the presence of the King and with an
ambassador as interpreter.

The espousal date had been fixed (though there
had been some argument over the wedding portion
demanded by England, Spain being of the opinion
that so large an endowment should only be expected
" with a princess who was deformed or of mean birth "),
when the death of the Pope flung everything into confusion once more, for now the new Pope must ratify
the dispensation granted by his predecessor ; in
vain the dismayed Prince pointed out that his father
was ill, that the people were murmuring at his long
absence, and that the marriage articles as signed in

England would be void unless he returned by a stipulated date. All that the King of Spain could suggest was that since Charles must needs go he should leave a proxy behind him to carry through the marriage, which could then take place immediately upon the arrival of the fresh dispensation. Urgent letters of recall made this the only possible action on Charles's part, so official business was concluded, the Infanta took the title of Princess of Wales and was bidden " carry herself in that quality towards all," and Charles sailed without his bride.

After an eight-months' absence he landed at Portsmouth " to the joy and comfort of all true-hearted subjects."

The Prince rode on to London, where a public holiday was declared in honour of his homecoming, and " no manner of work was done but the carrying and recarrying of wood to make bonfires, 108 of which were lighted between St. Paul's and London Bridge. Links were lighted around the Cross, one for each year of the Prince's age, and a bishop delivered a sermon from the text :

" ' When I shall come out of Egypt and the House of Jacob from amongst the barbarous people.' "

It was borne in upon Charles that part of the rejoicing was because he had come alone.

But in Spain two English tutors had been appointed to give an intensive language course to the Infanta in the intervals of ordering her trousseau, and the English Ambassador, who had been driven to pawn his wife's jewels to meet the expenses of the Prince's sojourn in Spain, was ordering liveries for the wedding. Nothing was needed but the letters from Rome. These came at last, and a Council was called in hot haste ; it was rumoured that the terms had been varied. Presently the matter was referred to Parliament, where James had to confess that he had been " deluded in the match."

Now came news that a messenger was to be sent to

Spain to explain that the King had been advised to break the " Treaty of the Match," since Spain would not restore the Palatinate, and that Charles was recalling his proxy.

London lighted bigger bonfires than ever in joy of the break and the Council continued its deliberations, for if the match with Spain was off another must be on, since the Prince required a bride—it was rumoured that Holland would offer a large sum if he would but marry there !

En route to Spain Charles had visited the French court, and a vision of a dancing princess had remained in his mind. Presently an emissary was dispatched and a new wooing begun.[1] The first overtures were not accepted too eagerly, and Charles's interest increased, but before anything was concluded James died.

" The same day in the afternoon Charles Prince of Wales, his only son then living, was proclaimed King of Great Britain, France, and Ireland with the general acclamation of all sorts of people as being a prince of admirable endowmenys of both mind and body. . . . He was now about 25, the most part of one year of which had been spent in Spain, where, although he was frustrated to the end for which he went, it gave him a tincture of travel and experience more worth possessing than the end he went for."

The coronet of a prince was exchanged for the crown of a king at a difficult time. The plague was raging with such intensity that Parliament was moved to Oxford, and a funeral, a marriage, a coronation, and a war made heavy demands upon the goodwill of the nation ; the new King required £300,000 to meet immediate needs.

Then, too, piracy was rampant off the English coast, and the Hollanders usurped our fishing rights and had to be " scoured off the high seas," yet when the King

[1] See *Her Majesty : The Romance of the Queens of England.*

asked for ship-money " a Mr. Hampden of Bucking-
hamshire " made trouble.

Presently a rumour spread to the effect that the
King intended to dissolve the House, and a petition
was prepared praying His Majesty to take no such
step.   When Charles declined to receive this, the
Commons employed propaganda methods, and the
King retaliated by issuing a proclamation against
the remonstrance.

Could men have read the handwriting upon the
wall, they would have seen the shadow of the scaffold
that was to be raised in Whitehall twenty years
later, when in a hushed silence the King emerged
from a window to lay his head upon the block, and
" such a groan as had never sounded " went up to
Heaven.

CHAPTER X

CHARLES STUART, PRINCE OF WALES (CHARLES II)

" Welcome God's Loan ! "—(Poem on birth of Charles).

CHARLES STUART, PRINCE OF WALES

Born at St. James's . .	May 29, 1630 (and declared Prince of Wales)
Titular King	January 30, 1649
Proclaimed King in Scotland .	February 5, 1649
Crowned in Scotland . .	January 1, 1651
Restoration	May, 1660
Crowned in England . .	April 22, 1661
Married (Catherine of Braganza)	May 21, 1662
Died	February 6, 1685

Descent

Charles I — *m.* — Henrietta Maria
|
Charles Prince of Wales (and others)
(Charles II)

CONTEMPORARY SOVEREIGNS

FRANCE : Louis XIII and Louis XIV.

CHAPTER X

CHARLES STUART, PRINCE OF WALES
(CHARLES II)

1630–1685

" HE is so ugly that I am ashamed of him," complained Henrietta Maria, ruefully contemplating her baby son, " but," she added, " his size and fatness supply his lack of beauty."

However, the birth of the Prince was the occasion of popular interest and enthusiasm, the more because men vowed that on this auspicious May 29 there was seen " a star at noon-day in the East. . . . Such a remark of Heaven's favour as was never before vouchsafed at any nativity except that of our Saviour." The less optimistic shook their heads at the sight " and left it to the astrologers to say whether the sign was a prophecy of good or ill." A few bold spirits earned unpopularity by insisting that the so-called star was the planet Venus.

A magnificent christening was arranged, for the Prince was the first direct male heir born to the Throne in England since Edward VI a century before.

Four chaplains with surplices and copes " in decent order " received him at the nursery door to walk beside the golden canopy under which he was carried into chapel. Bishop Laud baptised him, two countesses carried his train, and a duke and duchess were proxy sponsors for the King and Queen-Mother of France, who had accepted the office of " gossips."

The duchess, who had arrived with a retinue of six women and " uncountable gentlemen," all in white satin and crimson stockings, began the shower of christening gifts by presenting the infant with a jewel worth £7,000, and extended her bounty even to his rockers ; a few days later the child was declared Prince of Wales. He developed into an " unthankful," self-willed boy, with a persistent affection for a block of wood, without which he declined to sleep at night.

The honour of knighthood came to the little Prince when he was seven years old ; he received the Order of the Garter and was installed at Windsor.

The Earl of Newcastle was appointed as one of the Prince's tutors, and began his duties by drawing up a paper of instructions in the form of a letter to his pupil :

" It is fit you should have some languages, though I confess I would rather have you study things than words. . . . I would not have you too studious, for too much contemplation spoils action, and virtue consists in that.

" Study history so that you may compare the dead with the living, for the same humours is now as was then ; there is no alteration but in names."

The Prince was bidden to look upon himself as God's deputy ; to be reverent at prayers in order to set an example to his people, and, all important, to be courteous and civil to everyone. " The outting off of your hat and making a leg please more than reward."

Another dictum was on the advantages of kindly speech. . . . Speak well of everybody, and when you hear people speak ill of others reprehend them and say something in favour of those spoken against. . . . The other way, which is railing, scorn, and jeering, is fitter for porters, watermen and carmen than for gentlemen. . . . Win people's hearts, and then you have all they have ; more you cannot have." As a prince, Charles must always be dignified, " for nothing preserves Kings so much as ceremony," and he should thank God for the vantage

CHARLES II.
From a picture of " The Children of Charles I," after Van Dyck, in the
National Portrait Gallery.

ground he had over other people. He must strive
to become a brave, noble, and just King, one whose
name should be immortalised by his brave deeds
abroad and his unspotted justice at home—" qualified
by your well-temper and mercy."

The Prince of Wales remained under this tutelage
for three years, and two of the Duke of Buckingham's
sons shared his lessons. Already the times were
disturbed, and for safety's sake the King kept his
elder sons with him whenever possible, fearing that
Parliament might seize them if his vigilance lessened.

At ten years of age Prince Charles took his seat in
the Upper House, and soon afterwards performed his
first public duty in carrying to the Lords a letter
from the King urging that Strafford's life should be
spared, or, if he must die, " it were charity to reprieve
him until Satedaie." Within the next few months
he saw something of the hydra-headed nature of a
mob. It cheered and blessed the King and his family
on his return from Scotland, where he had been
making an effort to " quell that country's mightie
distemper," then murmured threateningly and
shouted for " Liberty " when, after the abortive
attempt to arrest the five members, Charles carried
the Queen and her children to the temporary haven
of Hampton Court. From here the Queen, eluding
Parliament, sailed across to the continent to seek
help for the King, taking with her as the ostensible
cause of her journey the Princess Mary,[1] who had
been betrothed to William of Orange.

In writing to his sister, Charles reported that his
father was " very disconsolate " by reason of the
absence of his wife and child, and the disturbances
in the kingdom ; " we are as merry as we may be and
more than we would sad," he added.

The King planted his standard at Nottingham and
the long-drawn Civil War began. From the frail
shelter of a hedge Prince Charles and his younger

[1] See *Royal Marys*, by E. Thornton Cook.

brother James watched the battle of Edgehill, so at twelve years old the King's son was called upon to lay his youth aside and make an abortive attempt to play a man's part. Oxford became the royalist headquarters, from which place Charles rode beside his father to share in the dangers of battles. The Queen joined them for a time, but the remainder of the family was in Parliamentary hands, and eight-year-old Princess Elizabeth was appealing to the Lords for fair treatment of her household.

The position grew worse, and Prince Charles, having been made Generalissimo of the forces, was sent to the west country to " unlog him," and made a difficult journey to Bristol, being short of both clothes and money.

There were marchings and countermarchings, a court set up in Cornwall, and divided Councils. The King had directed that the Prince should be sent out of England should the danger of his capture by the Roundheads appear imminent, and fear now drove his guardians to carry him to the Scilly Isles, where the little group landed to face new difficulties, for the island could not feed them, and letters from the King made it clear that he still feared for his son's safe keeping.

London's streets were lit by bonfires of crucifixes, " popish books and pictures," and Parliament sat long hours debating the problem of the King's eldest son, " having been informed that he was in some straits for provisions."

In the end it was agreed that a joint letter should be sent, signed by representatives of both Houses and written " in a loving and tender way," inviting Prince Charles to place himself in the hands of Parliament, which body would then decide where he might reside, and appoint him such councillors as met their approval.

When the document reached the little court in Scilly it was read as more of a summons than an invitation, but all bent themselves to the drafting of a suitable answer, which was carried to London by a trumpeter.

From this, Parliament learnt that while the Prince had " a great and earnest desire to be amongst you, if we might have an assurance that it would prove an expedient towards a blessed peace and the composure of these miserable distractions," he would do nothing without his father's approval, and asked that his messenger might have a safe-conduct to go to the King.

Next day a fleet of over twenty Parliamentary ships approached St. Mary's, but were driven off by a storm which raged for twenty-four hours, during which the Council sat in almost continuous debate, until brought to a unanimous decision by Charles's production of a letter from his father which had been written soon after Naseby and given to him for use in an emergency.

" My late misfortunes remember me to command you that which I hope you shall never have occasion to obey," wrote the King. " It is this. If I should at any time be taken prisoner by the rebels, I command you (upon my blessing) never to yield to any conditions that are dishonourable, unsafe for your person, or derogatory to regal authority upon any consideration whatever, even though it were for the saving of my life."

The letter seemed to crystallise the position and emphasise the danger of Prince and King. Without a dissentient voice it was agreed that Charles should go on to Jersey, and, the decision once made, all were in haste to start and leave the discomforts and dangers of Scilly.

So to board, and Charles took the steering-wheel of *The Proud Black Eagle.* Jersey welcomed him with open arms, and her people scattered flowers in the Prince's path when he walked to church. The weeks passed swiftly, and Charles held a court on borrowed money and won all hearts. He was not yet seventeen, and it was his first taste of kingship.

But anxious guardians knew that their Prince was not safe, and some urged that he should move on again either to Ireland, France, or Denmark.   There came a letter from the King, written in the hope that it would find Charles with his mother, and expressing the belief that the Prince being out of reach of the rebels would ensure his own safety.   Then came news that the King had left Oxford and gone no man knew where, and Henrietta Maria wrote from St. Germains :

" Come, and come quickly, for certainly your coming hither is the security of the King, your father.   Therefore make all haste you can to show yourself a dutiful son and a careful one to do all that is in your power to save him, otherwise you may ruin the King and yourself. . . . There is no time to lose, therefore lose none but come quickly."

Charles waited impatiently for a favourable wind. It came at last, but the boats put out, the wind changed and they were beaten back.   In the lull Charles vowed that they must go if all had to bend to the oars.   Then the breeze sprang up again and blew them merrily over the waters.   A landing was effected in a cockle-shell boat under the very nose of an enemy ship.

Charles rode on to Paris and his mother, to whom the King had written begging her for love of him to let the world see that she made no effort to " alter the prince's conscience."

For a few weeks questions of precedence absorbed France to such a degree that she could give no welcome to the fugitive, but at last he was bidden to Fontaine-bleau, and to the relief of the English royalists was received " as civily as could be."

The Prince played his part well and " behaved himself so handsomely that he hath gotten the love of all that have seen him, both men and women," ran one report, but even in this the keynote of life as lived at St. Germains was sounded.   " Though his entertainment hath been noble, there has been nothing

either by present or addition to the Queen for his
subsistance.''

Two difficult years dragged by, and financial matters
grew worse and worse : " The Queen's pension hath
been reduced, and the Prince has nothing but what
his mother gives him.'' Poverty-stricken himself,
Sir Edward Hyde could do little to help, and was
oppressed with fears for the Prince's safety, believing
that "there were those in France who desired the
misery of England.''

With a heart torn with anxiety for the husband
she loved, Queen Henrietta Maria worked and planned
for him and her son. Perhaps she could advance
the cause by marrying Prince Charles to Mademoiselle
de Montpensier, heiress and daughter of the Duc
d'Orléans ! But La Grande Mademoiselle was three
years older than Charles, and though she would flirt
and dance with the penniless exile whose father was
being hunted from pillar to post, she refused to view
him as an eligible *parti*, and Charles's hurt dignity
would have carried him into the French army, but the
move was vetoed as being a step beneath his position.

Then came news that the King had given himself
up to the Scots at Newark and had been handed
over to the English ; it fell like a bombshell on the
court at St. Germains. For the Queen's emotion
there was no outlet except prayer, but Charles seized
the chance offered to him by a revolt of part of the
English fleet, and sending his unwilling brother
James ashore for safety's safe, he sailed away to bottle
up the mouth of the Thames and capture homeward-
bound merchantmen, so stirring London that the city
petitioned for the King's release and a cessation of arms.

For a brief moment the young Prince saw success.
He dispatched a messenger explaining the purpose
of his actions, and calling on all loyal men to rise and
join him, and asking £20,000 as ransom for the ships
he held.

Now came Lauderdale with a suggestion from

Scotland that Charles should join the Scottish forces about to enter England.

A Council was held as the Prince lay in the Downs, but when it was decided that he should leave the fleet and go to Scotland the sailors rebelled and insisted that an attack should be made on Lord Warwick's ships in Lee Roads, and it was impossible that this should be done without Charles, or men would say that they had no Prince.

Charles went among them himself, " none other durst," and explained the impracticability of entering Lee Roads at the moment, since they were short of provisions, and that it was best for him to go to Scotland, " but no rhetoric would alter the mad multitude from their decision, since they believed that they could destroy Warwick's fleet and make us mistress of the seas. . . . The two biggest ships set off, so the Prince's ship followed contrary to the sense of all sea commanders. Warwick came out, the fleet made towards him in fighting posture, he retreated and we followed till darkness fell, when all anchored. Next day, no sooner were all within fighting distance than the wind sprang up, and the sands being dangerous we had to cast anchor till the morning, when all the victuals being spent we had to make off towards Holland."

So ended Prince Charles's gallant effort, and while he had hovered in the Downs Preston had been fought and the Scottish effort had failed.

Holland received her unwelcome guests and volunteered an allowance of 1,000 guelders a day for ten days, after which all must shift for themselves.

The Fates solved the problem, for the Prince fell ill of smallpox, the sailors mutinied for lack of pay, and the " fleet " dispersed itself without orders.

France was now in turmoil and could offer no asylum, but Mary of Orange stepped into the breach and gave a welcome to her penniless brother. The King (whose rescue from the Isle of Wight Charles

1685]

had failed to effect) was under no illusions as to his own position, and now wrote an earnest letter to the son he hoped would succeed to his throne, " and become as great a prince as your father is a low one, your state as much stablished as mine hath been shaken, for our subjects have learnt that victories over their princes are but triumphs over themselves and so will be the more unwilling to hearken to changes hereafter.

" The Englishmen are a sober people, however, at present infatuated," he continued and went on to warn his son that this might be the last word he could write to him.

" If God give you success, use it humbly and without revenge, and, if He returns you to your rights upon hard conditions, whatever you promise—*keep* and do not think anything in this world worth obtaining by foul means."

In despair Prince Charles appealed first to one and then to another. Surely Louis XIV would move on the King's behalf ? Would not the States-General make an effort to save his father's life ? For himself he wrote to Fairfax, sending a sheet of paper blank except for his own signature ; Parliament might fill in what terms it would.

He received no answer.

On a February morning Charles heard himself addressed as " Your Majesty," and realised that the sentence passed upon his father had been put into effect. Had he known it, he himself had been proscribed, for on the day following the execution of King Charles I Parliament had read a third time an Act prohibiting the proclaiming of any person to be King of England, and had ordered the post to be stopped till letters could be prepared advising the world of the passage of this act : " Whereas Charles Stuart, King of England, being, for the notorious treasons, tyrannies, and murders committed by him in the late unnatural and cruel wars, condemned to death, whereupon . . . pretences may be made unto the Kingly office to the hazard of the public peace. . . . Be it enacted and ordained that no persons whatsoever shall proclaim, declare, or publish, or any way promote Charles Stuart (son of the said Charles), commonly called the Prince of Wales, to be King . . . without the consent of the people in Parliament . . . under punishment of death."

There had followed a debate touching the disposal of the King's body and his George and Garter, " whether they should be sent to his son " ; the motion was " carried in the negative."

Scotland, a-simmer with wrath at the treatment meted out by England to her Scottish-born King, proclaimed his son in Edinburgh, but sent Commissioners to make it clear that this signified nothing until he had subscribed to the Covenant.

Charles, whose mourning had been provided by his sister's husband, the Prince of Orange, had no funds for an expedition to Scotland, and, moved on from Holland after the murder of a Parliamentary agent who had come to negotiate an Anglo-Dutch alliance, wandered back to Jersey, where new Scottish overtures reached him, and he hastened back to Breda to accept all conditions.

He agreed to " put away all papists from him, to admit the justice of the Covenant and maintain it to the utmost," and allowed it to be set down in uncompromising words that he had now " recovered from the snares of evil councillors " and henceforward would do nothing but with the approval of Kirk and State.

He sailed for Scotland, but found that further signatures were required to yet more humiliating documents before he was permitted to set foot on Scottish soil.

The crown seemed in sight, and the nightmare years of poverty, dependence, and exile were vivid in his mind, so he signed and discovered that those who had sought him had deceived both themselves and him.   The women of Scotland might give their jewels for his crown, but Cromwell came marching nearer and nearer, and Charles, " narrowly watched by serious Christians," was called upon to take part in various ceremonies on a day of public humiliation for the sins of the royal family.   By no other reasoning could the Scots account for the weight of the Lord's hand upon them.

Miserable months dragged by, but if Charles was required to listen to as many as six sermons in a day and forced to receive a deputation of divines come to rebuke him for card-playing, he was crowned at Scone on New Year's Day (1651).

Cromwell's   triumphs   continued,   so   Charles attempted a bold counter-stroke by marching into England, but met disaster instead of victory, and at Worcester his army was completely routed.

" Save the King ! " cried the loyalists, but Charles had gone no man knew whither, and a price was on his head.

Clad in a leather doublet, cloth breeches, and a green jerkin, with hair cropped so close that fellow-travellers took him for a Roundhead and claimed his sympathy on a rumour that " Rogue Stuart " was taken, Charles wandered about the countryside. He tried to reach London but found it impossible, then doubled back towards Wales, then strove to reach the coast, helped, now by one and another of those who penetrated his disguise, and vowed that they would go to death rather than betray their King.

One day, hidden in a friendly oak, he watched Cromwellian soldiers searching the wood ; on another, as Will Jackson, a tenant's son, he rode as attendant on a lady.

Shoreham was reached at last, and a sailor was found bold enough to make the run to France carrying " a person of quality who had escaped from Worcester." There was an awful moment when he recognised the

King, but avowing his belief that he was doing God
and the country a service, he decided to carry out
his contract.

Charles landed in the clothes of a common sailor,
and Mary of Orange welcomed him in secret, not
daring to betray her brother's whereabouts to those
around her. She gave him clothes and money, and
he went once more to join his mother in the stricken
court at St. Germains, supported by the bounty of
the King of France. But Cromwell's star was in
the ascendant, and the exile found himself moved on
from country to country and looked upon as an
unwelcome guest. His younger brothers, James
Duke of York and the Duke of Gloucester, joined him.
Princess Elizabeth had died in Carisbrook Castle,[1]
and the trio of brothers held court in Brussels, Bruges,
and Antwerp, till the younger princes, more fortunate
than their elder brother, found employment in the
Spanish army. Charles had sent ambassadors to
every court in Europe in the vain endeavour to get
military help and financial aid, but kings, like
princesses, turned deaf ears. Even Frances Cromwell
was denied him as a bride.

Cologne, which had welcomed him upon his arrival,
would give him little credit after two years, and he
went the weary round of Bruges, Brussels, and Breda
more once, distributing I.O.U.'s to royalists—" I do
promise to repay as soon as I am able."

During these lean years Charles would have found
it difficult to exist at all if it had not been for the
" King's dues " levied by Prince Rupert on ships
captured in his buccaneering expeditions. As it was,
the English Intelligence Agents were able to report
that " the titular King of Scots is in necessity . . .
his cooks and backstairsmen complain that they
cannot go on in the providing of his diet. . . . The
titular King of Scots is in so low a condition that
he is forced to eat his dinner in a tavern, not having

---

[1] See *Royal Elizabeths*.

the commodity of dining at home. . . . Charles
Stuart has left Paris; he made the more haste
because a servant of his was fallen upon and beaten
even in his master's place of abode at the Louvre,
and he was besieged there by bakers, butchers, and
other tradesmen of all sorts in whose books he is
very deep."

Sir Edward Hyde, on whom fell the task of paying
postage on the King's letters, confessed himself as
being in debt " for all the meate I have eaten this
three months, and that to a poor old woman who is
no longer able to trust." He often went " cold for
want of clothes and fire."

Cromwell's death raised fresh hopes among the
loyalists until a messenger sent to England in disguise
(on the proceeds of pawned Orders) brought back a
dispiriting report, and Charles learnt that he must
wait still longer.

At last came news that his portrait was being openly
displayed in London, where men were eager for a
king once more.

A declaration was drawn up from the " court "
at Breda, addressed to " All our Loving Subjects."

" If the general distraction and confusion which
is spread over the whole Kingdom doth not awaken
all men to a desire and a longing that these wounds
which have so many years been kept bleeding may
be bound up, all we can say will be to no purpose,"
wrote Charles, then went on to stress his desire
for peace and offer a general pardon to all who
within 40 days would announce their desire to
return to the loyalty and obedience of good subjects
" except any as shall be excepted by Parliament."
He promised, too, full liberty of conscience, " because
the passion and uncharitableness of the times have
produced several opinions in religion."

Through the intermediary of Sir John Grenville
this declaration was carried to England together with
letters to General Monk, the commander of the

English army, to the Speaker of the House of Commons, and to the Lord Mayor of London.

Parliament met on April 25 (1660), and General Monk, as member for Devon, took his seat and surveyed proceedings in silence for five days before he caught the Speaker's eye and rose to announce that he had received a letter from the King, and that Sir John Grenville was waiting with an epistle addressed to the House.

Called forward by general acclamation, Sir John advanced to the bar of the House and delivered his letter. The Speaker stood up " bare-headed, and all the members uncovered likewise while the message was read with reverence and respect."

Sir John retired, while a unanimous House decreed that a Committee should be appointed to prepare an answer which should express the great joy and thankfulness of the House at His Majesty's offers. And it seemed that the Lords were of the same mind as the Commons.

Sir John was summoned once more and escorted to the Upper House to receive the thanks of the Peers, " and to-morrow," he wrote to Charles Stuart, waiting at Breda, " I am to receive the same of the Commons. In fine two letters are being prepared, one from either side of the House, full of expressions of loyalty and duty, which I am ordered to convey to your majesty and to be accompanied by some members of the Lords and Commons with letters of credit for your majesty's present supply."

Already bells were ringing and bonfires lighted, and Sir John was presented with £500 with which to buy himself a jewel as a reward for being the bearer of so gracious a message ; a few months before he might have been sentenced to death had it been known that he had seen the King.

Lords and Commons assembled at Westminster Hall Gate and stood bareheaded while the Herald gave forth an agreed proclamation :

" Although it can no way be doubted but that
his majesty's right and title to the Crown and Kingdom is and was every way completed by the death
of his most royal father of glorious memory without
the ceremony of a proclamation, yet, since proclamations in such cases have always been used,
it is thought advisable to conform to precedent . . .
and we therefore, Lords and Commons now assembled
. . . together with the Lord Mayor and Aldermen
of the City of London, do according to our duty and
allegiance, heartily, joyfully, and unanimously
acknowledge and proclaim that immediately upon
the disease of our late sovereign lord King Charles,
the Crown of England . . . did descend and come
to his most excellent majesty King Charles II."

A similar proclamation was read in other places
while " the people gave great shouts, bells rang, great
guns and small shot a great many volleys, and the
city was full of bonfires and great joys." And then
nothing was thought of but to make such preparations
as were necessary for his majesty's reception.

There was much to do. An address had to be
prepared to be carried to Breda by the members of
Parliament who had been chosen to attend on Charles
with Sir John Grenville. As passed it ran :

" Dread Sovereign, your faithful subjects the
Commons of England have sent us hither (twelve
of their number) to wait upon your majesty, and by
their commands we are here, prostrate at your royal
feet, as all would have been if their duties had not
required their attendance in England. . . . Their
hearts are filled with veneration for you and a confidence in you and a longing for you. All the people
of your land are praying for you and sending up
one prayer to Heaven—God Bless King Charles the
Second. . . . Long Live King Charles the Second
and pray his speedy return ! "

In all haste a Committee was appointed to compile

lists of those necessities which must be in readiness
at his majesty's coming. He must have " a rich
bed, to be of velvet embroidered with gold or laces,
a high chair of state, a footstool and two cushions
all suitable to the bed, satin quilts and fustian quilts,
a down bolster, a pair of blankets and 6 pairs of
Holland sheets (24 ells of cloth to a pair) for the
present. There must be table linen too, and damask
napkins for his majesty's table—with a like number
for each duke if they eat asunder, but if they eat
together half the proportion."

There were bills to be prepared and passed. The
fleet needed new flags and the arms of the commonwealth must be taken down—" it would never do
to let his majesty find this emblem adorning the
Speaker's chair "—and information should be obtained
concerning the whereabouts of once royal jewels and
pictures, the crown, sceptre, and robes of state in
order that as much as possible should be restored.

Hardly was all in train before word of the King's
landing at Dover was received, and now a breathless
messenger announced that Charles II had ridden on
to Canterbury, where he had heard sermons, and
would be in London on the morrow.

The Lord Mayor and his aldermen met their
sovereign on the outskirts of the city, and " the streets
were hung with tapestry in honour and testimony
of the people's joy at the restitution of their King
. . . and no sooner did he come to Whitehall than
the two Houses of Parliament solemnly cast themselves at his feet with vows of affection and fidelity
to the world's end. In a word, the joy was so universal
that his majesty said, smiling on those about him :
' He doubted it had been his own fault that he had
been absent so long, for he saw nobody that did not
protest that he had ever wished for his return.' "

To assist the newly returned King, the Duke of
Newcastle, who had drawn up instructions for Charles's

youthful guidance, now drafted a paper of suggestions.
Charles should amuse his people and ever remember
that the great study and learning for Kings was not
books but men. Venison should be sent to lords
and powerful men at Easter—or still better to their
ladies. . . . " Keep clear of Rome . . . master
London—master that and you have the whole kingdom,
—disarm it, but hide your forces, for the people love
not the cudgel. . . . The Universities need purging.
That which hath done most harm is the abundance
of Grammar Schools and Inns of Court . . . these
should be cut down by one-half, since they only
teach boys to become clerks instead of farm labourers
and mechanics. . . . Your royal father always needed
money. . . . Put money in your purse, keep it, and
avoid Parliaments. . . . When you are rich and call
a Parliament your Majesty is master."

Crowds flocked to court eager to kiss the King's
hand, and with them came a stream of petitions
from those who had been ruined in the royalist
cause, one from a man who had lent him 10s. on his
six weeks' wandering about England in disguise,
another from the widow and five children of a farm
hand who had guided him out of Worcester and had
been hanged as a result.

There were bills to be met for clothes provided for
his soldiery nine years before ; an appeal from a
man, who, on account of his efforts in the Stuart
cause had been " tost and trampled upon and tried
for his life eleven times " ; and a request from the
Earl of Dorset that he might be granted the estate
of the first noble to be attainted of high treason,
since his late mother had superintended the Duke
of York's education without recompense. Even the
doctor who had ushered Charles into the world
appeared among the claimants with a request that
he be appointed court physician.

The King found himself with hardly leisure to eat,
so many pressed about him, and he was sometimes

required to " stroke " six hundred persons a week, so great was the throng of those who believed that the touch of a royal hand would cure their ills.

It became necessary to promulgate a new set of ordinances to regulate the King's household :

" The Knight-Martial shall cause his men to attend daily to punish and remove vagrant persons, rogues, and all sorts of beggars and uncivil, uncleanly, and rude persons. These are not to be permitted to lurk anywhere in our house.

" As for those who come to be healed, they must only be allowed to come on certain days of healing, not to flock when they would, as hitherto, which is not only noysome but might be very dangerous in time of infection.

" To the end that our house be a place of civility and honour we are obliged to renew the ancient order that if any of our people in the household be noted to be a prophane person of outrageous behaviour, a drunkard, swearer, bankrupt, or so vicious and unmannerly that he be unfit to live with civil and virtuous company, he is to be examined, and if found incorrigible shall be banished accordingly.

" All cupbearers, carvers, and Sewers before they give attendance upon the King's person must wash their hands.

" The King's bed is to be made at due and convenient hours.

" The Gentleman Usher is to see that no man of whatever degree shall be so hardie as to come too near the King nor stand under the Cloth of State under the degree of Baron, except the Clerk of the Closet and the King's physician, nor to lean on the King's bed, nor to approach the cupboard where the King's cushion is laid, nor to stand upon his carpet.

" The Gentleman Usher is to give warning when the King heals and is to be there to keep good order.

" The lean days were past. Charles Prince of Wales was King indeed."

CHAPTER XI

JAMES FRANCIS EDWARD STUART

'The young blooming flower of the auld Royal Tree.''—SCOTTISH SONG.

JAMES FRANCIS EDWARD STUART

Born at St. James's .   .   .   June 10, 1688 (and gazetted Prince
                                   of Wales)
Proclaimed King (in France)   .   September 16, 1701
Married by proxy (to Princess
    Clementina Sobieski)   .   .   May 28, 1719
Died in Rome .   .   .   .   January 12, 1766

Descent

Charles I — *m.* — Henrietta Maria
|
James II (and others) *m.* (2nd) Mary Beatrice of Modena
|
James Francis Edward Stuart (and others)

CONTEMPORARY SOVEREIGNS

ENGLAND : William and Mary, Anne, George I, George II, and
George III.

FRANCE : Louis XIV and Louis XV.

CHAPTER XI

JAMES FRANCIS EDWARD STUART

1688-1766

In the summer of 1687 James II and his Queen, Mary of Modena, went to make their prayers together at a shrine in Wales, and a few months later a royal proclamation decreed a day of public thanksgiving, when all true Englishmen and women were asked to pray that the Queen might become " a joyful mother of children, that angels should watch over her, and the King live to see his children's children around his throne."

The possibility of the birth of an heir to the King, whose unpopularity was on the increase, caused dismay among the non-Catholics, who could not face with equanimity the prospect of a Catholic Prince succeeding a Catholic father.

Four years before, when the Queen's last child had been born, the town-crier sent out to order the lighting of bonfires for the official rejoicing had added the warning message that those who failed to celebrate would be fined; now it was certain that many would pay rather than make festivity.

On Thanksgiving Sunday few of those who attended church brought with them the Special Prayer that had been issued for the occasion :

" It is strange to see how the Queen's being with child is everywhere ridiculed as if scarcely anybody believed it to be true!" wrote Lord Clarendon. "God help us!"

As the months passed, whispered innuendoes sounded louder and yet more loud, while daring spirits sang ribald songs almost within the court precincts, nor were jeering voices silenced when a prince "well formed and of full size" was born on Trinity Sunday.

"Why," it was asked, "had Queen Mary insisted upon being carried to St. James's late at night? Why had she selected for her lying-in a room with a door near her bed-head?   Above all, why was not Princess Anne present, as she should have been at the advent of an heir?   Bah!   The 'prince' was no prince, but a come-by-chance child who had been introduced into the Queen's bed in a warming-pan!"

But the handwriting on the wall was not read by those in the circle gathered about the rejoicing King and Queen.

Oxford poured out commemorative verses and drew a parallel between the new-born Prince and his great predecessor, Edward the Black Prince, born on a Trinity Sunday three hundred and fifty years before. The Lord Mayor and Corporation of London attended early to present the royal infant with a purse of gold and kiss his baby fist.   Rome rejoiced at the assurance of Catholic continuity, and the Dauphine of France sent the promise of an amulet, which the Prince must wear around his neck when teething, as had done the royal children of France with great benefit to themselves.

Announcements concerning the Prince's progress appeared in the court circular.   Now he was being carried daily to take the air in the public parks, and now he had given audience to favourite foreign ambassadors.

At five weeks old he was the medium of the presentation of a petition to the King.   When it was found that the document his baby fingers had clasped prayed an increase in the number of hackney cabs plying in London (from 200 to 400), the increase in revenue therefrom to be devoted to the "feeding and breeding of foundling children, the anti-Stuart Party found significance in this precocious solicitude for illegitimates."

JAMES FRANCIS EDWARD STUART AND HIS SISTER, PRINCESS
LOUISA MARIA THERESA.
From a picture by N. de Largilliere in the National Portrait Gallery.

Since the Queen's [1] other children had failed to grasp life firmly, it was decided that the Prince of Wales, who seemed " a brave and lusty boy," must run no risks. Eighteenth-century science decided that milk must be omitted from his diet-sheet, and that he should be fed with barley-flour gruel spiced with currants, and well dosed with many physics.

Very soon the court news retailed that the Prince had " the grippes," and that doctors, nurses, and midwives were gathered in consultation around the royal cot.

The reports grew worse and worse, and King and Queen posted down to Richmond, where the Prince lay, hardly conscious. Taking the initiative, the Queen seized upon the deep-bosomed, buxom young wife of a tile-maker and carried her into the nursery, where her services produced such excellent results that the tone of the court news changed :

" The prince has taken the suck and is better ! "

But society was shocked. " The nurse was fetched in in her cloth petticoat and waistcoat, in her shoes and no stockings ! " wrote scandalised retailers of gossip, but admitted that she was to be " rigged out by degrees so that the surprise may not affect her in her duty."

And now the Prince developed so rapidly that the suspicious-minded declined to believe that he was the puny child they had seen a week before, and while one party held to the warming-pan story, a new *cabal* told a tale of the substitution of a living child for a dead, and even the christening of the Prince did not still their clamour. This took place in October, and to the jubilation of the Catholics the Pope accepted the office of god-father.

But three months before a memorial had been dispatched to William of Orange praying him to save England.

---

[1] For her story see *Her Majesty : The Romance of the Queens of England.*

James knew his danger and watched the wind with anxious eyes, knowing that so soon as it veered to the east his son-in-law might make a landing. He had fought against the belief that such perfidy was possible, as he had turned a deaf ear to the innuendoes concerning his son. Now, William of Orange waited with his army ready to invade James's Kingdom, and " the Queen's character was being blackened by the most execrable falsetys that Hell itself was capable of inventing ! "

Action had to be taken. An Extraordinary Council was called at short notice, and, though Princess Anne was " industriously absent," the Queen-Dowager, Catherine of Braganza, attended, as did the Lords, Spiritual and Temporal, the Lord Mayor and Aldermen, the King's Council, and the King's judges.

The King addressed the assembly, telling it that malicious enemies had so corrupted the minds of his subjects that some now doubted whether " the son with which God hath blessed me is but a supposed child." But mercifully the birth could be proved, for " by particular Providence scarce any prince was ever born where so many people were present." In all sixty-seven persons had been in the Queen's chamber.

James went on to point out that a particular danger now threatened the country whenever the east wind blew, and that he who had risked his life for the nation in the past intended to do so again, " feeling the more bound now that I am King," so had summoned this Council to prevent doubting people deluging the kingdom in blood were he " exposed to accident." Determined to make all safe alike for his child and his country, he now called upon the witnesses of the Prince's birth to give their evidence.

The Queen-Dowager was the first to offer testimony, and forty others followed, the accoucheur whom the King had knighted at the Queen's bedside, the great ladies who had pressed close around the Queen in

her " good hour," the woman who had carried in the
coal-filled warming-pan, the lords and officers of
state ; and their depositions, being sworn, were deposited in the archives.

Believing that he had secured his son's succession,
James turned to deal with the Prince of Orange, who
landed at Torbay a fortnight later, but since London
was seething with discontent, the little Prince was
sent to Portsmouth, there to take ship for France
until the threatened danger had been overcome.
On arrival at the coast the child's startled guardians
were told that the law of England forbade the heir's
departure unless sanctioned by Parliament.

James was stricken by the discovery that even
the navy could fail in loyalty to him, and ordered the
Prince to be brought back to London, dispatching two
Catholic regiments to escort him.

But the guardians, having decided that Portsmouth
was a danger spot, started towards London before the
troops arrived, missed both the escort and an Orange
ambush, and succeeded in placing the Prince in his
mother's arms once more.   London's temper was now
at fever height, and when the Catholic regiments rode in
they were set upon by the mob and disbanded by force,
" every man being driven off to shift for himself."

There was no time to lose. If the Prince might
not leave the country openly, he must be smuggled
forth, so decided James, and despite the Queen's
tears he decreed that she as well as James Francis
Edward must leave England.

Relying upon the King's promise to follow her
within twenty-four hours, Mary of Modena stole away
from the palace in disguise, crossed the Thames by
ferry, lurked under a Lambeth wall with the six-
months-old Prince wrapped like a bundle of washing,
and eventually reached Gravesend, where a boat
awaited her.

News of her escape was soon published :

" The Queen went down the river yesterday

morning (December 10, 1688) with the Prince of Wales, and it is believed that she has gone to France. The King went this morning, and the Prince of Orange will be at Oxford this night."

But James was not allowed to escape so easily. He was captured and brought back to London while the mob rioted ; responsible citizens assembled at the Guildhall and decided to welcome William, who was coming to save them from popery " at much expense and the hazard of his own person."

The Protestant Prince reached London and took possession of the King's palace, when, by intention or otherwise, James's captors, having hustled him out, relaxed their vigilance, and he fled, leaving a written message to the effect that he would return when the eyes of the nation were opened to the error of its ways, and it would agree to permit liberty of conscience for all.

From the haven of France James drafted despatches explaining his " withdrawal " while Parliament sat in Grand Committee to determine whether the crown was " vacant." Had the King " gone voluntarily away ? " Was he " demised." Backwards and forwards raged the debate till after weary hours a resolution was submitted to the House :

" Resolved that King James the Second, having endeavoured to subvert the Kingdom by breaking the original contract between King and people . . . and having withdrawn himself out of the Kingdom, has abdicated the government and that the Throne thereby is become vacant." To this the Lords' concurrence was desired, and a fresh debate ensued, for the Upper House inclined to the use of the word " desertion " as against " abdication," but the Commons held their ground, for James had " renounced to be a King according to the law—such a King as he swore to be at his coronation . . . and had set up another kind of dominion, which is to all intents an abdication."

And now the question of another king was raised.

Consistency urged that if the rule of a popish king
endangered the country, there would be danger in
accepting a popish prince. Then one bolder than
the rest took the plunge. The throne was vacant
and must be filled :

"Consider of it a thousand years and you cannot
cast your eyes upon a person so well fitted to fill it as
the Prince and Princess of Orange. . . . With such
monarchs on the throne posterity would never be
subjected to the danger of popery and the arbitrary
exercise of power."

Ten days later William and Mary attended at
Westminster to accept the tender of the crown.

Once again France was called upon to offer an
asylum to an exiled King and Queen of England.

The Prince of Wales grew out of babyhood in the
Château of St. Germains, where his sister Louisa Maria
Theresa was born. The pair became the idol of the
Jacobites who sought a refuge in France and were
taught to give their pocket-money to the almost
penniless loyalists who had faced ruin in the Stuart
cause.

At two years of age James Francis Edward saw
his father depart for Ireland, and climbed on his
knee to comfort him after the tragedy of the Boyne.

The exiled King invested his son with the Order of
the Garter, and in honour of the event an inn outside
the Château gates hung a new sign, showing the
four-year-old Prince in the full glory of his insignia.
He was too young to realise the disaster of La Hogue
(May 23, 1692), when James saw the French fleet
burnt, or even the possibilities brought about by the
death of Mary of Orange or the bearing upon his own
destiny of the Peace Congress held at Ryswick (1697).

James drew up a protest warning princes of the
dangerous precedent created by the recognition of
"the Usurper of Our Kingdom," and urged all sovereigns to band together in a common cause, but the

Treaty was signed, and neither James nor Mary
Beatrice would accept the olive branch held out by
William, who undertook to recognise the Prince of
Wales as his heir provided that he was sent to England
and accepted Protestantism ; their son's soul must
not be jeopardised even for a kingdom, nor would they
entrust his body to the guardianship of a man whom
they held to be guilty of treachery.

When he was twelve years old, this Prince who had
known so little of royal pageantry had his great day.
He rode in state to Notre-Dame to make his first
communion, and a medal showing his portrait was
struck for circulation amongst the royalists.

A few months later James II was stricken with
illness, and all the resources of the Jacobites could
not provide sufficient money to send their King to
take the cure at Bourbon.

Louis XIV responded to the Queen's appeal, but
the waters failed in their purpose, and the dying man
was brought back to his pitiful " court," wherein
it was still believed that when William of Orange
died England would recall her King to his own.

But James died first, comforted by the assurance
that France would continue to protect his wife and
children and recognise his son.

" Remember," he told the boy, who could not
stifle his tears at the sight of his father's blood-
stained bed, " you must never put the crown of
England in competition with your eternal salvation.
There is no slavery like sin, and no liberty like service
to God. . . . If Providence wills that you shall sit
upon the throne of your ancestors . . . govern your
people with justice and clemency. . . . Kings are
not made for themselves but for the good of all
people. . . . You are the child of vows and prayers.
Behave yourself accordingly."

An hour later the young Prince heard himself
proclaimed at the gates of St. Germains. He was

Prince of Wales no longer, but titular King James
the Third of England and Eighth of Scotland.[1]

English loyalists attempted to make a similar
proclamation in London, but a mob dispersed the
pursuivants. Scotland was in a different mood, for
the Union hung over her, and few Scots welcomed it.
For her part she would receive the Prince and thwart
the Hanoverian projects. But Mary Beatrice was
more mother than Queen, and saw her son as one too
young for such a venture. She was responsible to
the nation for his safety ; the Scottish lords must
come again when James was older.

William of Orange died six months after James,
having given his dying assent to the entailment of
the crown on the Protestant heirs of Sophia of
Hanover, grand-daughter of James I.

Anne ascended, and James Francis Edward, often
known as the Chevalier de St. George, remained at
St. Germains dreaming of the time when he should
come to his own, and studying the letter of advice
James II had drawn up when his son was four years
old, and he himself was making his last futile attempt
to regain his crown :

" For my Son the Prince of Wales.

" Kings, being accountable for none of their actions
but to God and themselves, ought to be more cautious
and circumspect than those in lower situations. . . .
Remember always that Kings, Princes, and the great
ones of the earth must one day give an account of
all their actions before the great tribunal.

"Do as you would be done by, for that is the Law
of the Prophets. . . . A King ought to be the father
of his people. . . . Endeavour to settle Liberty of
Conscience by a law—'twas a great misfortune to
the people as well as to the Crown, the passing of
the Habeas Corpus Act. . . . Our blessed Saviour
whipt people out of the Temple, but I never heard
He commanded any should be forced into it.

[1] See *Their Majesties of Scotland.*

" Beware of the forbidden love of women, of all the Vices the most bewitching and the hardest to be mastered, if not crushed in the very Bud. . . . This vice carries its sting with it as well as all others, and with more variety it hath that which is common with the others, which is that one is never satisfied, and no sooner has one obtained one object (and that very often at the expense of one's health, estate, honour, and reputation), but one desires change and exposes himself again to all the former inconveniences. . . . Would but Kings and Princes consider and take warning of these kinds of dangerous women, then they would sooner take a Viper into their bosoms than one of these false and flattering creatures.   I wish to God that all men of all sorts would reflect on what I say on this subject.

" Make it your business to know the true constitution of the government that you may keep yourself, as well as Parliament, within its bounds, and in the next place study the trade of the nations and encourage it by all lawful means ; 'Tis that which will make you at ease at home and considerable abroad.   Preserve the mastery of the sea, for without that England cannot be safe.

" Be very careful in choice of your chief ministers . . . they must not only be men of good sense and sound judgment, but of great probity and well founded as to Christianity. . . . Have a great care of permitting a loose-liver, or one that shows himself profane, or atheistically inclined, to insinuate himself into your confidence ; they will all fail you in time of trouble, for how can you expect that those that fly in God's face every day can be thoroughly true to their King ? . . . Have a care how you trust a Latitudinarian ; they are generally atheists in their principles and knaves in their natures . . . as for trimmers, they are generally cowards and want sound judgment.

" When it shall please God to bring you to full

age of discretion, do not forget the good instructions you have received."

The Chevalier celebrated his eighteenth birthday by writing to the Scottish Jacobites.

" If I were once among you, which I so much desire and hope to be some day, I shall make it my business to give you proofs of my kindness and gratitude for all you have done for me," he wrote, and Scotland was in a mood to listen. She would accept even a Papist king rather than the hated Union : " For God may convert him or he may have Protestant children, but the Union can never be good ! "

An emissary sent out by Louis brought word that the time was ripe. James girded on his sword and sailed, but only to be intercepted by an English fleet of superior strength and driven back. All in vain he urged that he might be dropped into a fishing-boat and left to land where he could. Once again it was decided over his head that his was too precious a life to risk, and he was carried back to France.

All that was left for him to do to prove his manhood was to join the French forces in Flanders, where at Oudenarde he fought in the ranks opposed to his rival George of Hanover.

Force had failed of its effect, so now James tried persuasion. " Surely," he wrote to his half-sister, Queen Anne, " you will prefer your own brother, the last male of our name, to the House of Hanover (the remotest relations we have), whose friendship there is no reason to rely on and who will leave the government to foreigners ! " But Anne saw James as " the Pretender," not as the Prince of Wales and heir to his father's throne.

Yet the Jacobites were gaining ground. On May 29 men were seen wearing an oak-leaf, and on June 10 (James's birthday) they went still farther and displayed the badge of the White Rose. Shouts of " No Hanover ! " were heard in the streets, and messengers bore word to France bidding the Prince come in all haste.

But Louis XIV lay dying, and James Francis Edward had no money.

Queen Anne died (August 1714), Hanover was ready, and Stuart was not. George ascended, Sheriff-muir was fought, and a price of £100,000 set on the Prince's head before he landed.

The Fiery Cross might gather in the clans and ladies pool their jewels to make him a crown ; the futile bolt was spent. James was persuaded into a fishing-boat and sailed once more for the land wherein he had grown to manhood. But even France could no longer offer him a permanent asylum, and he wandered on to lodge himself successively in Avignon, Florence, and Rome supported by a pension from the Pope.

Thirty years later James was to see his son depart to make yet another bid for the crowns of England and Scotland. He died (1766) six years after the sixth usurping monarch had mounted the throne he claimed as his.

CHAPTER XII

GEORGE AUGUSTUS, PRINCE OF WALES
(GEORGE II)

" Young Hanover brave ! "—BALLAD BY CONGREVE

GEORGE AUGUSTUS OF HANOVER

Born at Herrenhausen (Hanover) . .	November 10, 1683
Married (Caroline of Anspach) . . .	September 2, 1705
Declared Prince of Wales (Letters Patent) .	September 22/27, 1714
Ascended	June 12, 1727
Died at Kensington	October 25, 1760

Descent

James I (VI of Scotland) — *m.* — Anne of Denmark
|
Elizabeth (and others)
|
Sophia (and others).
m. Ernest Augustus and became Electress of Hanover
|
George I (and others)
|
George Augustus (and another)
(Naturalised by Act of Parliament 1705)

CONTEMPORARY SOVEREIGNS

ENGLAND : Charles II, James II, Mary and William of Orange Anne, and George I.

FRANCE : Louis XIV and Louis XV.

CHAPTER XII

GEORGE AUGUSTUS OF HANOVER

1683–1760

GEORGE AUGUSTUS, later to become the second in the line of England's Hanoverian kings, was the great-great-grandson of James I. His mother, Sophia Dorothea of Celle, who had been married much against her will, was seventeen years old when her child was born. At twelve years of age, George Augustus passed into the hands of his grandmother the Electress Sophia, since his mother had been sent as a prisoner to Ahlden, where she was to remain for over thirty years ; her name was struck out of the state prayers, and all mention of her was forbidden, but George Augustus never forgot her. She made the only touch of romance in his life until one hot June (1705) he rode out from Hanover at midnight with a solitary gentleman-in-waiting beside him.

The secret of the Prince's journey had been well kept, and, though rumours flitted about, none knew where he had gone, though all guessed that he was seeking a wife.

That same June the little court of Brandenburg-Anspach was asked to receive an elderly Hanoverian nobleman and his young companion. They had arrived from Nuremberg carrying impeccable credentials and the two were made welcome during their short stay.

The court was thrilled when a few days after the departure of the guests a messenger arrived bearing a letter explaining that the younger of the two visitors was the Electoral Prince George of Hanover, who,

now having seen the Princess Caroline of Anspach,
was " seized with affection and desire " so great that
he desired to marry her forthwith.

Caroline was summoned, to be told that she had
charmed and delighted the young Hanoverian to
such a degree that he would consider it " the height
of good fortune to obtain her for his wife." She
showed proper surprise both at the proposal and the
identity of the knight-errant, " never having imagined
that anyone in Hanover had so much as thought of
her as a bride for the Electoral Prince," but the
hand of God was so plainly visible in the whole affair
that she felt bound to accept, she being an orphan
and staunch Protestant, and could only hope that
the Electoral Prince " would not find himself deceived
in the favourable opinion he had formed of her."

Within three months the marriage was accomplished, and Caroline left her brother's court for that
of Hanover, where her girlhood's training in diplomacy
stood her in good stead. Her mother-in-law was
twenty miles distant, in captivity, but her place was
more or less openly filled by a succession of ladies,
all of whom Caroline was expected to receive.

The Electress Sophia welcomed her grandson's
bride and saw to it that she, as well as George
Augustus, learned to speak English. Under her
rule the two prepared themselves to be King and Queen
of England and made welcome the stream of English
who, after the passing of the Act of Succession, came
visiting the court of Hanover and sent back glowing
reports of the younger generation, although they
found the Elector himself " but a proper-middle-siz'd
well proportioned man . . . not addicted to any diver-
sions besides hunting."

Periodically, a wave of anxiety would submerge the
Electress Sophia, George Augustus, and Caroline, for
too often rumours would reach Hanover that Queen
Anne's sympathies were veering towards St. Germains,
where her half-brother lived in exile. Perhaps,

GEORGE II.
From a picture by T. Hudson in the National Portrait Gallery.

despite the Act of Succession, she would find some way of bequeathing her crown to James Francis Stuart !

Jacobean songs were being sung far too loudly to please Hanoverian sympathisers :

" Bring in the bowl, I'll toast you a health
  To one that hath neither land nor wealth ;
  The bonniest lad you ever saw is over the hills and far away.
  Over the hills and over the dales—no lasting peace till he prevails ! "

Anti-Jacobites sent a hint that it would be wise if a member of the Hanoverian family could take up residence in England, since Queen Anne's death might occur any day, but the Elector George Louis, father of George Augustus, would make no move.   Thirty years before he had visited England as a suitor for the hand of Anne, in whose eyes he had not found favour, and had retained no pleasant memories of the country or its inhabitants.

It would be a dubious pleasure to rule over such a king-killing, fickle nation.   Within his own life-time had they not tired of the Republic they had established at high cost, welcomed first the son of the King they had murdered, and then (having driven his brother off the throne) a Dutchman: Worse, they had submitted to being ruled by a woman. Should the crown come to his mother or himself it would be accepted—but without enthusiasm.

Electress Sophia viewed the position with different eyes.   At her mother's knee she had learnt of the glory of England, and in the penurious days of her girlhood at The Hague she had been thrilled by the romance of the Restoration, for in her veins ran Stuart blood.   She would see to it that her grand-son's rights were not jeopardised by reason of his father's obstinacy.

A few years before Queen Anne had created Prince George a Knight-of-the-Garter and Duke of Cam-

bridge, so now application was made for a writ
in order that the Prince might take his seat in the
House of Lords. But Anne saw through the man-
œuvre, and, vowing that the very sight of George
would drive a nail into her coffin, declined to send
the writ. The affronted Elector took up the gage
and pointed out that in his opinion the British navy
was a frail bulwark against a Jacobean invasion
so long as James Francis Stuart lurked in the Duke of
Lorraine's dominions.

Queen Anne returned a vigorous reply, and the
Electress Sophia, too old and frail to withstand what
she saw as a death-blow to her ambitions, died
suddenly in Caroline's arms a few days later.

Within two months Anne followed her, and, while
Stuart supporters hesitated, Hanoverians acted under
a Regency which had been appointed as a provision
against such a contingency by far-seeing William of
Orange.

The right high and mighty Prince George was
declared " the lawful and rightful King of Great
Britain, France, and Ireland," while the Regency
issued a discreetly worded announcement to the
effect that his Majesty was hastening over " to
employ his utmost care in putting this kingdom into
a happy and flourishing condition."

" All the King-killers are on my side," said George
I, grimly, and came, but not for some weeks. He
brought his son with him ; Caroline and her children
were left behind, perhaps for safety's sake.

London was reached, and Prince, not King, caught
the people's imagination. There had been no Prince
of Wales in England since the days of Charles the
First, except the baby son of James II, who had
been carried out of the country rolled up like a
bundle of washing, and was now wandering penniless
upon the Continent issuing proclamations and protests that few would read.

As for George Augustus, travellers had sent home

good reports of him : " He has a very winning countenance, is middlesiz'd like his father, well made and of a manly aspect and deportment. He speaks gravefully and with the greatest earnestness imaginable. . . . Care has been taken to furnish him with such accomplishments as are fit for a gentleman, and these acquired parts, with a generous disposition and virtuous inclinations, will deservedly render him the Darling of our People."

All pressed to see him, and each man told the next of the Prince's gallant deeds. Had he not fought with the British troops under Marlborough and distinguished himself at Oudenarde when a mere lad, as commemorated by Congreve :

> " Young Hanover brave
> In this bloody field I assure ye,
> When his war-horse was shot,
> He valued it not,
> But still fought on foot like a fury ! "

The admiration was mutual. Soon it was reported that the Prince had said the English were " the handsomest, the best shaped, the best mannered, and the lovingest people in the world " ; the sure road to his favour was to tell him that he was like an Englishman.

At the first Privy Council the King, laying stress on his son's filial piety, created him Prince of Wales, and a flood of odes burst upon the town dedicated to the popular favourite, " heir alike to his father's virtues and his throne."

The Coronation went off fairly well, though the Thames rose to such an unprecedented height that there was fear of Westminster Hall being inundated, and it was rumoured, among those outside, that when the King's Champion rode into the banqueting hall and cast down his glove challenging anyone to deny the right of George I to the throne, some Jacobite had snatched it up and disappeared into the crowd with the gage before a capture could be effected.

But all contretemps were forgotten in the burst
of enthusiasm that enveloped Caroline, Princess of
Wales and first lady in the land (since Sophia Dorothea
was still a prisoner), and the three little princesses
she brought with her from Hanover. Frederick
Louis, the only son, had been left behind by order of
the King.

It was many a year since three generations of
royalty had been in existence in the direct line of
succession, indeed, not since the time of that hero
of chivalry, the Black Prince.

This was consolation for the only too evident fact
that the King hated England and all things English,
from the language to the oysters, and was counting
the months until he could revisit Hanover. As his
popularity waned, that of the Prince and Princess of
Wales increased ; there were gay nights at the opera,
crowded Drawing-rooms and musical parties, and
such throngs in St. James's when the Princess and
her children went for morning strolls that King
George vowed he would turn the place into a turnip
field, and Caroline (forgetting to be tactful) declared
the place " stank of people," and drove away through
the fields to Kensington Gardens. As for Sundays,
never had the Chapel Royal been better attended,
and so much " ogling and tittering " went on between
the court beauties and the court gallants that it was
decided to board in the pew in which the maids-of-
honour sat so that they could neither see nor be seen !

But all was not as tranquil as it seemed. Those
who had once scrambled for Hanoverian favours and
sung—

> " King George our Defender
> From Pope and Pretender ! "

now whistled Jacobite songs :

> " The man in the moon may wear out his shoon,
> By running after Charles's wain,
> But all to no end, for the times will no mend,
> Till the King enjoys his own again ! "

Oxford took to wearing the White Rose, and in Scotland prayers were asked for " a young gentleman that either was, or would be soon, at sea."

James Francis Stuart made a landing in the north, and George I offered a reward of £100,000 for " the Pretender " dead or alive. An anonymous author published a pamphlet proclaiming the doctrine that to take the life of an usurper in aid of a rightful prince was not murder, and London's citizens saw troops encamped in Hyde Park; there were street fights when in retaliation for the burning of the Pope and Stuart Prince in effigy the Jacobites tried to retaliate by preparing a duplicate of George as the *pièce de résistance* in an even greater bonfire.

But James Stuart was driven into flight, and news of Sheriffmuir reached London with incredible speed. Within five days the battle messengers entered the metropolis, and soon, captured Jacobite leaders were being led through jeering mobs while small boys carried warming-pans before them as a reminder that, in days of adversity at least, people still doubted the authenticity of the Prince they had followed to disaster.

Yet more tragic were the processions of prisoners who, too poor to purchase pardons, were sent off in gangs to work on West Indian plantations.

But the unrest continued till verbal allegiance was extracted from all and sundry. Officers would surround a church and administer the oath first to the officiating clergyman and then to his congregation; publicans applying for renewal of licence would find such withheld until they had proved themselves, in word at least, loyal subjects of King George; one recalcitrant " was whipt from Somerset House to Haymarket till he cried for the House of Hanover."

At last George shook the dust of England from his feet and sailed for the land of his birth, leaving the Prince of Wales not Regent, as he had hoped, but Guardian-and-Lieutenant-of-the-Kingdom.

Halcyon months followed. The Thames was fashion's highway, and sometimes boats were so closely packed that rowing became impossible, and with the royal family smiling and happy in their royal barge the mass of boats would drift slowly with the tide.

When the Prince and Princess of Wales moved to Hampton Court, making the journey by water, the court followed, and there was much " taking of the air " on the river, glee singing, water picnics, and dining in public, till an indignant King returned to stage a pretty family quarrel.

A new little prince born to the Princess of Wales was the unconscious cause, for the King appointed his son's *bête noire*, the Duke of Newcastle, as one of the child's sponsors, and the enraged parent shook his fist in the Duke's face !

A duel seemed inevitable, so by the King's orders the Prince was confined to his room, or rather to his wife's, since Caroline (who was still in bed, after the birth of the child) refused to let her husband out of her sight ; so shared his arrest.

Letters flew backwards and forwards, but it was not for some years that an eager public was permitted to purchase copies of them in the form of a two-penny broadsheet, attached to a memorandum from the King :

" As soon as the young Prince was born, the King informed himself of what was customary in like cases in the Kingdom with regard to the ceremony of baptism, and having found by the registers that when it was a boy the King was god-father and named the second from one of the chief lords of the court, he offered the honour to the Lord Chamberlain. He named for the office the Duke of Newcastle, and His Royal Highness the Prince of Wales was so chagrined at which that, as soon as the ceremony of baptism was over, being no longer able to contain his resent-

ment, he came up to the Duke of Newcastle and
gave him very vigorous language.

" The King was in the chamber, but not near enough
to hear what the Prince said to the Duke, who was
obliged to repeat this to His Majesty. His Majesty
then sent the Prince a message ordering him not to
go out of his own apartment until further orders.

" On Saturday the Prince writ a letter to the King,
and on Sunday writ another, but His Majesty not
having found them satisfactory, and having besides
many reasons for being discontented with the Prince's
conduct in several other particulars, signified to him
yesterday evening that he must go out of the Palace
of St. James's."

A message from the King :

" The Vice-Chamberlain is ordered to go to my
son and to tell him from me that he and his domestics
must leave my house. He is likewise to tell the
Princess from me that notwithstanding my orders
to my son she may remain at St. James's until her
health will suffer her to follow her husband, and he
is moreover commanded to tell the Princess from me
that it is my pleasure that my grandson and grand-
daughters remain at St. James's where they are.
The Princess is permitted to come and see them when
she has a mind, and the children are from time to
time permitted to go and see her and my son."

" Sir," wrote the Prince, " I received with all
submission Your Majesty's commands confining me
to my appartement till Your Majesty should signify
your further pleasure to me. So great a mark of
Your Majesty's displeasure surprised me extremely,
never having entertained a thought of Your Majesty
unbecoming a dutiful son." He went on to point
out that though he had felt it a hardship that the
Duke of Newcastle should be appointed a sponsor,

he had submitted, but that the sight of the duke taking the vows had stirred him to ungovernable wrath; hence his unfortunate outburst, which he begged His Majesty would look upon as a private matter.

A second letter was more definite : " Sir, I hope you will have the goodness to excuse me if in the condition I was in when I took the liberty of writing to Your Majesty I omitted to mention that I shall show no resentment to the Duke of Newcastle upon what has passed."

And now a third epistle : " Sir, I have just now obeyed your orders, having left St. James's. The Princess left with me, and our servants shall follow with all imaginable expedition."

A borrowed house offered temporary accommodation to the ejected Prince, and here Caroline wept daily for her children while the scandal swept the town.

> " The King then took his grey goose pen
> And dipped it o'er in gall . . .
> Take hence yourself and eke your spouse,
> Your maidens and your men !
> Your trinkets and all your trumpery
> Except your *children* ! "

The new-born Prince fell ill, and doctors warned the King that nothing could save the child's life except maternal care. It was sent to Kensington, where Caroline could have access to it without annoyance to His Majesty, but she gathered the baby into her arms too late.

There remained, the three Princesses at St. James's and Frederick Louis growing up alone in Hanover, so the Prince of Wales invoked the aid of the law, and twelve of the most learned judges in the land sat in long debate arguing the respective claims of King and Prince in regard to the latter's children. In search for precedents they ranged over a thousand

years of history, and called to witness the shades of
Edgar Atheling, Mary of Modena, and Richard of
Bordeaux.

The question before the court was : " Whether
the education and care of the persons of His Majesty's
grandchildren, the ordering of their place of abode,
the appointment of their governors . . . attendants,
and servants and the care and protection of their
interests when grown up, belonged as of right to His
Majesty the King of this realm, or to the Prince of
Wales."

The Lord Chief Justice and nine out of the twelve
judges decided on the ground of precedent that the
King held right of marriage over his grandchildren,
and from this argued that, since education was of
greater consequence than marriage, His Majesty must
pertain this right also. The Lord Chancellor and
the eleventh judge were in a minority of two ; he
lost his chancellorship and the Lord Chief Justice
received an earldom !

The feud lasted for four years, during which time
the Princess was permitted to see her three little
daughters only on Sunday evenings.

Leicester House became a centre of fashion and,
as the King believed, intrigue. The intensity of his
feeling against his son was discovered by Caroline
years later when going through the dead monarch's
papers. Among them was a draft scheme under
which the Prince of Wales was to have been kidnapped
and sent off to America. Under these conditions it
was guaranteed that he should " never trouble again."

A formal reconciliation was effected at a time when
Princess Anne, being ill " of the small-pox," a message
from the King sent through his favourite Turkish
valet gave Caroline permission to see the child daily.
Returning from St. James's one afternoon, she
encountered the Prince of Wales hastening to the
Palace ; his father had consented to receive him as

the result of a submissive letter written at the instigation of Sir Robert Walpole.

The interview was brief, for the King was almost incoherent and could only ejaculate : " Your conduct !—your conduct ! " But the populace showed pleasure, and when the Prince's chair was seen to have a Beefeater escort, a crowd assembled to cheer its delight at the visible proof of restored royal favour.

A Drawing-room put the official seal to the reconciliation, but one of the inner circles described the scene as looking like a set battle piece—" the King's court was all at the top of the room, and the Prince's hung about at the bottom behind him. . . . The Prince looked down and behaved prodegious well and the King cast an angry look that way every now and then. One could not help thinking it was like a Dog and Cat, whenever the dog stirs a foot the cat sets up her back and is ready to fly at him. . . . Such a crowd as was never seen, for not only curiosity but interest had brought it together."

The hollowness of the reconciliation became public when the King next went to Hanover, and instead of giving his son an official position left the country in the care of a Council of Regency. Even worse, in Caroline's eyes, was an official notice in the *Gazette* informing the world that during His Majesty's absence the Drawing-rooms would be held by His Majesty's grandchildren.

In high dudgeon Prince and Princess of Wales withdrew from Leicester fields and drove away down the footpad-infested roads to the seclusion of Richmond.

And to Richmond rode Sir Robert Walpole carrying the news of the King's sudden death near Osnabruck. George Augustus, disturbed in his afternoon nap, came hurrying out, breeches in hand, to receive the messenger.

He was proclaimed King next day, but too late to carry out his boyhood's dream of freeing his mother and bringing her to England ; for Sophia Dorothea's [1] long captivity had come to an end and she was dead.

All he could do was to display the portrait of her that he had kept hidden during his father's reign.

Eighteen months later Frederick Louis, the Hanoverian-born son of George Augustus and Caroline, took the packet boat from Holland to Harwich, posted to Whitechapel, and travelled thence to St. James's Palace by hackney coach. Once more, England had her Prince of Wales.

[1] See *Her Majesty : The Romance of the Queens of England.*

CHAPTER XIII

FREDERICK LOUIS PRINCE OF WALES

" Fresh as a rose but newly blown and fair ! "—ODE TO THE PRINCE.

FREDERICK LOUIS OF HANOVER

Born in Hanover . . . . . February 4, 1707
Created Prince of Wales . . . January 9, 1729
Married at St. James's (to Princess Augusta
of Saxe-Gotha) . . . . April 26, 1737
Died . . . . March 20, 1751

Descent.

George II — *m.* — Caroline of Anspach

Frederick Louis (and others)

CONTEMPORARY SOVEREIGNS

ENGLAND : Anne, George I, and George II.
FRANCE : Louis XIV and Louis XV.

CHAPTER XIII

FREDERICK LOUIS OF HANOVER

1707–1751

WHEN George I was called to assume the crown of England, he decreed that his grandson, Frederick Louis, should remain behind in Hanover. So the seven-year-old boy was left under the charge of governors and tutors to maintain the state of an electoral prince and hold Drawing-rooms for the élite. Before he had entered his 'teens he could " drink as deep as any German baron," and his helpless tutors wrote of his many misdeeds to his parents, who were equally powerless to act.

" But these are mere page's tricks," said Caroline hopefully.

" Would to heaven they were ! " cried an exasperated governor. " They are the tricks of grooms and scoundrels."

Fourteen years elapsed before Frederick Louis followed his parents to England. Other children had taken his place in their hearts, and they summoned him unwillingly when pressure was brought to bear by the English Ambassador, who discovered that the young heir was about to plunge into secret matrimony.

On one of George I's periodical visits to Germany he had selected Princess Wilhelmina of Prussia as a suitable bride for his grandson after having made a critical examination of her by candle-light. All was in order save the necessary signatures, when the King died, and Frederick Louis, finding the matter hanging fire and discovering that the match was not approved

by his father, George II, proposed to the Queen of
Prussia that there should be a secret wedding. She
welcomed the project, but in her excitement dropped
an incautious word to the English Ambassador, who,
in duty bound, sent a hasty warning to England.
Frederick Louis was summoned by his parents, and
Wilhelmina for her part, having been soundly whipped,
was sent to bed.

The Prince spoke English with difficulty, and found
himself a stranger in his own family. He was loaded
with debts, which his father refused to pay, was
bereft of a bride, and kept short of money. No one
wanted him except the country which had long been
dissatisfied that the heir to the crown had had no
English training.

" He is the most agreeable young man it is possible
to imagine without being the least handsome," wrote
one lady after a presentation at court. " His person
is little but well-made and genteel. He has a liveliness
in his eyes which is indescribable and the most obliging
address that can be conceived. The crown of all
his perfections is the great duty and regard he pays
the King and Queen," she continued " . . . as if
obliging them were the greatest pleasure of his life.
They receive it with the utmost joy and satisfaction,
and the father's fondness seems to equal the tender-
ness of the mother, so that, believe me, the world
never produced a royal family so happy in one
another. Pray God long to continue it ! " she
added piously, so perhaps a ray of doubt had crept
across her mind while penning the eulogy.

A few years later King and Queen were in full
agreement when Caroline exclaimed :

" My dear first-born is the greatest ass and the
greatest liar and the greatest canaille and the greatest
beast in the whole world, and I heartily wish he were
out of it ! "

Life at St. James's became more and more difficult
for the Prince of Wales, who still nursed the griev-

FREDERICK LOUIS.
From a picture by J. B. Van Loo at Windsor. By gracious permission of
His Majesty The King.

ance of his broken romance with Wilhelmina, but as debt piled on debt he cast about for a means of finding both happiness and wealth. The Duchess of Marlborough became a confidante, and a marriage between the Prince and her favourite granddaughter was suggested, for Lady Diana Spencer would then be dowered with a hundred thousand pounds. The Prince welcomed the project, arrangements were made for a secret ceremony at Windsor—and once again the Fates were unkind, for Sir Robert Walpole discovered the plot.

Insult was added to injury in the eyes of the frustrated Prince, for while he was left unmarried with his increasing pile of debts, the Princess Royal was provided with a bridegroom and received a substantial grant from Parliament.

In his indignation he launched an ultimatum demanding that he should be allowed to do military service on the Rhine, and that steps should be taken to provide him with both an established income and a suitable bride. His military ardour was quenched in haste, and no move was made in either of the other directions until it was rumoured that Prince Frederick intended to apply to Parliament, when the King offered him £50,000 a year, which was half the desired amount, and the matter became the sport of politics.

Family dissensions were suspended for a time when the King wrote from Hanover that he was arranging a match for his son, and the Queen began to order wedding garments for herself and " jewels for the Princess of Wales."

Frederick Louis was told that if he turned over a new leaf, and accepted the selected princess, his debts would be paid. He still hoped for Wilhelmina, and argued that a union with Prussia would be advantageous, but wrote a dutiful letter undertaking to accept any princess considered suitable for him.

A Prussian marriage was the last thing possible at the moment, for diplomatic relations between the

Kings of England and Prussia were strained to such a point that a duel had been proposed. Both were eager for it, and the dramatic encounter was forgone only when the would-be combatants were forced to realise that they might become the laughing-stock of Europe.

So it was Princess Augusta of Saxe-Gotha, and not Wilhelmina of Prussia, whom the Prince of Wales hastened down to Greenwich to meet. She proved " neither handsome nor ugly, neither tall nor short, but had a lively pretty countenance."

Crowds assembled to watch the two when they dined together in public and " took the air " on the river, but there was some dismay when it was found that the Princess could speak no English ; her mother had decided that Augusta need not trouble to learn such a barbarous language, since, the Guelphs having been twenty years on the throne, the best circles would undoubtedly speak German.

The marriage took place on the day following Princess Augusta's arrival at St. James's Palace, but not before she had been the witness of a desperate family quarrel.

Some question of precedence having arisen, it was decreed that the younger members of the family should dine alone together, whereupon Prince Frederick pointed out that he and Princess Augusta should be seated on chairs while his sisters must use mere stools. The meal waited while the battle raged, for the stubborn princesses refused to enter the room until the offending stools were removed and chairs introduced for all.

The wedding was an evening affair, and for that hour at least family dissensions were suspended.

Prince William, Frederick's younger brother, in whose favour the parents would willingly have disinherited their elder son, so far as the crown of England was concerned, disrobed the bridegroom, while

" his majesty did him the honour to put on his night-shift."

Meanwhile, the Queen and Princesses were performing similar offices for Princess Augusta, and laying aside her " virgin habit of silver "; then, she being in bed, the King brought in the Prince, attired in a nightgown of silver and a lace cap; when the quality were admitted to see the pair sitting side by side.

" The King wore gold brocade and the Queen was in plain yellow silk faced with pea-diamonds and other gems of immense value. It was observed that many of the rich cloths were of English manufacture ; the few which were French did not come up to them in richness or goodness."

Duty accomplished, the King went off to refresh himself in Hanover, leaving the Prince to discover the unsatisfactory nature of his allowance and the fact that no proper provision had been made for his bride.

The youthful Augusta nursed her most cherished doll at the palace window, to the horror of society, while the Prince fought for his rights, pointing out that he had sacrificed himself by demanding marriage, " though the Princess was the best and most agreeable woman in the world," and now it was the duty of the nation to stand by him.

The Opposition sided with the Prince, and a hot debate took place on the motion for an address to the King praying him " in consideration of the high rank and many eminent virtues of the Prince and Princess " to settle £100,000 a year on his son out of the revenue that had been cheerfully granted.

Some held it as extraordinary that Parliament should presume to prescribe to His Majesty what provision he should make for his own children ; others, that the Prince must be considered as emancipated and out of the family by virtue of his marriage.

" The use of the word ' emancipation ' in such a connection infers a state of slavery ! " objected a

back-bencher, but the Government guns were heaviest.
The King's prerogative must not be encroached upon.
. . . "The King must not be accused of injustice to
his eldest son, to do so might lessen the esteem the
people have and ought to have for his majesty and
make them think he is no longer fit for rule over us,"
cried a fiery orator. "Indeed," he went on in glorious peroration, "the consequences of such an act
might be fatal. For my part, if I were in a foreign
nation, and learnt that such a question had been
brought into the Parliament of Great Britain, I
should expect to hear by next post that Parliament
had deposed the father and set the crown on the head
of his son!"

He won. There was a majority of 30 against the
motion.

But as the King lingered on in Hanover he fell
from favour, and the popularity of the young Prince
and Princess increased.

"Lost, stolen, or strayed," notices were affixed to
the Palace walls, and the public remained unmoved
when a great storm blew up and for a space it was
believed that the King was drowned.

The Queen was in despair, and the Princesses vowed
that they would leave the palace "at grand galop"
if and when the Prince came to rule—but a message
arrived that George had not sailed.

"The King is safe!" cried Caroline, but few
rejoiced with her, and a pamphlet entitled *The Lost
Mutton Found; or the Royal Fly-by-Night* found
a ready sale.

A few months later a fire in the Temple gave the
Prince an opportunity to show his best side, and as
he worked to subdue the flames more than one man,
recognising the nation's heir, cried, "Crown him!
Crown him!"

The gloves were off with a vengeance, and the
fight for a larger income waxed stronger, while the
Prince dropped judicious hints as to future benefits.

But before anything was achieved a family con-
flagration occurred that set all other quarrels in the
shade.   The King had decreed that the Prince's child
should be born at Hampton Court; the Prince was
determined that the event should take place at St.
James's Palace.

One night, after an evening spent at cards, Princess
Augusta was carried into a coach and a furious drive
began.

"Courage! Courage!" cried the Prince to the
moaning girl.   "A quelle sottise!"

St. James's at last.   With tablecloths to serve as
sheets the Princess was hurried into bed, and most
fortunately the Lady-in-Waiting had had twenty
children of her own.   Presently a child was born, "a
little atom of a girl about the bigness of a good large
toothpick-case!"

News of the arrival was sent to the King and Queen,
still peacefully asleep at Hampton Court.   In fury
Caroline arrived to see for herself that no permanent
harm had been done to the Princess, and to tell the
Prince plainly that had he produced for her inspection
"a fine jolly boy instead of this poor ugly little she-
mouse," it would not have been accepted as genuine.

The King's wrath increased as he reflected upon
the way he had been hoodwinked, and history repeated
itself.   As he himself had once been turned out of
his father's house and home, so now he sent orders
to Frederick Louis commanding a withdrawal so
soon as mother and child could be moved.

"This extravagant, undutiful behaviour in so
essential a point as the birth of an heir to my crown
is such evidence of your premeditated defiance of
me and my authority, and of such natural rights
belonging to your parents, as cannot be excused by
the pretended innocence of your intentions nor palliated
by specious words," wrote the King.

Until the Prince "withdrew his regard from those
upon whose advice he had been acting and returned

to his duties" he should not be allowed to reside in the Palace, nor would the King receive any reply "till your actions manifest a submission that may incline me to pardon that which at present I most justly resent," wrote George II.

The messenger deputed to read the King's letter to the Prince reported that he received it "very civil and decent."

"I hope to God that I shall never see him again!" said the Queen.

"Thank God that to-morrow the puppy will be out of my house," added the King.

The break was complete. Copies of the correspondence that had passed between the King and his son were sent to the various ambassadors, and those who waited upon the Prince received warning that they would not be received at court.

The Queen's wish was fulfilled; she never saw her son again, for when she lay dying he was refused admission to her, the King seeing nothing but hypocrisy in his attentions.

Public opinion concerning the Prince varied: When Philip V of Spain objected to the presence of a British squadron off his coasts and declared war on England, the Prince joined the procession as it marched into the city crying for a "Free Navy" and "No search!" and drank success to the war at the Rose Tavern near Temple Bar; the people cheered him. But when the King turned down once more his son's further application for military service and went in person to lead his army, the position changed, and it was George II, not Frederick Louis, waiting to receive him back, who became the national hero.

Driven into inaction, the Prince lived the life of a country gentleman at Kew or watched his children give amateur plays at Norfolk House, till he died with startling suddenness as the result of a blow from a ball.

"Dead, is he ? " said George II, sitting over his card table. " Why, they told me he was better."

> " Here lies Fred,
> Who was alive and is dead.
> Had it been his father,
> We had much rather.
> Had it been his brother,
> Still better than another !
>
> Had it been his sister,
> No one would have missed her.
> Had it been the whole generation,
> Still better for the nation.
> But since it's only Fred—
> There's no more to be said."

So wrote a popular poet of the day, voicing the sentiments of the people.

CHAPTER XIV

GEORGE WILLIAM FREDERICK
(GEORGE III)

" This complete and wondrous man ! "—ODE BY POET LAUREATE

GEORGE WILLIAM FREDERICK

Born (Norfolk House, St. James's Square)	May 24 O.S., 1738, June 4 N.S.
Created Prince of Wales . . .	April 19, 1751
Ascended	October 25, 1760
Married Charlotte of Mecklenburg-Strelitz	September 8, 1761
Died	January 29, 1820

Descent

George II — *m.* Caroline of Anspach
|

Frederick Louis Prince of Wales (and others)
m. Augusta of Saxe-Gotha
|

George William Frederick (and others)

Contemporary Sovereigns

France : Louis XV, Louis XVI (guillotined), Louis XVII (nominally), Napoleon Bonaparte, Louis XVIII.

CHAPTER XIV

GEORGE WILLIAM FREDERICK (GEORGE III)

1738-1820

THE third Prince of Wales of the Hanoverian line was born at Norfolk House, St. James's Square, where his parents had set up a rival court when exiled from the Palace by reason of a family feud. He made a hurried advent about five o'clock one June morning some twelve hours after his mother, the Princess of Wales, had been walking in St. James's. The baby showed a weak hold on life and was given an immediate baptism; years later the question arose as to whether a bishop who had been born a dissenter could validly baptise an heir to the crown. And if George III was as bad as unbaptised, could he be regarded as the temporal head of England's established church ?

But this trouble was in the womb of the future. For the moment the vital question was the keeping of life in the frail little frame, so a stalwart, fresh-coloured young countrywoman was fetched in as foster-mother. To the dismay of the court this young person took the newly born scion of the royal house to bed with her and stood her ground, arms akimbo, when reproved.

" And why for not—the poor lamb ! " she cried indignantly, and vowed that officials who dared to interfere with her method might nurse the boy themselves. Etiquette was vanquished, and the Prince throve.

Twelve months later he was advanced enough to receive a troop of boys who came marching in military formation to kiss the fist of the year-old Prince George and appoint him their honorary colonel.

Babyhood slipped by while Princess Augusta added to her family, and every year George found himself elder brother to yet another brother or sister.

There might be war between the rival courts of King and Prince, but the royal children knew little of the trouble as they played at baseball or push-pin, appeared with the dessert to recite noble sentiments to admiring visitors, or, after careful coaching by a leading actor of the day, won plaudits for the private theatrical performances in which the Prince of Wales delighted. " Rule Britannia," was heard for the first time on one of these occasions.

At seven years old, a fair-haired, bright-complexioned boy, George, with his brother, passed into the hands of tutors ; Latin, music, fencing, water-colour drawing, mathematics, and elocution were the chief studies of the royal children. If, at eleven, Prince George could not write English, we have it on the authority of his governor that he had a pretty gift for Latin verses.

Now came an ordeal, for the King had decided to bestow the Order of the Garter upon his grandson, and the Prince of Wales, having ushered the boy into the royal presence, lurked behind the door, interjecting hints as to his deportment. A happier birthday treat accorded the princes was an expedition on the Thames when they went to see a boat-race from Whitehall to Putney, for which Prince George had offered a prize.

Two years later the death of Frederick Louis Prince of Wales flung his son into the limelight, for George II was nearing seventy and in the ordinary course of nature must be succeeded by his grandson at no very distant date.

The training of the heir became the nation's concern, and Prince George was endowed with his father's title and summoned to stay with the King

GEORGE III.
From a picture by Allan Ramsay in the National Portrait Gallery.

at Hampton Court in order that his attainments
might be considered. He failed to make a good
impression, and had his ears boxed before he escaped
to his mother, to pass through the hands of relays
of governors and tutors. "Hold up your head,"
said one. "For God's sake turn out your toes,"
commanded another. The perpetual changes stirred
the Prince to rebellion, and at last he turned upon
his tormentors vowing that if he were bereft of his
few remaining favourites he would burn his books
and decline to learn.

Princess Augusta looked on helplessly. "I don't
know what they teach him, but nothing of much use,
I am afraid." She wished her son less childish for
his age, but reflected that he was "a very honest
boy," and bent her energies to keeping him unspotted
from the world by depriving him of companionship
other than that afforded by his brothers and sisters,
for "the young people of the day are ill-educated
and so vicious that they frighten me."

Tentative attempts were made to broaden the
Prince's outlook by escorting him to different manu-
facturing centres, and on a red-letter day he was
taken to Woolwich to see the launching of a battle-
ship, but too often such excursions were made under
the guidance of the Duke of Cumberland, upon whom
the Princess of Wales looked with a fear which she
had communicated to her son in his childhood. The
drawing of a sword by the Duke made the boy flinch.
"What can they have told him of me?" cried
the horrified Duke; but it was years before the
Prince's fear could be eradicated.

At last public disapproval of the education provided for the heir became vocal. Pamphlets were
circulated, and the goaded tutors fell to quarrelling
among themselves, the many accusing one of tainting
the Prince's mind with Jacobitism. The King set up
a commission of inquiry, and yet another governor

was appointed. For the moment the Prince was too interested in the introduction of the Georgian Calendar to protest (it had the odd effect of depriving him of his birthday, and crowds of people as indignant as himself were parading the streets shouting, " Give us back our eleven days! "); in later years he described this new appointee as " a depraved and worthless man. Nor was the governor's opinion of his young pupil much more complimentary. He found George " uncommonly full of princely prejudices contracted in the nursery and improved by the bedchamberwomen and Pages of the Back-stairs."

The new régime decided that the Prince of Wales must be withdrawn from his mother's petticoat influence, and in the hope of developing the boy and ruling him through a wife, George II made tentative advances to a Brunswick princess on his grandson's behalf.

Princess Augusta viewed the project with alarm and objected that at seventeen the Prince of Wales was too young to marry. She was indignant that such a momentous decision should have been taken without her concurrence, and felt convinced that the Brunswick princess, of whom she knew nothing except by hearsay, was entirely unsuitable.

" Such a creature will not do for George," she assured those around her, and went on to discourse upon her son's character. " He is not a dissipated boy, but good-natured and cheerful with a serious cast of mind, and those about him know him no more than if they had never seen him." She knew that he was not quick, but as against this he was " applicable and intelligent." Though she held herself incompetent to judge of his " book-learning," she felt sure it was " small," but did not consider this her fault, for she had once suggested to a tutor that the Prince should be " informed about the constitution," but the gentleman had declined to give the instruction, " fearing to arouse the jealousy of another."

When the Prince of Wales attained his majority, the King made yet another attempt at rescue by offering him £40,000 a year and a residence at Kensington, but George, while accepting the allowance, declined to leave his mother's immediate circle, although he agreed to set up a household of his own, and with Lord Bute as a companion set about acquiring polish by travel. He visited Edinburgh incognito, and went as far north as the Isle of Bute.

But " bigoted, young, and chaste " though the Prince might be, he was growing up, and now startled those around him by falling in love with a pretty Quaker maiden whose uncle kept a linen draper's shop not far from St. James's.

Gossip ran rife. Some said the Prince had married her, others, that he had paid a complaisant husband to give the girl the shelter of his name and had then carried her off to immure her in a house with a high-walled garden.

Be the truth what it may, Hannah Lightfoot disappeared from her relation's ken.

Public affairs now began to attract the Prince's attention. When war broke out between England and France he chafed against remaining at home while his grandfather went abroad, feeling that heading the Commission which gave the royal assent to bills in the King's absence was too small a part to play.

He shared in the rejoicing over the capture of Quebec, but on the King's return slipped back once more into the rural life at Kew with his mother and her brood.

Then one autumn morning a note was put into the Prince's hand as he went out on his morning ride. George II was dead.

Princess Augusta was the first to hear the news :
" George, be a King ! " she had dinned the phrase
into her son's ears, and now the time had come to
act ; he was twenty-two, and no man knew of what
metal he was made.

At an early interview Walpole found George III
" a charming young King . . . with every appearance
of being good and amiable in everything, having no
view but that of contenting all the world."

Lady Hervey's first impression of the new sovereign
was equally flattering : " I have a moral certainty
that he was in his nursery the most honest, true, good-
natured child that ever lived. . . . What the child
was the man most certainly is."

But George III was to startle his ministers and
the country at a very early date, for after the Cabinet
had drawn up a careful " speech from the throne "
for delivery by the King, George, entirely on his
own initiative and in his own hand, interpolated a
paragraph :

" Born and educated in this country, I glory in the
name of Briton and the peculiar happiness of my life
will ever consist in promoting the welfare of a people
whose loyalty and warm affection to me I consider
as the greatest and most permanent security of
my throne."

The young King was not to be a cipher in the
hands of his ministers after all.

Another sensation occurred when the clergy were
forbidden to preach laudatory sermons concerning
the King in the King's presence, and a third on the
publication of a royal proclamation " for the encouragement of piety and virtue, and the punishment
of prophaneness, and immorality." In this, military
men were called upon to set a particular example to
the nation.

An eager throng attended the Drawing-rooms, and
soon it was seen that these too were changed from

1820]   "TELL LADY SARAH . . ."   227

those held in the last reign. They "lost their appearance of a lion's den, for the sovereign no longer stands in one spot dropping bits of German news, but walks about speaking freely to everyone!"

Yes, all agreed that a young King was an asset—but then again a bachelor King was an anomaly; one whispered to another that there would be a change before long, for already the youthful monarch's attention had been caught by Lady Sarah Lennox, a seventeen-year-old beauty and a great grand-daughter of Charles II. In the long summer days, when he turned his horse's head towards Kew, Lady Sarah was invariably discovered in the charmingly rural pastime of tossing hay in the ground of Holland House, which bordered the way by which the King rode.

All London was agog when at a Birthday Drawing-room the King advanced the suggestion that the forthcoming coronation would be a finer sight if a Queen as well as a King could be crowned, then sent a message to Lady Sarah Lennox, saying he was sure she would " grace the ceremony in the properest manner." There had been much talk of a wedding of late, and for his part he thought an English match would be better than a foreign one— " Pray tell Lady Sarah I said so ! "

No wonder court circles hummed with interest and Princess Augusta took alarm.

King George was plunged into state affairs, while an anxious ambassador journeyed over Europe seeking a suitable and Protestant princess. The hand-kerchief fell at the feet of bewildered Charlotte of Mecklenburg-Strelitz [1] and George laid aside his dreams. Calling a special meeting of the Cabinet, he announced his intentions, " and scarce six men in England knew of the existence of the princess he named."

[1] See *Her Majesty: The Romance of the Queens of England.*

The winds were adverse, but after nearly being driven on to the Norwegian coast Charlotte landed at Harwich, having taken ten days to make the journey from Cuxhaven; when the waves were highest the Princess had sat undismayed, plucking at her guitar strings and learning to sing " God Save the King."

" She has come after many false alarums," reported a contemporary letter writer, and the noises of the coaches, chars, horsemen, and the mob that has been to see her passing through the parks is so prodigious that I cannot hear the guns."

" She is not tall nor a beauty," said Walpole, " but she looks sensible and is remarkable genteel."

A fortnight later even greater crowds thronged the streets, for the youthful bridal pair drove to their crowning. In preparation for the event a band of patriotic citizens had sallied forth to cut down the gibbets on which the rotting bodies of executed criminals hung in clanking chains, but they had not been able to finish the work, and many still remained to taint the air. The thronging sightseers ignored such things, as they ignored the press-gang at work in the crowd around the Abbey; it was many a long year since London had had such a pageant.

" Sir," said the Archbishop. " Will you accept the oath taken by your predecessors ? "

" I am willing," answered the King.

" Will you solemnly promise and swear to govern the people of this Kingdom of Britain and the Dominions belonging to her according to the statutes of Parliament and the laws and customs of the same ? "

" I solemnly promise so to do."

" Will you keep peace and godly agreement according to your power ? "

" I will keep it."

" Sir, will you to your power cause law, justice, and discretion in mercy and truth to be executed in all your judgments ? "

" I will."

" Sir, will you hold, grant and keep, the rightful customs which the commonalty of this your kingdom have, and will you defend and uphold them to the honour of God as much as in you lieth ? . . . "

" I grant and promise so to do."

" God Save the King ! "

The coronation banquet followed the crowning, and the King's Champion rode into Westminster Hall mounted on the charger which George II had ridden at Dettingen, when for the last time an English king led his troops in battle. Men said that among those who watched was Charles Edward Stuart, the " Young Chevalier."

Next day, with the excitement behind them, credulous folk began to shake their heads and whisper forebodingly. Evil would befall the nation, for had not the best jewel fallen from the King's crown immediately after the crowning ? What could such portent mean but dire disaster ?

Twenty years later people remembered the omen.

George III set himself to learn his new duties while Charlotte grappled with the difficulties of the English language and gave birth to the first of her fifteen children.

" Our next monarch was christened last night, George Augustus Frederick," wrote Walpole. " The Queen's bed, magnificent and in the best of taste, was placed in the drawing-room. Though she did not receive in form as yet, all who presented themselves for the baptism were admitted. . . . I kissed the hand of his great-great-grandfather."

Young bloods might scoff at a royal pair who found pleasure in playing cribbage together night after night, but in the prosperous years the nation liked to watch the ever-growing queue of little princes and princesses following the parents in the bi-weekly walks at Richmond or on the terrace at Windsor Castle. It found pleasure too in the sight of the King dining in public, even though he " ate plain," preferring abstention to " growing diseased and old."

When bad times came, it was felt that this King would understand his people's troubles, and they deluged him with petitions. Hatters complained that they were being ruined by reason of the influx of foreign goods, and weavers protested against the rising figures of imported silks and velvets ; when the King went to give the royal assent to a prohibitory bill, they cheered him to Westminster and back.

But the bad times continued, and taxation had to be increased till visiting foreigners declared that there was hardly an hour in the day when the English were not subjected to duties : " at 8 a.m. they use taxed soap with which to wash, at 9 a.m. taxed sugar is eaten, at noon the hair must be powdered with taxed starch ; taxed salt is used to savour the meat in the evening meal. Porter (drunk to raise the spirits) is likewise taxed, as are the windows by which light enters their houses, and the candles that guide them to bed."

Yet money and yet more money was needed, and there seemed to be but one untouched source of supply—America.

Plans for the imposition of a Stamp Duty which it was expected would bring in £100,000 were advanced and approved. Parliament passed a resolution :

" It is just and necessary that a revenue be raised in Your Majesty's Dominion of America for defraying the expenses of defending, protecting, and securing the same."

The Act passed through a thin House with hardly

a dissentient vote, and in due course a bewildered
nation heard that the New World was aflame with
indignation, and that copies of the offending Act of
Parliament were being hawked about the streets
of New York emblazoned with a Death's Head in
place of the Royal Arms. Consignments of stamps
were seized and burnt, while Boston's flags flew at
half-mast and muffled bells tolled.

In England, divided Councils sounded and merchants
cried that they must go bankrupt, since America
refused to pay them. In America, representatives
of nine of the colonies drew up petitions and memorials
to King, Lords, and Commons.

Parliament met : " His Majesty recommended such
resolutions as might tend at once to preserve the
rights of the Legislature over the Colonies and to
restore to them the harmony and tranquillity which
has been interrupted by riots and disorders."

" I am more and more grieved by the accounts
from America," wrote George III. " This is undoubtedly the most serious matter that has ever
come before Parliament ; it requires more delibera-
tion, candour, and temper than I fear it will meet
with here."

The Repeal Act was carried, but prefaced by a
Declaration affirming the right of the British Parliament to make laws binding on British colonies, but
the Quakers of Philadelphia accepted the olive branch
and, as a symbol of their loyalty, undertook to wear
new suits made from British cloth on the King's
birthday.

The need for money remained, and a year later,
when the army estimates were under debate, it was
argued that America, like Ireland, should support
her defenders, and that it was unfair to British tax-
payers that no levy should be made on the colonies.
Overseas, the smouldering indignation flamed afresh,
and year by year as the trouble between England

and America increased so too did the disagreement between the King and his eldest son. At times, when waves of unpopularity engulfed him, George III looked towards Hanover, believing that he would be the last King of England.

News of rioting in Boston consequent upon the imposition of a tax on tea reached England when the House was in session. Members leapt to their feet to decry the very idea of the colonists putting up a fight—that was talk with which to frighten women and children! Others caught the Speaker's eye to protest against yielding to threats. Did England show a faint heart, it would mean that the seat of government had shifted from the tight little island in the North Sea to Philadelphia.

A divided House adjourned for Easter, and Generals Howe, Burgoyne, and Clinton sailed for Boston; on an April day (1775) the first shots were fired.

As the position developed, conflicting petitions were showered upon the puzzled King. London prayed him to bring about a cessation of hostilities, but the Universities of Oxford and Cambridge were urgent that the war should be continued.

" I deplore with the deepest concern the miseries which a great part of my subjects in America have brought upon themselves by an unjustifiable resistance to the constitutional authority of this Kingdom," answered George III.

The struggle went on, but wisdom came slowly. In 1782 a demand arose in the Commons for an address imploring His Majesty to end the war with America; it was lost by a majority of one.

Ten months later provisional articles were signed in Paris by which Great Britain recognised the thirteen colonies as free and independent states.

Parliament met, and the King made his announcement: " In thus admitting their separation from the Crown of Great Britain I have sacrificed every consideration of my own to the wishes and opinions of my people. . . . I make it my humble and earnest prayer to God Almighty that Great Britain may not feel the evils which might result from so great a dismemberment of the empire, and that America may be free from those calamities which have formerly proved, in the mother country, how essential is monarchy to the attainment of constitutional liberty. . . . Religion, language, interest, affection may, and I hope will, prove a bond of permanent union between the two countries."

" Did I lower my voice when I came to that part of my speech ? " asked George III.

The strain had been great, and those who had known of the King's temporary breakdown two years before were watching him anxiously. Then, he had found relaxation in his young family, in going about among his people, and in the writing of the agricultural pamphlets which had helped to earn him his nickname of " Farmer George." " The ground, like man, was never meant to be idle," he was wont to say. " If it does not produce something it will be overrun with weeds."

Now, his eldest son was a thorn in the flesh and the others were absent, the three younger members of the family having been entered at a German University.

The King's mental state grew worse, though he struggled gallantly. At a levee his incoherent conversation frightened many, and repercussions were felt next day, when stocks fell alarmingly.

Lord Thurlow, who was much disturbed, urged that the Sovereign should retire to Windsor and take care of himself, but the King turned upon him with indignation.

" You too, my Lord Thurlow, forsake me and suppose me ill beyond recovery ! But whatever you and Mr. Pitt may think, I that am born a gentleman shall never lay my head on my last pillow in peace and quiet while I remember the loss of my American colonies ! "

Worse was to follow. The distraught King presented Mrs. Siddons with a paper blank save for his signature, and the final crash came when the arrival of the Prince of Wales stirred his father to an outburst of ungovernable fury.

Parliament debated the Regency Bill while the Prince took control at Windsor, the weeping Queen shut herself up in her own apartments with the six princesses, and the King raved.

There were tragic months before George III recovered, to be confronted with the problem of Catholic Emancipation in a world disturbed by the French Revolution.

" I can give up my crown and retire from power. I can quit my palace and live in a cottage ; I can lay my head on a block and lose my life, but I *cannot* break my coronation oath," said the distraught King. " If I violate my vow," he told the Queen and frightened Princesses, " I am no longer legal Sovereign over this country."

The new French Republic sent an ambassador to inquire whether England was to be regarded as hostile or neutral, and England gave bold answer : " If France wishes to maintain peace between the two countries she must refrain from violating the rights of her neighbours."

While conversations were proceeding the tumbrils rolled through the streets of Paris and the King of France passed to the guillotine.

Diplomatic relations were suspended, the ambassador was bidden to leave the country within eight days, and France declared war on England and Holland ; during the ensuing struggle France once succeeded in making an abortive landing on British soil (1797). Never again till the bombardment of Scarborough and Hartlepool in the Great War were

English men and women to be driven from their homes by enemy attack.

But when Napoleon (whose " impious pre-eminence could not be of long duration " according to the King's firm faith) pitched his camp at Boulogne the nation was aroused and gave ready heed to the royal proclamation enjoining economy of food. All masters of households were enjoined to see to it that the consumption of bread was reduced by at least a third, and the population was instructed as to what must be done in case of serious invasion.

If the descent were made on Essex, Chelmsford was to become the King's headquarters, for George III was determined to head his forces. Should Kent have to meet the brunt of attack, the military would occupy Dartford, while the Cabinet withdrew to Worcester, to which town the Queen would travel also, together with the nation's treasure, under volunteer escort. The Tower was to offer safe storage to bank-books, and stores from Woolwich were to be securely hidden in the heart of England, to which they would be shifted by canal. It was also decreed that no news was to be published other than that supplied by the state to accredited news-writers by the Government. Such arrangements compare very favourably with those issued a hundred and twenty years later.

But then, as in the twentieth century, sea-power saved the nation. Trafalgar was fought, and the navy's prey was nineteen ships of the line.

When details came to hand men gloried to learn that the *Victory* and the *Téméraire* " were so close on top of the enemy ships that in the hottest hour of action British sailors had to desist from fighting to pour buckets of water on enemy flames lest all should be involved in destruction, an instance of cool deliberate bravery without parallel in the annals of English history."

But George III was old and frail. He could not wait to see the end, and a few years later there came another tragic breakdown. The Regency Bill passed (1811), and the Prince of Wales gathered up the sceptre that the weary King let fall while there yet remained nine years of darkened life before him.

CHAPTER XV

GEORGE AUGUSTUS FREDERICK
(GEORGE IV)

" The First Gentleman in Europe."

GEORGE AUGUSTUS FREDERICK

Born at St. James's Palace . . . August 12, 1762
Created Prince of Wales by Letters Patent August 17, 1762
Married Caroline of Brunswick . . April 8, 1795
Became Regent . . . . . February 5, 1811
Ascended . . . . . . January 29, 1820
Died . . . . June 26, 1830

Descent

George III — *m.* — Charlotte of Mecklenburg-Strelitz

George Augustus Frederick (and others)

CONTEMPORARY SOVEREIGNS

FRANCE : Louis XV, Louis XVI, Louis XVII (nominally), Napoleon Bonaparte, Louis XVIII, and Charles X.

CHAPTER XV

GEORGE AUGUSTUS FREDERICK (GEORGE IV)

1762–1830

" THE Prince of Wales is a charming little creature! Surely, if ever the birth of a prince was ushered in with favourable omens, his is; he is born at a time when the glory of British Arms is at the highest pitch that ever it was known before. He had not been in the world more than an hour when nearly a million of treasure taken from the enemy passed in a procession of twenty loaded waggons underneath his windows, and before he was six days old news arrived of one of the most important victories that have been obtained during the war—that of Havannah."

So ran a contemporary letter, while another enthusiastic, if slightly inaccurate supporter of the Hanoverian dynasty, pointed out that the infant had arrived on the forty-seventh anniversary of the accession of his house to the British throne, " which it was hoped he would fill (in due process of time) with a lustre not inferior to his predecessors."

The news of the birth of a prince was carried to the King at Buckingham House, which had been recently purchased for the Queen, and the fortunate messenger received a reward of £500.

Twelve days later George Augustus Frederick, Prince of Wales, was put on view in the Queen's chamber, and ladies in batches of forty, having been warned to " tread softly," were invited to see him reposing in his cradle, which stood on a daïs behind a light gilt railing.

A couple of white-clad young ladies stood one on each side of the cradle to rock it when desirable, and at the foot sat a nurse with a crimson cushion held ready to receive the child for occasional presentation to his mother.

Such crowds thronged the precincts in their eagerness to be admitted that those not fortunate enough to have the entrée grew envious, and denounced the whole affair as " un-English."

Before his third birthday arrived the well-drilled little prince received and, what is more, addressed his first deputation :

" I thank you for this mark of duty to the King and wish prosperity to this charity," he said clearly, to the relief of those responsible for his training, but it was felt that the risk was too great to be incurred a second time.

At seven, clad in scarlet and gold and wearing the insignia of the Garter, the Prince of Wales and his yet more juvenile sister, the Princess Royal, held their first Drawing-room. A few months later he passed into the hands of tutors, and with a life alternating between Buckingham House and Kew, began his serious education.

Eight hours a day were devoted to study, and both the Prince of Wales and his younger brother (despite his titular bishopric of Osnabrück) were flogged by the King's orders " whenever necessary." This treatment continued until they were old enough to combine and resist by force.

One of the Prince's instructors (he was hanged later for forgery) set him exemplary exercises in penmanship, and George Augustus Frederick bent over his copybook writing laboriously such sentences as :

" Learn, generous prince, what's little understood,
The godlike happiness of doing good ! "

GEORGE IV.
From a picture by Sir T. Lawrence in the National Portrait Gallery.

So trained, the sentiments he expressed in letters written to a select few won the admiration of all readers :
" I will try to imitate as far as I am able the examples that I love, Papa, mama, and my dear Lord whom I assure of all my friendship."

In the intervals between more exacting studies, Prince George and his brothers dug, planted, sowed, reaped, threshed, and ground the grain grown in their own garden, and watched it being made into delectable loaves for the schoolroom meals.

At twelve years of age the Prince of Wales could sing, was said to be fluent in foreign languages, and danced the minuet " as well as ever I saw," according to Mrs. Delany. He was good also at games ; indeed his enjoyment of rounders attracted the attention of a visiting American and brought about the introduction of the game into New England.

Two years later an astute governor was prophesying that his charge would become " either the most polished gentleman or the most accomplished blackguard in Europe; perhaps both."

Already the Prince was chafing at leading-strings and demanding a separate establishment. By the time he had reached his majority, steady pressure brought him a suite in Windsor Castle and a few rooms in Buckingham House, with a promise of Carlton House in the future. The King allowed his son an income equal to what he himself had had at the same age, but this was quite insufficient to one who was to win for himself the title of " the first gentleman in Europe." To add to the Prince's discontent the Country had added to the imbroglio with America a war with France and Spain, and instead of being given a military command he was left to learn the theory of fortification with his brothers in Kew Gardens.

Denied an outlet for his energies, Prince George flung himself into the pleasures of the town under the guidance of his uncle the Duke of Cumberland, and became the leader in masquerade frolics. He learnt to drink hard and play hard, and once lost £500 on a wager as to whether twenty geese or twenty turkeys would win in a walking race to Brighton.

Then one night at Drury Lane " Perdita " of *The Winter's Tale* flashed a glance at him across the footlights, and the Prince succumbed to the fascinations of the beauty, who at twenty-one was the toast of the town.

The young actress had seen life from a difficult angle. Her father, an American and the captain of a whaler, had made a practice of family desertion. Mary had married at sixteen a husband who retired to a debtor's prison, leaving his young wife to support herself and a child as best she could. With Garrick's assistance she found her way to Drury Lane, and now, wonder of wonders, came a letter from the Prince of Wales together with the double gift of a portrait and a heart inscribed " Je ne change qu'en mourant! "

There were romantic moonlit meetings when " Perdita " lurked on the island between Brentford and Kew till Prince " Florizel " signalled that the coast was clear. There were capitulations, impassioned letters (to be purchased later by the King for £5,000), and a bond to be redeemed when the Prince came of age. (But twelve months before this " Perdita " had suffered eclipse.)

The Prince had burst his bonds with a vengeance. From the day when he attended the Queen's birthday Drawing-room in a pink silk coat with white embroidered waistcoat, and took his seat in the Lords in black velvet powdered with gold and hair " very full frizzed " he had been accepted as a leader of fashion. If Beau Brummell captivated society by introducing starched neck-kerchiefs, the Prince created a sensation with a new shoe-buckle one-inch-long-by-five-broad, and the exquisites would spend hours together discussing the art of the toilet; at twenty-one the Prince was spending £10,000 a year on his clothes.

Small wonder that the paternal allowance proved inadequate, even before the appearance of "Perdita."

Weekly levees at Carlton House, card parties, "select" suppers, all helped to pile up a load of debt, and money slipped yet faster through the Prince's fingers when Charles Fox became his mentor; a man thirteen years his senior who could play cards for twenty-two hours at a sitting and lose £500 an hour without perturbation.

At twenty-three the Prince of Wales owed £160,000. How could it be otherwise, he argued, when "with the strictest economy" his expenses were double the amount of his income?

"May I suggest, Sir, the idea of your marrying?" asked Lord Malmesbury, the tactful intermediary. "It would, I should think, be most agreeable to the King, and I am certain most grateful to the nation."

"I will never marry," vowed the Prince of Wales. "My resolution is taken on that subject and I have settled it with Frederick [Duke of York]. No! I will never marry."

"Give me leave, Sir, to say most respectfully that you cannot have come to any such resolution," persisted Lord Malmesbury. "You *must* marry, Sir. You owe it to the country, to the King—to yourself."

"I owe nothing to the King," cried the Prince. ". . . Frederick will marry, and the crown will descend to his children."

"Till you are married, Sir, and have children you have no solid hold on the affections of the people, even while you are Prince of Wales," answered Lord Malmesbury. "But if you come to the throne a bachelor, and his Royal Highness the Duke of York is married and has sons to succeed, your situation, when King, will be more painful than it is at this moment."

Referring the Prince to the pages of history for illustrations of the truth of his remarks, his lordship begged leave to withdraw.

" Adieu, God bless you," said the Prince thoughtfully.

The *affaire* which weighed upon his mind was infinitely more dangerous than that with " Perdita " with her tragic background, for he had lost his heart to Mrs. Fitzherbert, of Richmond, a lady of some social position who, twice widowed though she might be, was still a girl in years.

Something of the truth had leaked out, and the nation was singing :

" On Richmond Hill there lives a lass,
More bright than May-Day morn ! . . .
I'd crowns resign to call her mine,
Sweet lass of Richmond Hill ! "

Mrs. Fitzherbert was no desperate young actress precariously dependent upon her own exertions who would make clandestine appointments by moonlight, and the Royal Marriage Act, passed twelve years before, lay like a flaming sword between her and the passion-racked Prince.

Under its ban " no descendant of George II, male or female (other than the issue of princesses married to foreign princes), shall be capable of contracting marriage without previous consent of the Sovereign —marriage without such consent would be void." There was one loophole, but it did not help the Prince of Wales. Should a royal prince over the age of twenty-five desire marriage and be refused by the monarch, he might apply to the Privy Council, after which, if within twelve months Parliament laid no embargo, the marriage might take place.

The passage of the Act had been fought phrase by phrase. Some saw it as a relic of the Star Chamber, others saw it as an intolerable burden on future generations, for, in due course of time, " the

descendants of George II might number a thousand
—where then were husbands or wives to be procured
for them ? "

"If the Pretender had been here he could not have
planned a bill more dangerous or more threatening
to the liberties of the people ! " cried one member,
and his neighbour denounced it as "an act to encourage adultery and fornication." It was an act
giving leave to the Princes of the Blood to "lie with
our wives while it forbade them to marry our
daughters . . . could there be greater servility than
to fetch a little family from Hanover and indulge
it in the scorn they had for marrying into our
families ? "

But the Bill had passed and here were the first-
fruits. Mrs. Fitzherbert would not weaken in the
stand she had taken ; if she were not wife she would
not accept the Prince's love. Once only did she
waver, and that, when friends carried her to Carlton
House to see the Prince lying blood-stained and faint
for love of her ; next morning, doubting her own
steadfastness, she fled the country.

Prince George determined to follow, and applied
for permission to live abroad on the theoretical
ground of economy, but the King proved adamant,
and his indignant son's love-making had to be
continued by letter. One epistle was thirty-seven
pages long, but it was over a year before Mrs. Fitzherbert could be induced to return, and then it was
whispered round the town that the Prince intended
to marry her come what may.

Charles Fox saw the danger before his young patron
and wrote warningly :

"If such an idea is really in your mind, and it is
not too late, for God's sake let me call your attention
to some considerations." . . . Was he aware that
marriage with a Catholic would bar him from the
throne, while if children were born of the union the
difficulties and dangers of the position would be

aggravated a thousand fold ? With all the gift of words that was his, Fox implored the Prince not to marry until he could do so legally.

"Make yourself easy, my dear friend," came the answer. "Believe me, the world will now soon be convinced that there not only is not but never was ground for these reports which have of late been so malevolently circulated."

Four days later a marriage between the Prince of Wales and Mrs. Fitzherbert was celebrated according to the rites of the Church of England. Two clergymen had refused to officiate ; a third succumbed to the temptation of a fee of £500.

For a century no one knew the truth, then archives were opened, and all men saw the wedding certificate Mrs. Fitzherbert had hidden away according to her promise, and also a will in which the Prince had bequeathed his property to Maria Fitzherbert, " the wife of my heart and soul, although by the laws of this country she could not avail herself publicly of that name. . . . Still, such she is in the eyes of Heaven and ever will be in mine."

The gay life went on, debts multiplied themselves in an astounding manner, and the Prince made Brighton fashionable. He would drive down tandem with six horses, a small postilion astride one of the leaders, drink his guests under the table, and return, taking the double journey in ten hours with one change of horses.

But clamouring creditors could not be staved off for ever, and one fine morning an execution was put into Carlton House. All sources of supply failed, unpaid workmen left the premises, the house was shut up, and the Prince lived here and there in borrowed houses. His horses, led by twenty grooms, were walked down Piccadilly and sold at Tattersall's. Now when the heir to the throne went to Brighton he travelled by common post-chaise.

An anonymous well-wisher published " A Warning to the Prince of Wales ! " It told him that " the nation which has seen your royal highness emerge from the nursery with paternal pride is now beginning to execrate the object it once adored," and bade him take heed. " Our acres will remain to us through every change that can possibly happen ; we have but to transfer our allegiance, but a revolution will send you to beggary and exile. . . . In such a moment of calamity you will not only find yourself without property, but without friends, for the vermin at present basking in the sunshine of your favour will be the first to abandon you to the rigors of your fate."

The nation was stirred, and political friends moved to introduce a Bill into Parliament, under which the Prince's accumulated debts would be paid and his income increased, but then a stiff-necked member took advantage of the opportunity to inquire if there had not been a breach of the Royal Marriage Act, and made it clear that a section of the House would consider a marriage between the Prince of Wales and a Roman Catholic as something approaching treason.

In a tense and crowded chamber Fox rose to give an assurance that the whispered story of a secret marriage was " a monstrous calumny, a base and malicious falsehood."

Other members sprang up to press the point home : did Charles Fox speak from authority ?

" Yes, from direct authority."

A relieved assembly turned its attention to the matter of the Prince's debts. A few nights later Sheridan rose in his place to deliver an involved oration on Mrs. Fitzherbert and her known virtue ; doubly faithless " Florizel " had had a wigging.

The King fell ill and the Prince hastened to take command at Windsor, " in consequence of which

there is NO command," wrote Lord Malmesbury. . . .
" Stocks have fallen, and the alarm of the people of
London is very little flattering to the Prince of Wales.
. . . People in all ranks seem to be sensible of the
calamitous effects to be expected as a result of his
Majesty's disaster, but as you may imagine there are
not wanting those who are thinking of extracting
good to themselves out of this misfortune ; I am old
enough to have been in a court on the demise of the
crown, an event which does not bring the virtues
of men more into light than the contrary qualities."
But the death of George III was thirty years
distant.

An anxious House searched for precedents and
received the reports of the King's physicians. Fox
leapt to his feet to point out that there was an heir
apparent of full age to exercise the royal power, as
was his right, during the King's incapacity, and across
the gangway Pitt confronted him on the constitutional
issue.

Week after week the struggle continued, and on the
eve of the passage of a restricted Regency Bill a
messenger arrived at the Bar with news that the
King was making rapid progress towards complete
recovery.

The Prince's load of debt grew heavier and heavier.
The Jews who had been eager to accept his I.O.U.s
now hesitated and offered higher rates. A trio of
the royal brothers even made a united effort to
borrow, offering on the accession of any one of them
not only repayment but an Irish peerage to accom-
modating financiers who took the bait ; dunning
tradesmen pestered the Prince of Wales in the streets
and bailiffs secured an entry into Mrs. Fitzherbert's
house and refused to depart till the Prince sold his
jewels and paid them.

Once it seemed as if fortune might await him on the
turf, for his horse " Baronet " flashed first past the
post at the Derby, but three years later his jockey

was warned off the course, and the indignant Prince, after pensioning the man in whose innocence he believed, withdrew from Newmarket.

There seemed but one way out, and the Prince took it by holding out the olive branch to his father and announcing himself as willing to marry. In an access of hope that his ne'er-do-well son was about to turn over a new leaf the King suggested sending " a confidential personage " to report on the Protestant princesses of suitable age and character, but the choice narrowed itself to two. Deciding that his mother's niece was probably even less preferable than his father's, the Prince decided on Caroline of Brunswick, although the character sketch sent by Lord Malmesbury was not laudatory : " She has some natural and no acquired morals, warm feelings, and nothing to balance them."

There was a proxy wedding at Brunswick,[1] after which Caroline was brought to England, and Beau Brummell was among the group who received her at Greenwich.

The day before Caroline's arrival the Prince rode to Richmond, and in the city bets were offered on the chances of the marriage taking place.

But Mrs. Fitzherbert gave no sign, and fortified with brandy the Prince played the part of bridegroom, though " looking like death " and requiring support. When " the lass of Richmond Hill " learnt that the ceremony was an accomplished fact, she fainted.

Princess Caroline lost any illusions she may have had on her wedding night. " I was the victim of Mammon," she said long afterwards. " The Prince of Wales's debts had to be paid, and poor little I's person was the pretence."

It was not an auspicious moment for securing some half-million, since the country was groaning under war taxation, and the people cried alternately for

---

[1] See *Her Majesty : The Romance of the Queens of England.*

" Bread " and " Peace." There was an acrimonious
debate when the enormous total of the liability was
realised, and indignant citizens published letters
pointing out that the sum required to clear the
Prince " would maintain 1,700 people for the natural
course of their lives." Others pressed for details
" of the disgraceful items which had swelled the
debts to a sum which renders your Royal Highness's
application for payment as preposterous as it is
indecent ! You will not answer—and the reason is
YOU DARE NOT ! ''

The latest popular ditty was hummed in the streets
more or less openly when the Prince passed :

> " O George, great Prince of Whales,
> Thy swallow never fails,
> Voracious Prince ! ''

Parliament compromised by granting the Prince
£50,000 for immediate expenses, such as the alteration
of Carlton House, and increasing his income to
£140,000 a year, but it was stipulated that a portion
of this must be set aside for the liquidation of liabilities,
and the Prince considered that he had sold himself
in vain.

Nine months later the child was born for which
the nation had paid so highly. The separation of
the parents, begun within three weeks of marriage,
was now made formal.

War seemed to offer the Prince an opportunity for
entering a different life, and he asked to be allowed
to undertake military service abroad :

" Death is preferable to being the only man marked
out as not being suffered to come forward on such
an occasion," he told the King. . . . " Were there
fifty princes or were I the only one it would be, in
my humble judgment, equally incumbent upon me
to stand foremost in the ranks at so decided a peril.
. . . My character with the nation, my honour, my
future fame and respect in life are now all at stake.

. . . I supplicate your majesty ! . . . What I solicit
is the certainty of active service."

But despite the precedent of the ages it was decided
that "military service is incompatible with the
position of Prince of Wales." Others might go, but
not the heir, though, "should the implacable enemy
so far succeed as to land, you will have an opportunity
of showing your zeal at the head of your regiment,"
replied the King. The Prince sought consolation
at the hands of Mrs. Fitzherbert, but as the burden
of war pressed heavier upon the country he made
another effort :

"Ought I not to share in the glory of victory
when I have everything to lose by defeat. . . . Every
motive of private feeling as well as public duty
induces me to implore your majesty to review your
decision and to place me in that position which my
birth, the duties of my station, the examples of my
predecessors, and the expectations of the people of
England entitle me to claim. . . . Hanover is lost,
England is menaced with invasion . . . Ireland is
in rebellion. Europe is at the foot of France."

But Nelson at Trafalgar saved the nation.

Once again the King's health failed, and this time
the Regency Bill passed. Supported by his six
brothers, the Prince of Wales produced for deposition
in the archives a certificate showing that he had
taken communion a few days previously, and repeated
the required oath :

"I do solemnly promise and swear that I will be
faithful and bear true allegiance to his majesty
King George."

"Never a huzza was heard nor a hat seen raised " ;
a hissing mob hovered at the Regent's coach wheels.

The " Delicate Investigation " was still in men's
minds. They could not forget that the Prince had
caused twenty-three Privy Councillors to ponder the
question as to whether the Princess of Wales had

borne an illegitimate child. Then the feeling of a
large section of the nation had been made evident in
an "Admonitory Letter" which had run into seven
editions; now it ventured to hoot. Three years
later public sentiment veered, and when a messenger
came riding post-haste to fling flags captured on the
field at Waterloo at the feet of the Regent, he found
himself the hero of a sudden burst of popularity;
it ended with the death of his daughter, Princess
Charlotte, "the Fair Rose of England," and sole heir
to the throne in the new generation.

"Where's your wife?" was shouted at the Regent
more than once as he drove to Parliament, for
Princess Caroline was wandering on the Continent.

The years of the Regency passed and the promise
of youth was fulfilled in manhood. Drinking hard
and eating heavily, the Prince came to turn the scales
at twenty-three stone ; for some time a contrivance
of trolley and pulleys had been required to enable
him to mount a horse and amble slowly round the
lawns. A popular cartoon portrayed the ruler as
"The Voluptuary."

There was jubilation when a child was born to
the Duke of Kent, for the nation saw her as probable
heir to the throne.

Since the Tsar of Russia was a sponsor, tact
decreed that the little princess must have Alexandrina
as her first name, with Georgina coming second, but
at the eleventh hour the Regent decided that "the
name of Georgina could stand second to none," and
in default of a better name the child was christened
Victoria.

George III died in the following year, and the
Prince Regent mounted the throne. One of his
first acts was to send word to Caroline that he would
provide her with an income on the condition that she

remained abroad and refrained from adopting the title of Queen.

The Brunswick temper flared, and Caroline took ship for England. On landing she was cheered all the way from the coast to the city.

" A great piece of news," wrote Lady Lyttelton. " The Queen is arrived and came yesterday to London openly to declare war against her enemies. . . . The Government have filled two enormous green bags with evidence of her guilt. . . . The country is all for the Queen, but she is to be tried, whether by Parliament or a Court of Justice nobody knows."

When a Bill was drafted under which the royal marriage would be dissolved, Caroline demanded to be heard at the bar of the House either by counsel or in person.

She drove to Parliament, alternately hissed and cheered, while cartoonists and pamphleteers reaped a harvest. A favourite print showed her seated on a scale with a paper inscribed " Public Opinion." The other half of the balance was in the air, though tugged at by the King and all his ministers, and John Bull looked on, saying, " I'll see fair play ! "

A pamphlet that had almost as great a sale was entitled " Half-a-Crown-Lost, or the Examination Extraordinary of a Hanover Gentleman " :

Q. " ' What is your family name ? '
A. ' G'—lphs.'
Q. ' Do you go in general by that name ? '
A. ' No."
Q. ' How are you designated ? '
A. ' My friends and people in general call me Double G . . . o . . . '
Q. ' I presume you are married ? '
A. ' I was some years back, but found it rather inconvenient.'
Q. ' Is your wife living ? '
A. ' I'm apprehensive she is, but I wish she was dead.' "

A hot August dragged to a close and the House sat into September. "Lamentable indeed it will be if the issue is favourable to the Gentleman at the end of the Mall!" said one and another in a fit of anxiety, but there were some whose faith never wavered.

One day cheering crowds watched "the navy of England" marching to Brandenburg House to present an address to the Queen. "There were thousands of seamen, all well-dressed and sober, the best-looking, finest men you can imagine. Every man had a new white silk or satin cockade in his hat, and they carried a hundred colours at least, inscribed with such sentiments as 'The Protection of the Innocent!' . . . . 'and there would have been thousands more,' said one of the marchers, 'but we would not let any man over forty come because we have so far to walk.'"

The Bill of Pains and Penalties was abandoned, and London went literally drunk with joy at what was considered the Queen's triumph, while Caroline drove to St. Paul's to offer thanks "for one saved from peril" and prepared herself for a final struggle.

"Your greatest enemy is dead, sir," said a minister, announcing the death of Napoleon to the King.

"Is she indeed, by God!" answered George IV, thinking of the Queen. The date of the coronation approached and "everybody is in rather a fright, for the King is determined to be crowned alone." Caroline was demanding her rights, and the mob was on her side.

George IV drove to the Abbey in safety, though here and there came a shout of "The Queen! The Queen!" or "Where's your wife?" But when Caroline reached the entrance she was repulsed by the soldiers on guard.

"There was no room for her, but only for the Vice-Queen, Lady Conyngham!" said a witty courtier.

A silent multitude watched Caroline drive away in tears. A week later she was dead.

The King made a royal progress. Ireland, Scotland, Hanover, all saw and acclaimed him.

Prince of Wales for over fifty years, and Prince Regent for nine, George IV reigned as King for ten years, and though when he died he left behind him bundles of letters from the eighteen women he had " loved," with innumerable locks of hair ; he wore Mrs. Fitzherbert's portrait round his neck on his death-bed.

One contemporary saw him as " a bad son, a bad husband, a bad father, a bad subject, a bad friend, and a bad monarch."   Another more kindly wrote of him as a man who had been " driven to occupy himself in trifles because he had found no opportunities to display his talents in the conduct of great concerns."

After George IV came William, to be followed by the young Princess Victoria, who would have been Georgina but for the Regent's pride of name ; until the birth of her son England knew no Prince of Wales.

CHAPTER XVI
PRINCE ALBERT EDWARD (EDWARD VII)

" Son métier était d'être roi."

ALBERT EDWARD PRINCE OF WALES (EDWARD VII)

Born at Buckingham Palace . . . November 9, 1841
Created Prince of Wales . . . December 1841
Married (at Windsor) to Alexandra of
  Denmark . . . . . March 10, 1863
Ascended . . . . . . January 22, 1901
Died at Buckingham Palace . . . May 6, 1910

Descent

George III — *m.* — Charlotte
|
Duke of Kent (and others)
m. Victoria Augusta of Saxe-Coburg
|
Victoria
m. Albert of Saxe-Coburg Gotha.
|
Albert Edward (and others)

Contemporary Sovereigns

FRANCE : Louis Philippe and Napoleon III.

GERMANY : Frederick William IV, William I (proclaimed German Emperor), Frederick I, and William II.

RUSSIA : Nicholas I, Alexander II (assassinated), Alexander III, and Nicholas II.

CHAPTER XVI

ALBERT EDWARD PRINCE OF WALES
(EDWARD VII)
1841-1910

On November 9, 1841, Queen Victoria asked for her journal in order that she might make an entry of importance :
" At 12 minutes to 11 a fine large boy was born. O, how happy and how grateful do I feel to that Almighty Providence who has really blessed me so peculiarly," she wrote, then lay back white and smiling on her pillows. It was only a few hours since her new-born child had been displayed to the official " witnesses."

" Is it a boy ? " asked the old Duke of Wellington anxiously when the nurse appeared carrying the baby.

" It is a *prince*, your Grace," came the loyal answer.

Not since the days of George the Third and " Good Queen Charlotte " had an heir been born to an English sovereign, and now the nation went mad with delight. Joy-bells were rung, bonfires were lighted, street merchants found a ready sale for miraculously produced " portraits of the royal infant " ; people crowded into the theatres and music halls mainly to join in singing the National Anthem ; the Archbishop of Canterbury ordered special prayers to be read and commanded her Majesty's printer to produce " a competent number " of these forthwith ; a London Gazette-Extraordinary appeared with the information that " Her Majesty and the Infant Prince are, God be praised, both

doing well; at the Lord Mayor's Banquet that night
a beaming Lord Mayor arose amid deafening cheers
to propose " health and a long life to the heir apparent
to the British throne," while " God Bless the Prince
of Wales " wavered across the Guildhall in illuminated
letters; and *Punch* (not six months senior to the
new arrival) produced a " poem " that swept through
the country :

> " Huzza !   We've a little Prince at last,
>   A roaring, royal boy.
> And all day long the booming bells
>   Have rung their peals of joy ! "

"He is a wonderfully large and strong child, with
very dark blue eyes and a finely formed but rather
large nose and a pretty little mouth," noted the
happy young mother.

Ignoring protests, she decided that her son was
to be called Albert, with Edward for a second name :
" You will understand," she wrote to her favourite
uncle, King Leopold of Belgium, " how fervent are
my prayers (and I am sure everyone's must be) to
see him resemble his father in *every* respect."

Five centuries before Edward III had granted the
Duchy of Cornwall to his small son, later to be known
as the Black Prince, entailing it on the heirs apparent
to the English throne, so that title now came to
Prince Albert Edward, and in addition, by reason of
the Union of Scotland and England, the Dukedom of
Rothesay and Earldom of Carrick; by right of his
father he was also Duke of Saxony.   When barely a
month old he was created Prince of Wales.

In January (1842) came the baptism, a magnificent
affair with two bottlesful of water from the Jordan
(one sixteen years old, " yet fresh and sweet ")
poured into the font.   The Queen was attired in the
Robes of the Order of the Garter and the baptismal
feast was held in the Waterloo Chamber, into which
the Principal Yeoman Confectioner wheeled a giant
christening cake 8 feet round and 4 feet high.

EDWARD VII.
From a print in the British Museum of a portrait by Richmond at Windsor.

" *Little* Albert (what a pleasure it is that he has that *dearest* name) behaved *so* well ! " said the Queen, oblivious of one awful moment when the baby Prince had made a gallant if ineffectual effort to snatch off the Archbishop's wig.

Almost at once the question of the Prince's up-bringing became a subject of paramount importance to both his parents, for some months before his birth Baron Stockmar, to whose advice the Queen and Prince Consort invariably listened, had written to point out that " a man's education begins with the first day of his life." Hence it was agreed that no time should be lost.

For the moment the actual safe-keeping of the Prince of Wales and his elder sister, the Princess Royal, was a matter of acute anxiety, for threatening letters often reached the castle. As a consequence the children's nurseries had to be guarded, and were secured from intrusion by intricate locks. Prince Albert invariably kept " the most important key of all " in his own custody.

Baron Stockmar was empowered to engage three governesses, English, French, and German, while Lady Lyttelton, one of the Queen's most trusted Ladies of the Bedchamber, assumed charge of the two precious little people, the Princess Royal and Victoria's first son. " The Prince of Wales," she decided, " to judge by his noble countenance and calm manner, is very intelligent and looks through his large, clear blue eyes full at one."

The nation's interest in the new baby was embarras-sing. When a journey to Walmer Castle was under-taken—the going was a hundred and three miles in nine hours—excited people lined the route clamour-ing for the Prince.

" Show him ! Turn him this way ! . . . Bless his little face ! " And one woman, bolder than the rest, actually snatched the child from his nurse's arms and kissed him !

The baby bore it all phlegmatically, but the little Princess Royal was more responsive. Sturdy "and round like a barrel," dressed in "garter-blue velvet, Brussels lace, and adorned with pearls and diamonds" she waved her hands and bowed to the delighted people in quaint copy of the Queen.

The inmates of the royal nursery were trained to be bilingual, so by the time the Prince was two and a-half years old he could talk both English and German, though he was "somewhat babyish in accent." He understood some French too, and took "outdoor exercise" strapped into a Spanish saddle on the back of a pony.

He was described as "generous and good-tempered, although with occasional stampings and passions" and as "exemplary in politeness. . . . He bows and offers his hand beautifully, besides saluting à la militaire quite unbidden."

The "stampings" continued into later years presumedly, for there is a penitent childish letter extant which runs :

"I do not know how it is that I am ever naughty, for I am much happier when I am good."

The "smallness" of the Prince was an oft-mentioned matter for regret in these early years, but at least the child had courage. Before his third birthday he was present at a military review, and revelled in the scene till the firing began.

"Soldiers go popping!" he exclaimed in dismay, then added warningly : "No more—I cry!" But finding his protests disregarded, he made a valiant effort at self-control and choked back the tears.

A year or so later he was considered old enough to go with the Queen when she distributed blankets and plum-puddings to the poor at Windsor, and then on a yachting cruise.

To his immense delight he was entered on the ship's ratings as a midshipman and was promoted to baggy white trousers. The sailors gave him

" nine-times-nine " when he appeared on deck in his brave attire, and he was allowed to order them an issue of grog.

When the *Victoria and Albert* anchored off Penzance, boatloads of eager people came out to cheer the little " Duke of Cornwall."

" Why do they call me that ? " asked the puzzled child, and was told of his famous ancestor the Black Prince whose titles he now bore. Did the boy's attention wander before the moral was reached ? " He must emulate the merits of that great prince so as to be equally beloved and remembered in the centuries to come."

The voyage continued, Wales was reached, and here the Dukedom was completely ignored. Instead, the boy waved his sailor hat while the people hailed him as " Prince of Wales "—and was bidden to remember Carnarvon Castle as the birthplace of the first holder of his title.

Last came Scotland, where the " fair-haired little lad of rather slender build " discovered that he was Duke of Rothesay.

He returned from the great adventure " very brown and less shy," to forget his royalty in such delights as a performing menagerie in the quadrangle of Windsor Castle, an interview with Tom Thumb, visits to the circus, and the ever-recurring family festivals.

Once the royal children were whirled off to Osborne in hot haste on the advice of the Prime Minister. Louis Philippe had been expelled from France, and there was serious unrest in England.

All unconscious, the little Prince and his brothers and sisters worked in their gardens and hammered their fingers in learning carpentry, while the Queen and Prince Albert consulted as to how the growing family could best be fitted to fill any station " high or low," and Lady Lyttelton wondered gloomily " whether there would be any princes left ten years hence."

" O merciful God, I thank thee for giving me rest during the night and refreshing me with quiet sleep. O Lord, grant that I may pass a good and happy day, and be obedient to all those set to watch over me. Bless dear Papa and Mama and give them the comfort of seeing me grow up a good child. Bless and keep my brothers and sisters and teach them and me to remember our Creator in the days of our youth, through Jesus Christ our Lord." So prayed the little Prince each morning, in happy ignorance of troubled days ahead when he should be considered old enough to begin definite training in kingship.

Among other works on education an anonymous pamphlet entitled " Who Shall Educate the Prince of Wales ? " had found its way into royal hands, and after being carefully considered had been forwarded to Baron Stockmar. All agreed that the education of all the royal children must be " thoroughly moral and thoroughly English," but in the case of the heir apparent it was vital that no mistake should be made. From him, at all costs, any symptoms of the vices of his ancestors must be eliminated, for had not the actions of certain princes of the past " done much to diminish the respect and influence of monarchy " ?

Baron Stockmar drew up " an Educational Discipline " which, applied to the little Prince with due thoroughness, should produce a wellnigh perfect King. To this end, at seven years old, he was placed in the hands of carefully chosen tutors, who were bidden to guide and train him " with unceasing vigilance." Sport and amusement, "if of a sober kind such as croquet," were permitted " in moderation," and it was intended that youthful companionship should be almost completely debarred, though later this rule was relaxed to the extent of permitting a chosen half-dozen Eton boys to visit their future King on Sunday afternoons under the eye of the Prince Consort.

1910] FIRST DUTIES

Public duty was the only excuse for an interruption of lessons. For instance, when the Queen fell ill of chicken-pox and could not open the Coal Exchange, the Prince Consort deputised for her and took with him the Prince of Wales and Princess Royal to " soften the disappointment of the people."

All London turned out to do the children honour, and the two quaint little figures went to the city in the State Barge. He, eight years old, in black velvet coat with gilt buttons, black trousers, white waistcoat, a turned-down collar, black scarf, and white peaked cap ; she, a year older, in a gay flounced green silk frock, a pink, quilted-satin bonnet with feather, a black-velvet-mantle and pale drab boots (!)

" Who taught him to read like that ? " whispered the awed children as the Recorder delivered his impressive address, and " Princey " glanced in bewilderment at his father when he heard himself hailed as " the pledge and promise of a long line of kings."

The Prince Consort, gathering his children for the processional march, bade them remember that they were " indebted to the Lord Mayor of London for this, one of the happiest days of their lives."

The " educational discipline " was being worked out according to plan, for kingship is no light burden. A classical tutor and chaplain were added to the circle, together with a special lecturer on political economy. For relaxation there were speech days at Eton and Harrow and lectures at the Royal Institute.

The Crimean War brought fresh duties to the nation's heir. He stood by the Queen when the Guards marched past Buckingham Palace before embarking ; he followed her through hospital wards. Eager to make a contribution to the Patriotic Fund, he and the other royal children bent over their drawing-boards, and while " Bertie " laboriously drew " The Knight," which fetched fifty guineas, the

cleverer Princess Royal composed " The Battlefield,"
a coloured masterpiece that sold for five times as
much.

At a special session of Parliament Prince Albert
Edward sat in a small chair beside his mother on
the throne. He went with her to Aldershot and
became fired with the desire to be a soldier ; he saw
her distribute the first Victoria Cross and helped his
father light a bonfire to celebrate the fall of Sebastopol.
He went to France when the Queen paid a brief
visit to Napoleon the Third and the Empress Eugénie,
and won all hearts when he danced in his kilt at
Versailles and knelt before the tomb of the great
Emperor.

The Prince was growing up, but yet fell far short
of the pitch of perfection to which he should have
attained under the " educational discipline."

Gravely anxious parents decided that the time had
arrived for him to be entrusted with an allowance and
permission to purchase his own hats and ties.   Liberty
to select his clothes came a year later with the stipu-
lation that he must wear nothing extravagant or
" slang."

As an experiment the Prince, under careful
guidance, was sent on a walking tour in Devon
strictly incognito, and for the first time in his life
found himself treated as of little consequence. At
one inn the host had " no time to bother with boys "
when he asked a question ; at another it was suggested
that, since the place was crowded, the " lad " might
shake-down on a sofa in a passage.

All too soon the identity of the tourists was discovered, and the Prince was mobbed by enthusiastic
well-wishers. An attempt to continue the experiment
in the Lake District was hardly more successful,
and after much consultation the Prince was sent
abroad for a short tour with four Eton boys as
companions, and a proviso that the " programme of
study " was to be pursued without deviation.

He returned in time to play his part at the wedding
of the Princess Royal and to undergo confirmation.
The prelude to this was an hour's questioning by
the Dean of Windsor in the presence of the Queen,
the Prince Consort, the Archbishop of Canterbury,
and two bishops. The ceremony itself went off
" with great solemnity," and the Prince Consort
hoped it had made " an abiding impression " upon
his son.

The Prince's desire for a military career was still
strong, but all were agreed that he was not sufficiently
prepared. Instead of going to Aldershot he was
sent to White Lodge, and Colonel Robert Bruce
(later General), was appointed as Governor with
instructions " to regulate the Prince's movements
and the employment of his time."

Bruce found that his charge had " a charm of
manner but was given to frivolous disputes "; however, he had a " fund of good sense and was anxious
to improve himself."

Others whispered that the young Prince was
" passionate enough and determined enough for an
autocrat."

Various memoranda were drawn up. The equerries
selected to attend on the Prince were bidden to pay
careful attention even to " what might appear
trivial." For instance, " the Prince's deportment
will be more watched and his attire more criticised
than that of other men " . . . he must never walk
with his hands in his pockets or slouch when sitting.
Manners, it was decreed, were of immense
importance—" a Prince must never say a harsh or
rude word to anybody. He should learn too to
acquit himself creditably in conversation, and to
be scrupulously punctual. It was hinted that those
around should teach him by example." " The Prince
of Wales must not only be a gentleman, but his
rank and position pointed him out as being the first
gentleman in the country."

The Prince was told that his equerries were to take and receive their orders from the Governor. As for himself :

" You will never leave the house without reporting yourself to him, and he will settle who is to accompany you."

Prince Albert Edward was eighteen ; when four years his junior, the Black Prince had fought at Crécy. As a birthday gift there came a colonelcy unattached and a letter from Windsor :

" A wide sphere of life now opens for you in which you will have to be taught what to do and what not to do, a subject requiring study far more important than any in which you have hitherto engaged. . . . Life is composed of duties, and in the punctual and cheerful performance of them the true Christian, true soldier, and true gentleman is recognised. . . . Your behaviour should be in strict conformity with the Church catechism. . . . You must learn to love your neighbour as yourself and do unto others as you would they should do unto you."

The Garter was promised for a later date.

The Prince put on his new uniform and went off " looking well and happy " to report himself at the Horse Guards.

Son métier était d'être roi.

The training went on. Edinburgh, Oxford, and Cambridge must all be called upon to give of their wisdom. So the Prince was sent north to master " history, law, and the practical application of science. If he was growing restive at this intensive training, so was the nation, and when *Punch* came forward to break a lance on his behalf the public hailed with enthusiasm a set of verses under title of " A Prince at High Pressure :

" O dear little Wales, sure the saddest of tales,
Is the tale of the studies with which they are cramming thee !
In thy tuckers and bibs, handed over to Gibbs,

Who for eight years with solid instruction was ramming thee. . . .
    In Edinburgh now, thy poor noodle perplext,
The gauntlet must run of each science and study. . . .

" Dipped in grey Oxford mixture (lest *that* prove a fixture),
    The poor lad's to be plu ₋ged in less orthodox Cam. . . .
  'Gainst indulging the passion for this high pressure fashion
    Of Prince's training, ' Punch ' would uplift a loyal warning ! "

But the Prince was working better than he had
done in previous hands, and presently the puzzled
Queen began to receive favourable reports of his
progress instead of reiterated complaints that he
was " incapable of concentration." In all haste the
Prince Consort went north to summon a conference
of tutors and map out a course of future study.

But perhaps *Punch* was responsible for a certain
slackening of tension. Occasional mild dinner-parties
were permitted, and twice a week the Prince went
to train with the Hussars.

One incident, small in itself, proved that the much-
schooled heir apparent had learnt the first step
towards ruling in that he could obey.

During a science lesson the tutor, Dr. Playfair,
washed his pupil's hand in ammonia and bade him
ladle out a handful of boiling lead.

" Do you tell me to do this ? " asked the Prince.

" I do."

The order was instantly obeyed.

Edinburgh now bid farewell to her Prince, and after
a brief interlude at Balmoral, where he shot his
first stag and captured a salmon, Prince Albert
Edward was started on his carefully guarded Oxford
career.

Sometimes he dined in Hall ; occasionally, warned
that he must not " take sides," he slipped in to listen
to a debate at the Union ; sometimes he attended
public lectures, but for the most part his studies
were private, or pursued with a few most carefully
selected companions.

Hunting was looked upon as "an encroachment on study," so was only rarely permitted; tennis and croquet served as "exercise." At the end of each term came a strict examination.

The Queen and Prince Consort held "that the nation had a clear and indisputable right to demand of the Prince of Wales that he make that use of his position for which it was given him, viz. for the general good and the welfare of the whole." Others might play, the Prince must never waste an hour, and neither must he show too much initiative.

Some little time after his confirmation they learnt that he was intending to attend a communion service at a date other than that on which they had agreed as suitable. The matter was taken up by the Prince Consort, who, after pointing out the two extreme points of view taken by communicants, advised that the Prince should follow the example of the Queen and himself in the matter : "We have decided to take it twice a year at fixed seasons." . . . "If you have a real yearning of the heart," go by all means, wrote the father. . . . "If the subject be indifferent to you, and your wish has been but a slight one, do not unnecessarily break our rule, knowing now the reasons upon which this rule rests."

The Easter vacation found the Prince visiting Belgium and Germany, where "Stockmar seemed pleased to see me," but the "Long" had its difficult and responsible duty.

When Canada had sent her soldiers to fight in the Crimea she had asked a favour—that someday the Queen would visit the Dominion. Victoria had answered that such a journey would be impossible for her, and Canada had pressed for one of the Queen's sons as Governor-General.

Then, the young princes were too young to fill such a post, but now Albert Edward was older than his mother had been when she ascended the throne,

and Lord Palmerston was urging that all precedent
should be broken and the heir apparent should go
as his mother's ambassador to drive the last rivet
into the mighty bridge which should span the St.
Lawrence, and lay the foundation-stone of Ottawa's
Parliament.

A suite was selected, a ship equipped ; he went
abroad " an eager, graceful, handsome boy interested
in everything," and the midshipmen gasped at his
retinue of " seven royal flunkeys," one of whom was
quickly nicknamed " Old Twenty Stun."

The voyage was to be longer than had been intended,
because no sooner was it known that the Prince
was going to Canada than James Buchanan, the
Democratic president, then occupying the White
House, sent a pressing invitation for the Prince to
visit the United States, and this it was agreed he
should do " to increase good feeling," though
travelling as Baron Renfrew.

There was little respite from study during the
fifteen days of the crossing, for piles of maps and
books dealing with the places to be visited were
displayed for the Prince's benefit, and work went on
" according to plan " while the Duke of Newcastle
drafted replies to the addresses that were to be
received.   These surpassed all expectations, for during
the first day in Newfoundland the Prince was required
to respond to fourteen.

Descriptive letters from " your dutiful and affectionate son Bertie " were dispatched to " My dear
Mama " at frequent intervals, and when he wrote
from Halifax the Prince thoughtfully enclosed a slip
of sweet-briar that he had taken from the ruins of
a house in which the Duke of Kent had once lived,
thinking the Queen might like it in memory of her
father.

The letters were supplemented by reports from
General Bruce and the Duke. " The Prince," they
were able to say, " performed his part with no greater

diffidence than was perfectly becoming." . . . He was
" pleased with everything, himself included."

As an interlude in the official round came a few
days at Niagara, when the Prince lived in a cottage
in the hotel grounds " almost like a private citizen " ;
for the first time since landing he could move " without a mob at his heels."

The Falls were illuminated, and gave him a thrill
in more ways than one, for Blondin had been com-
missioned to walk across a rope stretched from the
Canadian to the American side, carrying a man on
his back. The distance was half a mile, and the
rope—two hundred and thirty feet above the swirling
waters—sagged in the middle, so that it had to be
descended and ascended. Thousands watched breath-
lessly and none with more tenseness than the Prince.
When Blondin had succeeded he came to suggest
that he should wheel the Prince across in a wheel-
barrow, and so enable " Baron Renfrew " to make a
really dramatic descent upon American territory.
Prince Albert Edward was eager to accept the
sporting offer, but his horrified guardians were prompt
with their veto.

Despite the good intentions of everyone to conform
to the Queen's behest that, while in the United
States, the Prince of Wales should travel as Baron
Renfrew, public enthusiasm knew no bounds once
he crossed the border. It was the first time an
English prince had visited the republic, and in their
eagerness to do honour to their guest Americans forgot
that he was the great grandson of execrated George III.

He was rushed to Harrisburgh to sit in the sacred
chair wherein Hancock had sat to sign the Declaration
of Independence ; he was escorted to Mount Vernon
to plant a chestnut tree beside the tomb of George
Washington ; he was entertained intensively at the
White House—" He may consider himself a lucky
lad if he escapes nomination for the presidency,"

observed a facetious reporter. They showed him West Point, and the General who was his guide proved to have been taken prisoner by the English in 1812.

Boston outdid Washington in her generous entertainment, and prepared a new version of England's National Anthem for the occasion :

> " Guard Thou the Kingdom's heir,
> Guard all his ways. . . ."

New York vied with Boston despite the protests of a few disgruntled Irish who protested that it was against the dignity of a sovereign people to pay court to a representative of monarchy. It gave him a ball whereat two thousand gate-crashers contested the floor with three thousand invited guests ; it organised a tremendous torchlight procession down Broadway, and, finest gesture of all, when the Prince attended Sunday service at Trinity Church prayers were offered up for the royal family.

The homeward voyage took twenty-six days, and all England was stirred to real anxiety before Prince Albert Edward landed at Plymouth, having celebrated his nineteenth birthday *en route* by dining with the midshipmen. It was a memorable dinner, for a waterspout took the gathering unawares, washed the mess president out of his chair, and soaked the entire company to the skin—at which no one laughed more heartily than the half-drowned and struggling Prince.

Within a week of his return this King-to-be was back at Oxford with every hour scheduled for work. Though " grown and more manly," freedom was not yet in sight for the much-trained Prince, who found himself transferred to Cambridge for the next term. He was chafing at the continuous discipline, and the Prince Consort found it necessary to pay many visits in an effort to keep the wheels running smoothly and convince his son that there was yet much to be learned before he would be fitted for his destiny.

As a delightful respite came a few weeks at Curragh —a compromise, since Aldershot was still vetoed— and some genuine military training.

With much pride the Prince led his own company past the Queen at a review.

" Bertie did not look so *very* small," wrote Victoria in her journal.

Even in her eyes Prince Albert Edward was growing up, and if he was not considered wise enough to be emancipated, he was verging towards a suitable age for marriage ; for marriage, like so many other things, was the manifest duty of this heir apparent who was " the pledge and promise of a long line of kings."

Some time before a list of " possible " princesses had been compiled which had been carefully scrutinised by the anxious parents and the Crown Princess of Prussia, who took a vivid interest in her brother's affairs—was he not one of her son's forty-two godfathers and godmothers ? First one, then another was ruled off, for much was asked of the future Queen of England. The Queen favoured a German bride, the Prince Consort inclined towards Denmark. Then, through a favourite lady-in-waiting, the Crown Princess heard a personal report of Princess Alexandra. She was said to be " beautiful, with lovely eyes and good teeth," also " tall and graceful " ; further inquiries were set on foot.

Little was said, but that year when Prince Albert Edward went to visit his sister a carefully casual meeting took place between him and Princess Alexandra, who " happened " to be going through Speier Cathedral. The Crown Princess wrote to her mother that " Bertie seemed greatly pleased."

But though marriage was in contemplation, the Prince had to be submerged in the student, and once more he was returned to Cambridge. Again it became necessary for the Prince Consort to pay frequent visits to his son. Returning from one of

these, he contracted a chill, and presently a startled
Prince was summoned to Windsor, where his father
lay dying, watched over by a stricken Queen.

The public now looked· to see the Prince stand at
his mother's right hand, but she, heartbroken and
desolate though she was, was convinced that her son's
training for the kingship was still far from complete.
She must guide him as well as rule her country, and,
above all, plans made by the Prince Consort must be
carried out; hence the Prince of Wales must sail for
the East with a carefully chosen suite all bidden to
" imbue him with a taste for useful pursuits and keep
before his mind the possibility that he might be
called upon to ascend the throne *at any moment.*"
Dean Stanley accepted the task of guide " with
vast reluctance and misgiving " ; General Bruce was
still the Prince's governor.

Prince Albert Edward rode through the streets
of Cairo on a donkey. He climbed the pyramids in
the early dawn and spent a Sunday at Thebes, where
the Dean preached to his tiny congregation in a
corner of the Great Hall of Karnak, while the " asses,
dromedaries, and their native attendants waited at
the other end." He landed at Jaffa and, following
in the footsteps of an English king, " saw Jerusalem
for the first time at the very spot where Richard
Cœur-de-Lion had hidden his face and prayed :
" Oh, Lord God, if I am not worthy to win back the
Holy City I am not worthy to see it ! " . . . He
wandered in Bethlehem and camped in the valley of
Jehoshaphat.

The tour was an unqualified success, and upon the
Prince's return the Queen could write : " Bertie goes
on being as good, amiable, and sensible as we could
wish."

But " good, amiable, and sensible " though the
Prince might be, and on the eve of marriage, the
Queen thought it necessary to appoint another

governor on the death of General Bruce a few weeks
after his return from the Eastern adventure.

And now Queen Victoria decided on a visit to
Coburg, her husband's early home, and the Prince
followed her in dutiful attendance. What more
natural than that Princess Alexandra, being on a
visit to Brussels, should be received by the Queen,
who gave her a sprig of white heather.

"Now I will take a walk with Princess Alix in the
garden," said the Prince, "and in three-quarters of
an hour I will take her into the grotto, and there I
will propose, and I hope it will be to everybody's
satisfaction."

It was.

The affianced pair celebrated the event by visiting
the field of the Battle of Waterloo on the morrow,
and soon joy-bells were ringing in England because
the heir apparent had taken another step on the
road to manhood, and was to marry a princess
beautiful enough to be the heroine in one of the
fairy stories Hans Christian Andersen himself had
told her.[1]

The world anticipated an early marriage, but to
the Queen's mind Princess Alexandra, like Prince
Albert Edward, required training for the position
she was to fill.

The Prince was dispatched on a Mediterranean tour
with his married sister and her husband in order that
he might be out of the way and the rules of strict
propriety be obeyed—incidentally he celebrated his
twenty-first birthday at Naples—while the Princess
Alexandra received an invitation to stay at Windsor
under the Queen's wing.

"May my dearly loved Alix . . . rightly and
consciously fulfil her future position, which will not
be quite easy," wrote her father, Prince Christian.
"Her chief aim and effort must ever be towards that
—to be the best and most loving of wives to her

[1] See *Her Majesty : The Romance of the Queens of England.*

future husband, and, at the same time, the obedient, tender, and affectionate daughter of his mother the Queen."

Those who saw Princess Alexandra while she was in residence at Windsor reported her as " full of spirits and courage and seemingly quite happy."

All went smoothly, and while Prince and Princess completed their training Marlborough House and Sandringham were arranged for their reception.

The Prince had a fleeting glimpse of his fiancée *en route* as she went back to say farewell to her own country. A few weeks later she returned to England for her marriage.

The last Princess who had come to wed a Prince of Wales was Caroline of Brunswick, who had had to be " smuggled in " while a Franco-Dutch fleet waited in the Channel eager to capture the prize. Alexandra of Denmark came escorted by father, mother, brothers, and sisters on the royal yacht *Victoria and Albert*, which was beflagged from stem to stern. The Prince of Wales greeted her and a million voices cheered her along the way to Windsor. " Looking like a rose," she was received into the arms of the Queen.

" A charming marriage ! " declared the guests.

" Dear Alix so lovely, fair, and above all else sweet and *good*," wrote the Queen.

There followed a week's honeymoon at Osborne, two days at Windsor, and then Prince and Princess were called upon to take up their duties.

" Both of them appear extremely happy," decided onlookers, and Londoners rejoiced in a wonderful season.

Soon such a wave of popularity engulfed the two that there came a whispered demand for the abdication of the Queen, who still hid herself away with her grief, but it received no encouragement from the heir apparent, who considered himself as her Majesty's first and most loyal subject. Despite his resolution,

" God Save the Prince of Wales " became a more popular song than the National Anthem.

Fresh troubles soon began. The Prince of Wales had been trained to work, and now there seemed none for him.

He asked to be kept informed of the trend of state affairs, but the Queen refused to countenance such a breach of precedent, for " Bertie lacked discretion." Thirty years passed before the point was conceded.

The Prince had been sworn as a Privy Councillor, but his presence was rarely required, and forty years were to elapse before, in the Queen's absence, he was called upon to preside at a meeting of the Council and use his influence towards the holding of the ring while America and Spain fought out their quarrel.

Ireland grew restive, and it was thought that a royal viceroy might have a soothing effect on Erin's sons. The Prince showed eagerness, but the Queen decreed that " the most distressful country " was " an unsuitable residence for a prince," and he had to remain at home.

The routine of life went on. Balls and garden parties were given and attended. Drawing-rooms were held, hospitals opened, foundation-stones laid. The Prince joined clubs and entertained shooting-parties at Sandringham, where a piper in Highland garb marched round the dinner-table every night " except Sundays " playing the bagpipes, and the host methodically weighed each guest on arrival, recording the result in a special book.

In a last attempt to obtain definite employment the Prince of Wales suggested that he should be attached in turn to each department of state so that he might obtain administrative knowledge ; this too was refused ; he took his seat on one of the cross benches in the House of Lords, and almost immediately received a warning against attending debates with any regularity !

Royal Commissions promised to afford a field of
usefulness, and the Prince studied such questions as
housing and old-age pensions, but when he volunteered
to serve on a third, concerned with industrial relationships, he was advised that the subject was " too con-
troversial " to be dealt with safely by the heir
apparent.

The years went on and children were born. The
first had made a premature arrival at Frogmore when
arrangements for his reception had been begun at
Marlborough House. The Princess had spent an
enjoyable afternoon skating, returning home in time
for tea. Suddenly it seemed necessary to send for
a doctor, and a Windsor physician was summoned
in haste; the child was born within a few hours of
his arrival.

The social whirl continued till the Prince became
involved in a scandal and was called upon to give
evidence in a court of law, which outraged public
opinion. The Princess had been ill, and the Queen
was brought to agree to an Eastern tour " provided
Sundays were observed as days of rest."

The two went via Copenhagen, where a family
party was gathered, as many as seven languages being
spoken around the dinner-table, and on to Berlin,
visiting more relations, Vienna, and the Orient.

The Prince of Wales saw the completion of a stage
of the Suez Canal and found it " an everlasting pity
that it is not in English hands, since it is our highway
to India." With the Princess and a small suite he
travelled up the Nile, explored ruins, and watched for
crocodiles. Hard on the heels of the royal flotilla
came " the man from Cook's." Often there would
come a warning cry : " The tourists are coming ! "
and cover would be swiftly sought.

The Franco-Prussian War found the Prince of Wales
eager to be true to his famous motto, " Ich Dien."
Could he not act as mediator between the Emperor

of the French and the King of Prussia ? " I would gladly do anything or travel any distance to stop it," he wrote to the Queen. But 1870 was "too soon " for intervention, and presently Napoleon III was a prisoner and the Prince was offering a welcome to the fugitive Empress.

With her coming a flash of revolutionary feeling spread to England, stirring the embers that had been kindled on the abdication of Louis Philippe, and even Victoria's throne seemed unsafe. . . . Then the Prince fell ill.

" Heaven has sent this dispensation of the Prince's illness to save us," wrote the Duke of Cambridge, for when the Queen's son lay at the point of death the nation forgot all else but its love for him, and later millions thronged the streets to cheer him on his way to the thanksgiving service at St. Paul's.

They cheered him too when he sailed to visit India, carrying messages from the Queen. On his homeward way he learnt of Disraeli's addition to her Majesty's titles, and vigorously objected to being converted into an " Imperial Highness."

" England is justly proud of many things, but at this moment she is prouder of nothing more than the Prince," said Disraeli suavely upon his return, and the Prince of Wales had found his life-work. His was to be the task of keeping the world's peace ; of travelling now to France, now to Germany, now to Russia as need arose, to soothe ruffled feelings, to attend christenings and marriages and funerals, to tie closer and yet closer the strings of relationships in this amazing family party which was Europe. And at home he was to be " the first gentleman in the land."

A year after the Prince's return from India the royal colours were seen on the turf, and presently the purple, gold braid, scarlet sleeves, and black velvet cap worn by his jockeys were to be well known. Within twenty years he was to win a million sterling.

Twice, while Prince of Wales, Derby crowds were to
cheer themselves hoarse when Persimmon and
Diamond Jubilee flashed past the winning post.
Once, as King, he was to lead in Minoru, who won
by half a head after a neck-and-neck race, while the
National Anthem offered the only outlet for the wild
enthusiasm of the delighted people.

At Cowes, year after year, he raced his own yacht,
and twice carried off the Queen's Cup. And always
he was the genial host to the Kings and Queens, the
Emperors and Tsars, the Sultans, Shahs, and other
royalties who paid ceremonial visits to the great
Queen who called so many of them kin.

When she celebrated her Jubilee thirty-two princes
of her own house rode in her *cortège* with the Prince
of Wales at their head.

In the long years of his apprenticeship four
sovereigns came to the German throne and three
Tsars were crowned in Russia. As a child he had
seen Louis Philippe and learnt of the fall of the
House of Orleans. He had watched the coming of
the Second Empire and the formation of the Third
Republic. He had dashed to Denmark to bring
home the Princess of Wales when her country was
under threat of war ; he had mourned at the funeral
of Alexander II, blown to pieces by a bomb;
witnessed the wedding of Nicholas II and attended
the confirmation of that " impetuous and conceited
youth, William of Germany."

He had known the Duke of Wellington and Sir
Robert Peel ; listened to Disraeli as he brought in
his first Reform Bill, and acted as pall-bearer at
Gladstone's funeral. He had poured oil on the
troubled waters between England and America when
they glared at one another across the Atlantic and
had wired a New Year's " Peace " message that
stirred two nations. Not for nothing did Disraeli
describe him as " a Prince who has really seen everything and known everybody."

On a grey evening the royal yacht, bearing the body of Queen Victoria, came out of the mist lying low over the Solent, above it and above the grey avenue of war-ships flags hung at half-mast. Albert Edward looked up at the royal standard above his head.

" The Queen is dead, but the King lives ! "

In quick obedience the flag was raised.

Eighteen months later the Archbishop of Canterbury addressed the great congregation which was assembled in the Abbey :

" Sirs, I here present unto you King Edward, the undoubted King of this realm. Wherefore all of you who are come this day to do your homage, are you willing to do the same ? "

Peers and commoners gave answer, the silver trumpets sounded, and outside booming guns gave the signal of the crowning.

" God Save the King ! God Save the King ! "

Then came Scotland's hour when King and Queen drove to Edinburgh Castle and received a sentry's challenge : " Who goes there ? "

" Edward VII, King of England, Scotland, and Ireland, demands admission."

A fanfare of trumpets, a squad of rushing men— the bridge was lowered and the guard of honour crossed at the double. High above them came the voice of the herald :

" Pass, King Edward VII."

Work went on. Edward VII journeyed abroad. Lisbon saw him, and in France murmurs of " Vive les Boers " changed to shouts of " Vive notre Roi ! " The Entente Cordiale was in sight.

A letter to President Roosevelt drew the New World closer to the Old.

" Edward the Peace-Maker " visited the Austrian Emperor and held out a hand to the Tsar on his tottering throne, despite the cry of protests, led by

Ramsay MacDonald, that royal recognition should be given to " a common murderer."

Under no illusions as to political undercurrents and the vagaries of diverse characters, the King asked Mr. Asquith whether the Cabinet " in its framing of the naval estimates had taken into consideration the possibility, he hoped the improbable possibility, of a European war." But still he travelled here and there, and played host to royal visitors, still he wrote to that wide circle of relations scattered over Europe.

" It is essential for the peace of the world that we should walk shoulder to shoulder," he reminded his fire-brand nephew in Germany.

The nine years of kingship ended before the house of cards fell. On May 6 (1910) he admitted that he felt " miserably ill," but set advice aside.

" Of what use is it to be alive if one cannot work ? " he asked; but as the hours passed he grew worse. " Work," he murmured half unconsciously . . . " work ! "

At midnight the crowds waiting silently outside the palace heard that the King was dead.

Cæsar, the little white dog that had never left his master night or day when travelling, had his place in the funeral procession, and as the black-robed Queen passed she stooped to pat his head.

CHAPTER XVII

PRINCE GEORGE FREDERICK ERNEST ALBERT (GEORGE V)

GEORGE FREDERICK ERNEST ALBERT (GEORGE V)

Born at Marlborough House . June 3, 1865
Married . . . . . July 6, 1893
Created Prince of Wales . . November 1901
Proclaimed King . . . May 9, 1910

Descent

Edward VII — *m.* — Alexandra of Denmark

|

George (and others)

CONTEMPORARY SOVEREIGNS

GERMANY : Kaiser William II (abdicated).
RUSSIA : Tsar Nicholas II (murdered).

CHAPTER XVII

GEORGE FREDERICK ERNEST ALBERT
(GEORGE V)

1865

GEORGE FREDERICK ERNEST ALBERT, later to become King George V, was born at Marlborough House on a Saturday morning in June (1865), arriving before the Secretary of State, whose duty it was to receive him.

The child was "nice and plump," according to Queen Victoria, although, as she added regretfully, "not very pretty."

A month later a special train took guests to Windsor for the christening. The little Prince was endowed with his fourth name to mollify his grandmother, who disapproved of George, "which only came over with the Hanoverian family. . . . However, if the dear child grows up good and wise I shall not mind what his name is," she added. After all, Prince George was but a second son, and two generations distant from the throne.

The children of Edward VII (then Prince of Wales) led a quietly happy life, counting Sandringham as their chief home. They were sent to bed early and expected to be up early enough to enjoy the fresh morning hours ; they learnt to ride on shaggy ponies and to enjoy long walks. Once a year they went with their parents to the family gathering in Denmark, when their beautiful mother became a girl again and they met cousins of half a dozen different nationalities.

Society saw little of the royal children, though once when Prince George was ten years old he appeared with his elder brother at a wonderful costume ball at Marlborough House ; the two went as pages in attendance on their mother, who drew all eyes as Mary Queen of Scots.

Long before this, regular lessons had been begun under a tutor, and periodical reports on the princes' progress were being made not only to their parents but to the Queen.

The Prince of Wales had decided that his sons' education was to be conducted on normal lines, and that, above all, they were to have companionship. Overruling the Queen's wishes, he sent the two elder princes to Dartmouth and Osborne ; they began a naval career on the *Britannia* before George was twelve years old. The sole concessions made to their rank was the attendance of a tutor and the assignment of private quarters ; in all other respects the younger boy at least shared the full work of the ship, and learnt to answer to the name of " Herring."

" Up at 6.30 ; cold tub; 7 a.m., roll call ; 7.10 a.m. drill; after which comes three hours of ordinary lessons." So ran the daily programme for four years till the brothers passed out and were sent to continue their training on the *Bacchante*.

When the nation learnt that a cruise to the West Indies was to be undertaken it took alarm, and Lord Beaconsfield pointed out the dangers arising from sending both princes on one ship. Perhaps he used less than his usual tact, for Queen Victoria was stirred to give immediate approval to the project, and informed her Prime Minister that " the question of the princes' cruise was NOT a Cabinet matter."

The *Bacchante* sailed, and Prince George's thirty years' sea-service began.

" *September* 26, 1879.—Passed the Lizard about 11 a.m. on a fine sunny morning ; the little wind

H.M. KING GEORGE V.

there is comes from the West, and we are going 6½
knots. . . . Lost sight of Land's End." So ran one
of the first entries in the diary the brothers kept
together for the next three years, while they learnt
visually, as well as by rote, the geography and
grandeur of the overseas countries that make Greater
Britain. They were young and imaginative enough
to thrill when they passed historic sites :
" Trafalgar Bay!—Here on October 21, 1805,
twenty-seven English ships of the line and four
frigates engaged thirty-three French and Spanish
ships of the line and seven frigates. . . . Nelson
was wounded a quarter-before-one and died at
half-past-four the same afternoon, only 47 years
old ! . . . A fine bright morning. . . . Mids drill
with dumb-bells before breakfast."

Palermo was sighted, and the *Bacchante* played her
first cricket match, " the first half of the alphabet
against the second " ; Prince George was to play
cricket around the Empire.

November brought the *Bacchante* to Gibraltar—
" it has now belonged to England for just three-
fourths of the time for which it belonged to Castile
before," noted the diarist, and settled down to " usual
school " before going ashore.

" *Dec.* 15.—Finished reading *Westward Ho!* for
the second time and suppose we are on the track of
those Northmen."

On Christmas Day (1879) the eager midshipmen
were on deck at 4 a.m. to see the Southern Cross
and catch their first glimpse of Barbados, whence put
out boatloads of negro washerwomen seeking trade.
One, a fine six-footer, claimed the Princes' laundry as
her established right, since she had previously " washed
for Prince Albert."

The brothers were immensely interested in the
history of the island, and that day's journal entry was
pages long : " They call it Little England, and in
the planters of Barbadoes we certainly find the earliest

type of the true English colonist," they wrote. . . .
" Cromwell did a good deal for the West Indies by
sending many of the Irish and Scottish prisoners
out as slaves. Seven thousand Scots, for example,
were sold to the planters after Worcester. . . .
Barbadoes is the last spot of English territory Nelson
trod upon in life," commented the princes, and were
shocked to find the island had " no decent Sailor's
Home ! "

Laying the diary aside, the two went off to drive
through the capital and attend a ball at Government
House, where they quickly noted the social gulf :
" Black men and women in the streets all day, white
men and women alone to be seen at night ! "

By the New Year Prince George had grown an
inch and put on 7 lb. in weight !

A few weeks later the *Bacchante* passed between
St. Lucia and Martinique. " We should be less than
Englishmen, less than men, if we did not feel a thrill
of pride while sailing here . . . the air seems full
of ghosts, the ghosts of gallant sailors and soldiers."
. . . The information that a harassed Colonial Office
in London had contemplated giving up the West
Indies moved the young Princes to wrath : " Was
it for this that the seas were reddened with the
blood of our own forefathers there year after year !
. . . Did all those gallant Souls go down to death in
vain ? " . . . Cromwell was approved once more,
since he had helped Jamaica to prosperity by decree-
ing that no tax should be placed on colonial produc-
tions for a decade. . . . " We are proud to think
that within a hundred years after England took
Jamaica it had become one of the richest places in
the world."

Young minds were expanding fast, and the science
of Empire development soon proved as fascinating
as cutlass drill, seamanship, gunnery, and torpedo
work to the middy-princes. Summer found them
in Bantry Bay with the half-yearly examinations

proceeding, " but all very jolly and meeting old
Britannia shipmates." To the delight of the
Bacchante a rumour had reached England that the
Princes had had themselves tattooed on their noses,
and a flood of indignant paragraphs were discovered
in the newspapers when mail reached the ship.

Even the most hide-bound Cabinet minister was
bound to admit that the preliminary cruise had
proved an unqualified success, so there were few
protests when a few months later the *Bacchante,* with
the Princes aboard, set off on a tour round the world
with the rest of the Training Squadron, scheduled
to visit South America, South Africa, Australia,
China, and Japan ; the diary was opened once more.

" *Oct.* 19 (1880). Coming out of Ferrol is the
time to read the last chapter of Froude's *History of
England*—The Armada. . . .

" *Nov.* 10. Manned and armed boats. . . . Mail
from England ; many parcels marked ' Not to be
opened till Christmas.' "

Just before Christmas came the excitement of
crossing the " line," and when Neptune boarded the
ship the Princes found it all tremendous fun, as
they were initiated into the mysteries of ducking.
" There is the duck courteous, the duck oblique, the
duck direct, the duck upright, the duck downright,
the shower duck, and the duck-and-the-drake."

A course was set towards South America. " We
are reading Squire's *Peru* and Prescott's *History of
the Incas* between drills, school-work, gymnastic
exercises, and cricket," which last proved " very
expensive " on account of the number of balls lost
overboard.

Now came January 8, " and a big cake in the
gun-room, as it is Eddy's birthday, who is 17
years old."

The weather had turned so cold that the midshipmen played duckstones on the quarter-deck to warm
themselves, " and such a gale that at noon today we

are just where we were three days ago, and forty-five miles further off our destination than we were yesterday. We are reading Lord Anson's account of doubling the Horn." . . . Still the gale went on : " We can't help feeling wonder at the invisible force of the wind and a sense of mystery about its persistent antagonism to us thus day after day."

But meditations were interrupted, and the minor thrills of life forgotten when off the Falkland Isles a message was received ordering the squadron to the Cape of Good Hope. Those on the *Bacchante* fell to arguing as to whether the demonstration was to be against Zulus or Basutos, and the curriculum was widened to include skirmishing.

As they voyaged on, sighting never a sail for 4,000 miles, the midshipmen felt as if they were negotiating the sloping edge of the globe and might well slip off the edge into space.

There was consternation in England—worse even than that occasioned by the report of the tattooed noses—and Queen Victoria announced that the princes had been sent to sea " for education and moral training, and it would be very wrong to let them become involved in a civil war. . . . In after years, when Georgie is older, and if his ship be obliged necessarily to take part in a war," she would agree with the Prince of Wales that his sons must play an active part. Now they were too young.

All unconscious of the royal fiat, the Princes waited in Cape Town, and, having discovered that the enemy was Boer, not Zulu or Basuto, played cricket; " the *Bacchante* was well-beaten by the Diocesan College," and acquired general information by visiting ostrich farms and making shopping expeditions, when they were shocked to find " everything very dear—oranges grown in the country cost 2d. each, and in a land teeming with cattle most of the milk comes in tins from Norway and Switzerland."

They climbed Table Mountain on foot, and discovered the town laundry—" native women pounding away at clothes in the stream and the whole place reeking with soapsuds and filth." The two decided that garments would emerge from such a process worse than they went.

A semi-official interview was arranged between the Princes and Cetewayo, the Zulu king, " a bloodthirsty old chap eager to wash his spears in the blood of the Boers. 'Let me go and I will do it now!' he urged, and broke off to send a message to ' his mother the Queen of England,'" as Victoria's grandsons recorded with delight. " The old chap weighs 19 stone, is 6 ft. high and possesses four wives each of whom weighs 16 stone or over, and all are dressed in Scottish plaids."

The royalties exchanged photographs, Cetewayo giving his in Zulu costume, " which is almost nothing at all."

" *February* 27.—A defeat at Laing's Nek. . . . We have kept as quiet as we could here, no balls or entertainments, for neither the people nor ourselves are at all in the humour for such things."

The *Bacchante* took up her station in Simon's Bay, and hope ebbed :

" We had expected that some of the Squadron would have been taken to Natal for service," came a diary entry. " We could have sent at least a thousand men. . . . As for demonstrations, for us lying in this secluded bay . . . well out of sight of the Dutch, who have scarcely known of our existence, it is a very hollow affair. We are patiently awaiting orders as to what is to be done next. . . . We have been of no use in any way as yet, to anybody but the beef contractor, whatever people in England may think."

Balm to sore hearts, the *Bacchante* won a cricket match by two wickets.

294 GEORGE FREDERICK ERNEST ALBERT

" *March* 19.—General Roberts is arrived and has
sailed again by the next boat, as they have changed
their minds since he left England, and there is to be
no more war. . . . Most of the troops brought at
great expense will have to return without landing,
and this squadron, brought half across the globe,
is to be sent away also, for they have no use for it
here." . . . These young midshipmen felt that they
could have managed the war infinitely better than
some of the statesmen in their grandmother's Cabinet.

Africa was left behind, and, sailing for Australia,
the *Bacchante* encountered high winds and stormy
seas. One night there was a crash in the darkness,
a cry—" Something's happened ! "—and laughing,
Prince George had to be extricated from the mêlée of
his cabin, wherein every article of furniture was
indulging in a game of general post.

" *April* 18.—Reading *Problems of Greater Britain*
from the ship's library.

" *April* 20.—Went on reading about free trade
and protection.

" *April* 21.—The Southern Cross again. All the
constellations are different except Orion ; it fills us
with a weird feeling of being in another world. . . .
Had a good game of prisoner's base. A stiff gale is
blowing, and the sight is magnificent with dense black
storm-clouds and a moon visible every few minutes.
The sea is like boiling foam."

Once again " something happened," but this time
not to Prince George alone, but to the *Bacchante*.
The rest of the squadron had disappeared in the
storm, and the stricken ship had to ride out the gale
as she could, then make rough-and-ready repairs and
set a course for the nearest port, nearly 400 miles
distant. So Albany, all unprepared, and not
Sydney or Melbourne, gave a first welcome to the
travellers, and entertained them for three glorious
weeks,

There was a cricket match "in which George played," the ship against Albany Union Club, "and we won by 7 runs," never-to-be-forgotten bush excursions, and an easy open-handed hospitality in which the Princes and their fellow-midshipmen revelled. Off on a kangaroo hunt, a party of nine found themselves housed (?) in a two-room shanty. Toilets were made in the open, and at night friendly visitors deposited two pailsful of milk at the door lest anyone should thirst.

All were astir at dawn and off on the hunt, to return to a glorious breakfast " of hot scones, butter, cream, fresh milk, jam, and minced kangaroo served in the farmhouse kitchen." Here too a simple religious service was held on a Sunday morning, and at dinner-time each Prince found a little wreath of roses laid around his plate " in memory of England."

Albany, the two decided, would make " a magnificent sanatorium for our troops from Southern India." . . . But here, as in Africa, the cost of necessities shocked them—" Bass's beer is 2s. a bottle ! "

So back to the *Bacchante* and lessons. Then a cross-country journey and the exploration of a mine over which they were shown by " true Cornishmen of real English bone and sinew with a straightforward look about their faces."

Everywhere the two met with a stirring welcome. " Of course, we know well enough that this is not got up for us, but is merely a sign of the warm attachment to England over the seas and all that name awakens and recalls in every British breast," they explained modestly in the diary.

Melbourne fascinated them : " The city is just as old as the Queen's reign ; it was then but a few wooden huts and a wooden church with a bell hung in a tree, and now it is as big as Manchester and the new Treasury Building, when finished, will be larger than our own in London. Government House reminds us of the Queen's house at Osborne. The ballroom is longer than the state ballroom at Buckingham Palace by 18 feet ! "

They joined in the celebrations commemorative of the birth of the colony of Victoria " when she was born to separate life from New South Wales, boldly cutting adrift and becoming mistress of her own destinies when only fifteen years old ! . . .

" Old colonists can remember when they tethered their cows where the Town Hall now stands, and fifty years ago the shore of Victoria was unknown to Europeans."

The story of the development of the youthful continent fascinated them, as did the result of their investigations into the condition of life in the New World—there was no poor rate, and every man could support himself if he would.

Then for an hour the two cast aside their books, forgot the responsibility of position, and became enthusiastic boys, for the armour once worn by Ned Kelly, the famous Australian bushranger, was produced—" and we put it on ! . . . It is made from ploughshares, and weighs nearly 87 lbs. . . . the helmet is like a round pot with the bottom knocked out."

The *Bacchante* sailed for Sydney.

" *July* 12.—Had Euclid examination paper to-day.

" *July* 13.—Trigonometry . . . we are rolling a good deal more.

" *July* 25.—Another practical navigation paper this forenoon."

Port Jackson won high eulogy—" it is like a combination of the English Lakes with the harbours of Dartmouth and Plymouth "—and now the Princes plunged into sightseeing. They examined refrigerating plants, they saw the cathedral, the foundations of which had been laid with fine faith when New

South Wales was in the diocese of Calcutta, and they
visited an outlying station, to become learned on the
subject of sheep and awed by the silence of the
bush : " In this stillness there seems to sound the
echo of the command given to the forefathers of
the human race when they stepped forth into a
solitary world. . . . The astonishing feature of these
plains is their capacity to receive millions, and,
swallowing them up, to wait open-mouthed for more.
Vast and silent, fertile, yet waste, field-like, yet
untilled, they have room for all the teeming multitudes
that have poured or can pour from England. Nature
has planted her hedgeless, gateless, free to all, a
green field for the support of half the human race."

" After England, Australia will always occupy the
warmest corner of our hearts," the Princes vowed,
deciding that " our Australian fellow-subjects consist
of the stoutest and staunchest of English, Welsh,
Scottish, and Irishmen who are showing at the same
time an amount of energy and activity in all the
branches of commerce, education, government, and
everything that makes a people great, which has
never before been surpassed in the whole course of
English history."

The cruise continued. Drill and routine lessons
were resumed, the ship's company being increased
by various pets such as kangaroos and wallabies,
but occasionally a diary entry betrayed a touch of
homesickness.

" *Sept.* 13, 1881.—At 4 a.m. this morning it
was 4 p.m. in England the day before, so here we are
in Tuesday while they are still in Monday.

" *Sept.* 14.—Just a year to-day since we left
Marlborough House. . . . Finished David's capital
little book on Buddhism."

Intensive reading prepared the travellers for a
happy week in Japan, during which Prince George

steered the officers' boat in a race. They knew
enough to marvel at the transformation that had
taken place in the lifetime of their host, the Mikado ;
they visited the shrines and temples, and rode through
the capital in jinrickshaws ; they discovered that the
Mikado's Minton dinner service was a duplicate of
that at Marlborough House, and saw the revolving
library, the contents of which might be " taken as
read " by students who turned it thrice on its axle.
Discarding their boots at a doorway, they became
guests at a Japanese banquet, squatting on knees and
heels while Japanese maidens plied them with strange
edibles served on lacquered plates and in lacquered
cups, " and of course we used nothing but chop-
sticks to eat with. . . . Next morning the remains
of the repast were sent to us, carefully packed in
wooden boxes and trays, on the same principle that
some of the City of London Companies give their
guests boxes of sweetmeats."

An indelible souvenir was secured in Japan, for
here the Princes achieved their long-cherished desire,
and were tattooed, though on less conspicuous parts
of their anatomy than noses.

Tattoo artists found it necessary to take up their
abode on the *Bacchante* and work night and day.

" One man mixes the colours and the other tattooes,
holding the instrument in the right hand and
grasping your arm with the left while he tightens the
surface of the skin on which the drawing is to be
made with finger and thumb. He first sketches the
outline in Indian ink and then pricks in the colour
with a little instrument that looks like a camel-hair
needle. We did not find the pricking hurt at all,
but this varies with different people and the different
parts of the body. . . . He does a large dragon in
blue and red writhing all down the arm in about
three hours. . . . The man who did most of our
party was beautifully tattooed over the whole of
his body," wrote the Princes with a touch of envy.

Meditating on the Japanese as they sailed away, the brothers noted them as " the most polite, civil, good-humoured, cheery, and hearty lot we have ever met."

China seems to have been approached with some misgiving, reading having revealed the fact that it was " a country of frequent revolutions. . . . In a little over twelve hundred years there have been fifteen changes of dynasty." But " the little boy-Emperor," aged ten, caught their imagination and sympathy when they discovered that, though he was regarded as the vice-regent of Heaven, he had to sit on his dragon throne for two hours daily, receiving reports from his Cabinet, while the Empress Dowager prompted him in his duty from behind a curtain.

They were startled to discover that although succession to the throne was hereditary in the male line, a sovereign had power to nominate his successor, also that Chinese hereditary titles decreased in each succeeding generation " from duke to marquis, to count to baron," so only lasted for a number of generations according to the class of the dignity. The fact that in China any honour won by a man redounded to the honour of his parents struck them as " a far more sensible notion than a son getting credit for his father's good deeds."

The diary was laid aside that they might go duck-shooting, but this proved " ticklish work, for it is scarcely possible to bring your gun to your shoulder without covering a Chinaman." . . . The experience set them to look up populations, and presently a diary entry records that " every fourth man in the human race is a Chinaman, and the British and Chinese between them own just half the world ! "

" *Dec.* 22.—Hong Kong, the creation of British energy, enterprise, and industry. Drizzling all day, but rowing before breakfast. Two examinations this forenoon, one in French and the other in steam."

These accomplished, Hong Kong was explored, and the Princes noted with dismay that there was not a single gun on the island that could pierce an ironclad, so the naval dockyards and 100,000 tons of coal were " absolutely defenceless ! " They fell to planning fortifications.

" *Dec.* 25, 1881.—The third successive Christmas Day away from England. Letters from Home.

" *Dec.* 26.—Turned out at 5 a.m. and kept morning watch. Ship's band played ' The Roast Beef of Old England.' "

Homesickness was combated by hard study, the tenets of Confucius were mastered, and the method of recruitment to the Chinese Civil Service became as an open book to these inquiring minds.

" *New Year's Day.*—Singapore founded by the prescience of Sir Stamford Raffles two-thirds of a century ago. Cricket—navy versus Singapore—the navy won easily."

March found the Princes climbing the Pyramids. " It makes your knees ache, but you can get to the top easily in a quarter of an hour."

And now Alexandria and mail from England " only six days old. The youngest we have had for a long time ! "

Aboukir Bay. " Victory," said Nelson, " is not a name strong enough for such a scene ! " What a strange multitude of reminiscences these lands awaken."

Syria. A camp was pitched outside the Damascus Gate, and awakening in the dawn, the Princes heard " little sparrows chirping in the dusk just as they do at home." The two wandered among holy sites, walked down the Via Dolorosa, passed the Garden of Gethsemane, and so along the road " by which, eighteen hundred years ago, our Lord approached the

Holy City. . . . We climbed Mt. Olivet, looked back on Bethany—that green knoll to the north may perhaps be Calvary."

In Jerusalem they were shocked from thoughts of Saladin and Richard Cœur de Lion by discovering that an armed Turkish guard had to be mounted in the Grotto of the Nativity " to prevent squabbles or worse between the two branches of the Catholic Church over the birthplace of the Prince of Peace ! "

June found the *Bacchante* creeping along the Sicilian coast. " Thermometer 78. Dead calm. We mids at our half-yearly seamanship examination.

" *July* 2.—Tangiers—part of the dowry Charles II got with his wife.

" *Aug.* 1.—Passed Finisterre . . . there is more of a feel of England about the air than we have been accustomed to for the last two years.

" *Aug.* 4.—At daybreak seven sail in sight and the wind is blowing straight off English land . . . the sight of Devon cornfields, grass lawns, and woods sloping to the sea makes every heart on board beat more quickly. . . . Salcombe Bay, Street, Stoke Fleming, the entrance of Dartmouth, Kingswear Castle, all stand out one after the other as clear as possible in the light of the setting sun. . . . We communicated with a little Brixham trawler and got some fresh English fish and a newspaper only a week old last Saturday. . . . As we near the Britain of the North Seas we should be unfaithful in our duty if we did not, above all, recall what we have seen and known of the Greater Britain of the Southern Seas.

" *Aug.* 5.—At 6 a.m. we passed Portland Bill. . . . The *Osborne* with the Prince and Princess of Wales met us off Swanage Bay. We saluted with 21 guns. The crew of the *Osborne* cheered, and our men cheered in return. . . . The Prince and Princess of Wales and our three sisters came on board the *Bacchante*. . . ."

Three days later the bronzed young travellers were confirmed in Whippingham Church : " God grant that you, sirs, may show to the world what Christian princes ought to be," prayed the Archbishop. " A great field lies before you."

The close companionship between the brothers was nearly at an end. Together, they went to the Continent for a few months' language study, then their paths diverted. The Duke of Clarence remained at home, while Prince George made an independent start in life ; for ten more years he was to sail the seas as a naval officer. As midshipman and sub-lieutenant he served on the North American and West India stations ; the Mediterranean Squadron welcomed him as a lieutenant. At twenty-six he took his first command in naval manœuvres ; two years later he was a captain. The successive steps followed : Rear-Admiral 1901, Vice-Admiral 1903, Admiral 1907, and Admiral of the Fleet 1910, but long before these were achieved the death of the Duke of Clarence had placed Prince George in direct succession to the crown, so making it necessary for him to abandon the sea as a profession.

The first outward sign of the change in position was the creation of the Prince as Duke of York, a title that had been in abeyance for over sixty years ; then, in the spring of 1893, came the announcement of the Duke's engagement to English-born Princess Victoria Mary of Teck, " A happy event which pleases everybody," said the Duke of Cambridge.

Queen Victoria saw the prospective bride as " a charming girl with much sense and amiability and very un-frivolous."

Children were born, the nation rejoiced at the lengthened line, and the Queen held her great-grandson in her arms.

The world moved onward, and there were stirrings overseas in the new lands the Duke had visited in his boyhood. Australia federated, and asked for

the honour of a royal visit. Queen Victoria approved,
having been greatly moved by the spontaneous
outburst of colonial loyalty occasioned by the South
African War.

When King Edward ascended the throne, one of
his first pronouncements was to the effect that the
Queen's wish should be fulfilled, and his son should
sail across the world once more. With him, for the
first time in history, went an English princess.

Gibraltar presented loyal addresses to Duke and
Duchess ; Maltese children sang the National Anthem ;
Ceylon assembled her soldiers, returned from the
South African War, that they might receive their
medals at the Prince's hands ; Singapore massed
5,000 of her children (European, Malayan, and
Eurasian) to cheer, while through her narrow streets,
canopied in brilliant silks, there wended, in honour
of the visitors, a monster procession of dragons,
fishes, serpents, devils, and vampires.

Young Australia sang a joyous song of welcome to—

" Great . . . Victoria's grandson,
Heir to the British throne ! "

And in a single morning 4,000 people pressed forward to shake him by the hand, while forty-seven
deputations lined up to present loyal addresses.

Through tirelessly cheering multitudes the Duke
and Duchess strove to obey the King's behest.

Eleven thousand miles from home the old ritual
was in force, for the Federated Parliament of the
youngest of the nations was patterned on the Mother
of Parliaments sitting at Westminster. Black Rod
attended, the Speakers were dignified in robes and
wigs, and the members of the House of Representatives came flocking to the Bar of the Upper House
to hear the Clerk of Parliament read the Letters
Patent, wherein King Edward VII, " trusting in the
discretion of our dear son," empowered him to do
all things necessary for the holding of a Parliament.

The Duchess touched a golden button, so flashing news of the opening around the world, and the Duke stepped forward to read a telegram just received from the King wishing Australia prosperity and happiness. That afternoon, when the daughter-Parliament sat in first session, Westminster sent greetings.

There followed a crowded month, in which the royal visitors laid foundation-stones, planted trees, witnessed processions, took the salute at military reviews, and distributed war medals.

"We cannot all be winners," said the Duke to young Australia . . . "but let both success and failure serve as stimulants to new endeavour. . . . We look to the rising generation not only to hold and keep what your forefathers have bequeathed you, but to push forward. If I may offer you advice, I should say, ' Be thorough, do your level best in whatever work you are called upon to perform . . . be loyal to your parents, your country, your King and your God.' " As he spoke a signal released 7,000 Union Jacks to fly above Australia's schools.

When the cities were left behind and the Duke and Duchess sat on kerosene tins in the shade flung by tall eucalyptus trees, while the billy boiled for bush tea, the ghosts of the young midshipmen of twenty years before must have stood very near : "This is Australia! Australia! Australia!" the brothers had said, roaming off to hunt kangaroo. Then Prince George had celebrated his sixteenth birthday in Albany; now, on his thirty-sixth anniversary, Sydney was to wish him "Many Happy Returns of the Day."

It fell to Adelaide to offer the prettiest welcome to the Duchess : she massed her students, who sang to their future Queen :

"There is a lady sweet and kind,
Whose winsome face so pleased our mind—
We did but see her passing by,
Yet we shall love her till we die ! "

Meanwhile, New Zealand was waiting impatiently with triumphal arches and singing children; and here Duke and Duchess broke fresh ground. At Rotorua there were strange scenes among the weird setting of the geysers, where the Maoris gathered in full battle array to sing a lament for Victoria and bring gifts to the Queen's grandson; barely two generations before had sovereignty over the islands been ceded.

" Here, in the presence of your Royal Highness, we confirm the acts of our fathers," vowed the chieftains. " Hear, O ye peoples, to-day we make a new treaty— new and yet old—inasmuch as we confirm the loyalty of our generation. . . . Hear, O Prince from the far ends of the earth, from remote Hawaiki across the seas or Kira. You have come to see these lands and peoples ; it is well, for by so doing you have drawn closer the bonds of love. . . . Welcome and farewell ! "

The South Island offered her visitors a Scottish welcome. Little Tasmania, second in age of the Australasian group, built her welcoming arches of apples and proudly stood forward her two sons who had won the first Victoria Crosses bestowed on colonials in the Boer War.

South Africa claimed attention, and, though once again the land was darkened by war, children, white and coloured, sang " God Save the King," and Zulu chiefs offered salutations to the son of the Sovereign.

Flags fluttered above the citadel of Quebec when the *Ophir* swept up the great waterway of the St. Lawrence with black cruisers in her wake.

" Bienvenu ! Bienvenu ! " cried ten thousand voices.

> " 'Tis the son of the greatest of England's sons,
>   Of the monarch of half the world,
> Who comes with a message of great goodwill
>   With the words of his Sire's decree,
> To Britons afar, that are Britons still,
>   In the Britains beyond the Seas ! "

306 GEORGE FREDERICK ERNEST ALBERT

On the Plains of Abraham, where nearly 150 years before Wolfe had won Canada for England, the Duke was required to review 4,000 troops, Canadians all, whether of French or British extraction.

And now a train became the royal headquarters for the month-long journey of 7,000 miles from seaboard to seaboard and back again, and all along that mighty route, wherever the royal train stopped, groups of Canada's children assembled to sing alternately " God Save the King " and " The Maple Leaf " :

> " In days of yore from Britain's shore,
> Wolfe the dauntless hero came
> And planted firm Old England's flag
> On Canada's fair domain.

> " Long may it wave, the emblem dear,
> Of ties that none may sever.
> The Thistle, Shamrock, Rose entwined
> The Maple Leaf forever !

> " The Maple Leaf, our emblem dear,
> The Maple Leaf forever !
> God save our King, and Heaven bless
> Our Maple Leaf forever."

Six crowded hours passed swiftly in Vancouver, then on went the royal travellers once more, to snatch a glimpse of Victoria (B.C.), back through the Rockies (Duke and Duchess rode on the cow-catcher through Hell's Gate), so on to Newfoundland, thence to England, a welcome by the Channel Squadron, and Portsmouth through stormy seas.

In all the amazing journey of 45,000 miles no foot had been set except under the shelter of the Union Jack save for the brief hour in Port Said.

London rose to welcome the first prince of her royal house to have gone round the world, and his creation as Prince of Wales " in consequence of the admirable manner in which he has carried out the task confided to him " met with acclaim.

" I only hope," said the Prince, " that I may be worthy to hold this ancient and honourable title," and at the ensuing Guildhall banquet he told the nation of the deep loyalty to the Crown of the Britons overseas, and also of their nascent nationalism. " We must send of our best to such lands," he declared, ". . . and the Old Country must wake up if she intends to maintain her own position of pre-eminence."

For a year or so the Prince of Wales remained at home except for ambassadorial visits to the Continent, but 1905 found him sailing off to India, and in 1908 he hoisted his own flag on the *Indomitable*, in command of a sea-going squadron off to take part in Canada's tercentenary celebrations. " The profession that I love so truly " was no idle phrase on the Prince's lips.

The years of training for the kingship were drawing to a close. In May 1910 George V came to the throne—an English-born monarch with an English-born consort, and the most travelled sovereign the world has known. He had visited Canada six times, Australasia twice, South Africa twice, and India once, to mention the outlying portions of the Empire alone ; he had laid foundation-stones and opened memorial parks in Newfoundland, Rangoon, Wellington (N.Z.), and Maritzburg.

One of the King's first messages was addressed " to my peoples beyond the Seas," and on the coronation stole, in addition to the Rose, the Thistle, and the Shamrock, there were worked the Dragon of Wales, the Lotus of India, the Maple Leaf of Canada, the Wattle of Africa, the Southern Cross for Australia, and the stars from New Zealand's flag.

" Almighty God, of His mercy let the light of His countenance shine upon your Majesty, grant you a prosperous and happy reign, defend and save you and let your subjects say, ' Amen.' God save the King ! " So prayed the Archbishop in the words Cranmer had used more than three centuries before.

Help was needed, and this the new-made King

knew full well : " The British Empire at the present time requires hard service from all its sons, and it requires the hardest service from those to whom the most has been given," he said years before the outbreak of the Great War.

Eighteen months later George V created precedent by sailing with the Queen for India. With a fanfare of trumpets the Chief Herald made announcement of the coronation at Westminster; then, beneath a golden-domed pavilion on the plains of Delhi, King-Emperor and Queen-Empress received the homage of the feudatories and subjects who passed before them in endless procession.

Hindus, Jains, Mohammedans, and Sikhs gave thanks in that an old prophecy was now fulfilled— " from across the ocean had come a race of men who would spread peace and justice and root out tyranny and oppression."

But the mills of the gods went on grinding.

CHAPTER XVIII

EDWARD PRINCE OF WALES (PRESENT DAY)

EDWARD ALBERT CHRISTIAN GEORGE ANDREW PATRICK DAVID (PRINCE OF WALES)

Born at White Lodge, Richmond . .	June 23, 1894
Created Prince of Wales (by Letters Patent)	June 23, 1911
Investiture at Carnarvon Castle . . .	July 13, 1911

Descent

George V — *m.* — Princess Victoria Mary of Teck.

Edward (and others)

CHAPTER XVIII

EDWARD ALBERT CHRISTIAN GEORGE ANDREW PATRICK DAVID

1894

THE patron saints of England, Scotland, Ireland, and Wales were evoked at the baptism of the twentieth Prince of Wales ; father, grandfathers, and great-grandfather and saints gave him their names, and for the first time in history a ruling Queen took into her arms her descendant in the fourth generation.

Since the birth of Edward VI, son of Henry VIII and Jane Seymour (1537), no other royal prince in direct succession to the throne had been born in England of British-born parents. Kaiser, Emperor, and Tsar sent their good wishes ; twenty-four years hence all were dead or exiled and the map of the world had changed.

Once more the golden bowl that had served as a royal font for three hundred years was filled with water from the River Jordan and Queen Victoria gave her great-grandson his seven names—Edward Albert Christian George Andrew Patrick David. The Union Jack and Royal Standard waved above the tiny gold coronet that surmounted the sugar cradle on the giant christening cake which was cut at the White Lodge, once a hunting-box of George II.

" He is a very fine healthy boy, 8 lbs. in weight," wrote the Duke of Cambridge in high good-humour.

A week later the House of Commons moved a congratulatory address to the Queen, but just as it was about to be passed, Mr. Keir Hardie, first member of the Socialist Party, sprang to his feet and an amazed House heard that he " and those he represented " were unable to join in this address :

" I do not owe allegiance to any hereditary ruler," declared Mr. Keir Hardie, ignoring interruptions, " and I consider that this resolution elevates to an importance it does not deserve, an event of everyday occurrence. . . . I have been delighted to learn that the child is a fairly healthy one, and had I had the opportunity of meeting its parents I should have been pleased to join in the ordinary congratulations, but when we are asked, as a House of Commons representing the nation, to join in these congratulations, then, in the interest of the dignity of the House, I take leave to protest. . . . It is a matter of small importance to me whether the future ruler of the nation be the genuine article or a spurious imitation. . . . We are asked to rejoice because this child has been born and that he will one day rule over this great Empire. . . . Up to the present we have no means of knowing what his qualifications for that task may be," persisted the honourable member, defying disapproval and forgetful that the princeling of whom he spoke was but five days old. . . . ' From his childhood upwards he will be surrounded by sycophants . . . and will be taught to believe himself a superior creature. . . . In due course, following the precedent that has been set, he will tour the world —and probably rumours of a morganatic marriage will follow ! ' he shouted above the jeering cries of those who visualised the unconscious infant in his cradle.

" As a matter of principle I protest against this motion being passed," he ended, " and if there is another member of the House who shares the principles I hold, I will carry my protest to the length of a division."

But Mr. Keir Hardie's was a voice crying in the wilderness, and " the Ayes " had it very decidedly.

A happy babyhood was followed by a happy normal childhood, spent for the most part between York Cottage, Sandringham, and York House, St. James's. Other children came to join Prince Edward in his nursery, there were ponies to ride in Windsor Great Park, yachts to sail .on Virginia Waters, and a fascinating model railway for diversion on wet days.

Queen Victoria died and, clad in white sailor suits, the seven-year-old boy and his younger brother sat at their mother's feet watching, wide-eyed, the pageantry of a coronation.

A lusty young nation was born overseas and the Duke and Duchess of Cornwall and York sailed on a royal mission, leaving behind them three half-tearful, half-indignant children. But the months which threatened to be so long when they loomed ahead passed with incredible swiftness, and presently the parents returned loaded with gifts for their little people from the children of the Overseas. Africa had sent three Basuto ponies, and Newfoundland a magnificent dog broken to harness, towards the purchase of which every child in the colony had contributed one cent.

Prince Edward was nearly eight years old. Lessons on ordinary lines had been begun some time before, special attention being paid to foreign languages and public speaking, but it was felt that he was now sufficiently advanced to pass into the hands of a tutor, and, with Prince Albert, begin to prepare for his first step into the outer world of boys.

The following years were as normal in their course as it was possible to make them, and Prince Edward's chosen treat on his eleventh birthday was a cricket match in the Home Park, when he and Prince Albert captained rival teams of youthful Etonians.

At thirteen he entered Osborne and was nicknamed " Sardine." At fifteen, Cadet Edward of Wales passed out and on to Dartmouth, and a short year later was summoned home to follow the coffin of his grandfather.

The throne was one step nearer, and though the Prince's sea-training continued, it was subject to interruptions ; King George V was crowned and his eldest son needs must lay aside his cadet uniform, and, coroneted, drive through streets thronged with cheering people to pay homage to his father in Westminster Abbey.

A king-in-the-making has many duties.   The Royal Naval College could not hold the heir apparent much longer, but at least he could dash back for the annual regatta, and, as coxswain, steer his boat to victory !

Slight, and young, and shy, Prince Edward was admitted to the Order of the Garter at Windsor as a prelude to the yet grander ceremony of his investiture as Prince of Wales.

Letters Patent had been issued from the Palace of Westminster, and now Wales called insistently, for the splendid pageant was to be staged amid the magnificent ruins of Carnarvon Castle, where, six hundred years before, the first English Prince of Wales had been born.   That Prince Edward had been presented to the Welsh people in his swaddling clothes ; this, the seventh of his name, arrived at Carnarvon in a midshipman's uniform.

Vociferous cheers greeted him when he introduced a few Welsh sentences into his first speech : " Already," so he told them, he had found " mor o gan yw Cmyru i gyd " (all Wales a sea of song), and that as they had greeted him with the word " Croesaw " (Welcome), he must answer them by saying : " Diolch o waelod fy nghalon i hên wiad fy nhadau ! " (Thanks from the bottom of my heart to the old land of my fathers !)

A fanfare of trumpets and a salvo of guns announced the Prince's entrance into the Castle.

Now the King's procession began to wend its way

through the narrow streets of the old city headed by
the pursuivants, Blue Mantle and Rouge Croix, and
the Heralds. King and Queen passed to the dais
while with all fervour of Welsh hearts the standing
thousands sang " God Save the King ! "

Garter-King-of-Arms summoned the Prince, and
the multitude waited in the sunshine. He came,
bareheaded, in short purple velvet surcoat, white
breeches and stockings and broad buckled shoes,
and before him walked four peers bearing the insignia.

As the Letters Patent were read, the King invested
his son with the purple ermine-trimmed mantle, girt
him with the sword, set the coronet on his head, the
ring upon his finger, and the golden virge in his
boyish hands.

Kneeling, the Prince made homage. . . . " I,
Edward Prince of Wales, do become your liege man
of life and limb, and of earthly worship, faith, and
truth I will bear unto you to live and die against
all manner of folk."

The King stepped forward, raised and kissed this
youthful liege man, all unknowing that three years
hence he would go forth, sword in hand, against his
countries' enemies, and placed him on the empty
throne on his right hand.

" The bowmen and pikemen of Wales followed
the Black Prince to Crécy and Henry of Monmouth
to Agincourt "; so ran Wales's first address to her
Prince. " The valour of Welshmen placed Henry
Tudor on the English throne . . . and so it comes
that on this historic day the people of Wales . . .
acclaim you their Prince and Leader. Long live
the Prince ! Long live the King ! "

A glance at his father and the Prince was on his
feet : " I thank you with all my heart for your
cordial welcome." . . . Yes, his Tudor descent, his
title and his name all bound him to Wales. He had
come to the land of his fathers, and he hoped that the
day would always be counted a happy one for the

principality in that it had brought a new friend, though a young one.

" I am *very* young," continued the Prince, " but I have great examples before me. I have my dear father and my dear mother, and good friends to help me, so, bearing in mind our ancient and beautiful saying, ' Heb Duw, hêb ddim, Duw a digon ' (Without God, without anything, God is enough), I hope to do my duty to my King, to Wales, and to you all."

" O Lord God of our Fathers, hear our prayers we beseech Thee, for Thy servant, Edward the Prince," prayed the Bishop of Bangor. . . . " Grant unto him, O Lord, wisdom and knowledge and an understanding heart."

With bent heads all listened to the benediction in Welsh : " Unto God's gracious mercy and protection we commit you."

Hand in hand King and Prince walked to Queen Eleanor's Gate, while the trumpets sounded, and when the guns ceased the multitude waiting below saw the shining sun-flecked figure of the young Prince, robed and crowned, standing shy and proud above them ; in the shadow of the hoary arch the King and Queen watched their son.

A roar of cheering sounded, and then with one accord the stirred people broke into their National Anthem :

> " Oh, Land of my Fathers, the land of the free,
> The home of the Talyn so soothing to me,
> Thy noble defenders were gallant and brave,
> For freedom their heart's life they gave.

> " Wales, Wales, home, sweet home is Wales,
> Till death be passed, my love shall last,
> My longing, my hiraeth for Wales ! "

A few days later the Prince took up his naval duties again, and sailed for a three-months' cruise on the *Hindustan*—a very junior officer at 1*s*. 9*d*. a day. He returned to bid farewell to the King and Queen, who were leaving for the Durbar, then settled down to hard study at Sandringham, since he was to go to Oxford in 1912. Before this, however, came three months in Paris, when the Prince shared the life of a distinguished French family. They were busy, happy months, for all doors opened to the eldest son of the King of England, even though officially he was merely Earl of Chester. One red-letter day he took part in the French naval manœuvres, on another he made a descent in a French submarine. By the time he dashed back to celebrate his eighteenth birthday at Windsor he had won golden opinions.

" He has the charm of an English boy, the tact of a Parisian, and the manners of his grandfather," said one *grande dame.*

The world was a peaceful place when in October 1912 the Prince of Wales donned cap and gown at Magdalen. He matriculated as a commoner, dined in Hall, attended lectures as an undergraduate, argued in the common-room, played tennis, squash-rackets, and polo, hunted, ran with the beagles, and drilled as a private in the O.T.C. till he achieved his corporal's stripe.

The vacations of 1913 found him in Heidelberg and Friedrichshafen, where he saw a Zeppelin in flight.

August 4, 1914, and the outbreak of the Great War ended the Prince's University career. On August 7 he was gazetted 2nd Lieutenant in the Grenadier Guards, and four days later he was in barracks and drilling with energy. Within a month his battalion was detailed for active service, but the indignant Prince was informed that as he had not completed his military training, " it was not considered desirable " that he should proceed overseas.

The blow was heavy, and the Prince rebelled. All young England thirsted to strike a blow in defence of maltreated Belgium, and he, " the King's liege man of life and limb," was denied ! From one to another he went, arguing and pleading.

" Death is preferable to being the only man marked out as not being suffered to come forward on such an occasion. . . . Were there fifty princes, or were I the only one, it would be in my humble judgment equally incumbent upon me to stand foremost in the ranks at so decided a peril." So had cried another Prince of Wales a hundred and fifty years before.

" What does it matter if I am shot; I have four brothers," insisted this Prince.

" If I were certain that you would be shot," explained Lord Kitchener, " I do not know that I should be right in restraining you. What I cannot permit is the chance of the enemy securing you as a prisoner."

The Prince was silenced if not convinced. Was the oath taken at Carnarvon to mean nothing ?

The arrival of trains loaded with wounded men became of daily occurrence, and eager thousands thronged Whitehall struggling to enlist. By November 17 the Prince's persistence had secured him appointment to the staff of Sir John French, and two days later he reached Headquarters.

Perhaps the part he was called upon to play was not what he would have chosen, but there was danger and discomfort everywhere in France in those days, even though the whole army might try to keep him in cotton-wool !

Now he was assistant transport officer, now the bearer of dispatches, and now he found himself detailed to escort the King on his Majesty's first tour of the trenches. Father and son stood on the contours of Agincourt.

The line knew him from Ypres to the Somme before the powers that be decided that the Prince of Wales must know more than one battle-front, so 1916 found him " kicking his heels " on the banks of the Canal with British, Australian, and New Zealand troops.

He was in France again when the King paid his

fourth visit. White through his tan, years older in an hour, he saw his father's horse rear and the King's fall and was sent to carry details of the disaster to the Queen.

For six months he served with the Italian army, leaving it to deliver a message in Rome :

" I have come to you from the front on which our soldiers are fighting shoulder to shoulder to uphold the same ideals and to defend the same inalienable rights. I come to you to bring you a message of encouraging sympathy from the King, my father, and his subjects in Great Britain and in the Dominions overseas."

Wider and wider grew the demand for the Prince's services. Carrying home dispatches for the Secretary of State for War, he took his seat in the House of Lords and fulfilled a score of engagements. He toured the industrial areas stirring with unrest, was lowered down Welsh coalmines, drove rivets into a ship on the Clyde, and walked through endless hospital wards where lay bandaged men ; but spend himself as he might, he felt, as others felt, that nothing was enough to give in the hour of England's need.

At the eleventh hour of the eleventh day of the eleventh month he entered Valenciennes with the Canadian troops ; after four years the guns were silent and the stricken earth ceased to tremble.

The Prince's twenty-first birthday had been passed unnoticed in the throes of the war, an official request having been made that all congratulations, public and private, might be postponed, and now England was clamorous. But, though he returned, the demands made upon him were not lessened. The Americans wanted him on the Rhine, the Overseas troops registered claim on claim, while London, Edinburgh, Plymouth, and a dozen other places were eager to give him the freedom of their cities.

A lithe figure in khaki, he marched through London

as a captain in the Grenadier Guards wearing on his breast the ribbons of the Military Cross, the Italian Croce di Guerra, and the Belgian Croix de Guerre.

The war strain was visible for all his youthful bearing. Was this the fair-haired boy who had stood shyly in the Welsh sunshine but seven years before ?

" The part I played was a very insignificant one," the Prince said modestly at his admission to the freedom of the city, and added that he felt sure he would never regret his service overseas.   " In those four years I mixed with men; in those four years I found my manhood. . . . When I think of the future and of the heavy responsibilities which may fall to my lot, I feel that the experience gained since 1914 will stand me in good stead."

The succeeding four years were to be almost as strenuous, if free from tragedy, for the training in modern kingship which had been interrupted by the Great War was to be continued on intensive lines.

He had done service in stained khaki on the battlefields of a world in arms " against all manner of folk." Now, as the King's liege man, he was to carry his father's message of thanks across the world. August 5, 1919, found the Prince steaming out from Portsmouth bound for a four-months' tour of Canada and a glimpse of the United States of America.

Newfoundland gave him his first greeting, and all along the ten-thousand-mile trail from Quebec to Vancouver and back, by train, boat, and motor, Canadians massed to cheer him, and everywhere he grasped the outstretched hands of ex-service men and comrades.

" I want Canadians to look upon me as a Canadian, if not actually by birth yet certainly in mind and spirit," he told his hosts, and added that he had made so many friends among the Canadian troops that he had no feeling of being a stranger in the Dominion.

For two and a half months a railway carriage was

to be the Prince's home. Fifty towns delivered loyal addresses, and half a million people thronged to the reception held in Toronto. By the time he reached Winnipeg his right arm had been put out of action, and had to be carried in a sling.

Ontario took him down cobalt mines, Saskatoon gave him an exhibition of rough riding, and wildly enthusiastic cowboys cheered themselves hoarse when the Prince mounted a bronco. Edmonton showed him a cattle round-up, Moose Jaw provided a few days' shooting. Within an hour of his arrival in Vancouver, 100,000 people were boasting that they had seen " our Prince."

The Redskins were as enthusiastic as their pale-faced brothers. Over two thousand had assembled on the plains near Calgary to welcome King George when he had come among them as Duke of York, all eager to remind him that they had never had any " wrong words " with Queen Victoria, who had promised them that not till the rivers ran dry and the sun ceased to shine should they be left without food. Now, high in the Rocky Mountains they hailed the Great White Queen's great-grandson as Chief Morning Star. The Blackfeet, not to be out-done, christened him Chief Red Cow, the Mohawks welcomed him as Dawn of the Morning.

Canada, so said the Prince, did much to make him realise both his privileges and his responsibilities. " I can only assure you that I shall endeavour to live up to that responsibility—and to be worthy of your trust," he said soberly.

Something of the enthusiasm of the pioneer caught him as he travelled over the endless plains, and before he left Canadian territory the Prince gave proof of his determination to return by purchasing a ranch in the foothills of the Rockies, a place to be run by ex-service men and stocked from his English pro-perties, where, every now and then, he would come to be " at-home " to " fellow-Albertians."

"Now that the war is over we have to keep up
that standard of patriotism and unity of which we
have shown ourselves capable during that long
struggle. We have got to keep it up all we know. . . .
We must not lose touch with one another, or we
shall lose all that we won during the four years of
our common action against the enemy." The purchase of the E.P. Ranch was one of the ways by
which the Prince intended to keep in touch with
Canada.

The first anniversary of Armistice Day found the
Prince of Wales on American soil. He had crossed
the frontier at Rouse's Point on the shores of Lake
Champlain, while rival bands played " God Save the
King " and " The Star Spangled Banner." Union
Jacks and "Old Glories" hung side by side and
many came from the surrounding districts to see the
royal visitor from over the Atlantic.

The eleventh hour of the eleventh day struck when
the royal train was in Baltimore, and the Prince
stood at attention for the Two Minutes' Silence.

This was the first official visit paid to the Republic
by a Prince of Wales, for Edward VII had travelled
incognito as Baron Renfrew, and the nation took him
to its heart.

"It's the smile of him," decided New York when
a way had been forced for his motor through the
solid mass of people in Broadway, and "the Democratic Prince " evoked cheer on cheer by standing
up in his car and saluting as he drove.

He visited the tomb of Washington, laid a wreath
on Roosevelt's grave, and attended, among other
things, a ball where fellow-guests of honour were the
descendants of those who had attended the similar
entertainment arranged for " Baron Renfrew " sixty
years before.

The *Renown* brought the Prince home, sure that
the welcome given him had been to the King's son

and heir, and was due to the same splendid impulse
which had made the whole British Empire stand and
fight together.

"Travel opens one's eyes and clears one's brain,"
he found, "and my recent travels have made me
realise the necessity and importance of close contact
and intercourse between the nations of the Empire.
. . . The British Empire is something far grander
than an Empire in the old sense of the word. . . .
I'm not sure but that what I have learnt about
Great Britain from the outside is not the most
valuable part of the last four months. . . . Believe
me, the restoration of world peace and happiness
depends largely upon Great Britain's example of
confidence and steadiness."

New Zealand and Australia were awaiting their
turn with impatience. They too had stricken and
disabled men eager to shake the Prince's hand and
children to cheer him.

He started via Panama, touched at San Diego, where
he was called upon to address an audience of 10,000
people, and crossed the Equator. April found him
in the North Island of New Zealand.

"A mighty war has shaken the world since the
King, my father, came to this place," he said to the
Maoris, who laid a chief's battle-axe at his feet.
"But the Maori people have held true to that oath
which they swore on the day he stood here. Your
warriors went forth to fight and conquer his enemies
in many distant lands ; I saw and spoke with them
often on the hard fields of Tu. Chiefs and people,
it is Queen Victoria's great-grandson who speaks to
you to-day. . . . Chiefs and people, I greet you from
my heart ! "

He travelled south, while at every town addresses
were showered upon him and in wayside clearings
children sang " God Bless the Prince of Wales."

As New Zealand had tried to out-rival Canada in

loyal enthusiasm, Tasmania and Australia set themselves to surpass New Zealand in fervour.

"Australia is proud of you!" was written large above Port Melbourne's first arch. "Good-bye, Digger!—Come back again!" shouted Sydney, where he celebrated a birthday. In Queensland motors raced beside his train for miles, and the telegraph poles cracked beneath their human loads; he crossed the border to the strains of "Auld Lang Syne" over a carpet of woven yellow wattle.

At Fremantle the entire population turned out to cheer, and Adelaide's streets were so densely packed that it was absolutely impossible for his motor to force a way through, and after delivering his speech from the roof of a building the Prince escaped by the back door.

"It is a miracle he has not been injured," decided those who had seen the enormous crowds assembled throughout the Continent to do honour to the King's son—this "junior officer who had played an inconspicuous part in the Great War," as he described himself. In a score of places people had paid a shilling a minute for the privilege of standing on a packing case to get a better view of him.

In nineteen crowded days the Prince had reviewed cadets, decorated returned soldiers, laid foundation-stones, shaken hands with the disabled, attended state banquets, addressed massed school children, walked from bed to bed in hospital wards, and in "rest" days in the back-blocks had hunted, enjoyed bush picnics, ridden forty to sixty miles on a cross-country cattle round up, and, entranced by the sight of power-driven clippers, had essayed to shear a sheep.

Louder and louder grew the cheers.

"What luck, Digger?" cried a friendly voice as the Prince drove off a race-course.

"Rotten!" came the quick reply, and no speech on all the tour brought him closer to the people's hearts.

" He has silenced criticism of monarchy for current
life-time," was the message sent " home."

A look in at Fiji ; a glimpse at Samoa in response to
a " prayer that the Prince would remember this
small branch of the great tree of Empire " ; three
days of surf-riding at Honolulu ; Trinidad ; on to
Antigua and cheering school children, white and
coloured, a brave welcome from Bermuda, and the
task was accomplished.

In October the Atlantic fleet met the Prince at
Spithead to escort him up the Channel.

One abiding memory he had brought back was of
the courage and self-confidence of the Australians—
" And I can assure you, you want both those qualities
to succeed," he added when delivering his message
from the New World to the Old. . . . " They were
always free and frank with me and let me know
exactly what they thought—and I hope they know
how I felt. I left them with a great lump in my
throat, and I look forward to seeing them again.

" I have come back with a grateful heart to all
those Britishers overseas who opened their hearts
to me."

Nine months later the Prince of Wales started on
his travels again. Malta, part of Britain by her own
request, had been constituted a self-governing colony
and asked him to open her Legislature. And the
King's son was bidden to carry the King-Emperor's
thanks to the Princes of the Indian States and the
peoples of India for help rendered in the World War.

Armistice Day (1921) found the *Renown* in the
Red Sea. At 11 a.m. her turbines stopped and she
drifted lazily in the heat while 1,000 officers and men
stood bareheaded for the Silence, their eyes on the
still figure of the Prince.

At Aden, Jewish, Arab, and English children sang
the National Anthem in their respective tongues.
At Bombay the reverberations of the guns were still

echoing when the Ruling Princes came aboard in their shimmering silks and jewelled turbans.

Gandhi's influence was strong, and there were many who urged that the tour should be abandoned, but, though a *hartal* had been ordered, excited natives flung themselves on the ground to kiss the dust through which the Prince's car had passed. " I want you to know me and I want to know you," said the Prince to the people of India.

In city after city he laid foundation-stones, opened war memorials and inspected returned soldiers. At Lucknow, the shop-keepers sent word that if the bazaars were closed they would supply any of the Prince's requirements " without payment," and in three days the *hartal* had faded out. At Allahabad, if the groups venturing into the streets were few in number, they cheered lustily.

Malcontents at 6 annas a day had been imported into Calcutta, but disloyalty evaporated in a burst of enthusiasm at sight of the Prince, and at the end of a spectacular pageant the crowds swept all before them, surging, in a roaring mass of thousands, to the very brink of the dais upon which the Prince stood.

Driving out from Delhi, delegates of the All-India Depressed Classes Conference were found assembled by the wayside. Like magic word flashed through the East that the son of the King-Emperor had deigned to salute the Untouchables when he stopped his car and accepted the address that had been prepared with misgiving.

The Ruling Princes offered their visitor banquets and days of sport in the jungle; the veiled woman ruler of Bhopal gave a gorgeous Durbar; and in Gwalior, George and Mary, the small son and daughter of the Maharajah, came hand in hand to welcome him. Only in Peshawar were the streets deserted, and the frontiermen, indignant that their character for hospitality should be sullied, made futile application for permission to fall on Gandhi's followers and " take the roof off the bazaar ! "

The Eastern tour continued : Ceylon, Malaya, Hong Kong welcomed the Prince with a mounting wave of enthusiasm : " Now that for the first time the Heir Apparent has vouchsafed us the signal honour of his visit, 'tis meet that the streets and lanes resound with song. . . . Reverently we admire your surpassingly youthful wisdom. . . . All the world looks up to your pre-eminent virtue. . . . You comforted your soldiers and shared their pain and hardships ; you were present at your post and shirked not pain or danger. Verily your merit o'ershadows the age and your fame covers the world ! " Perhaps it was fortunate that this address was in Chinese.

Japan sent out aeroplanes to shower tiny Union Jacks over the *Renown*, each supported by a balloon. " Banzai ! Banzai ! " cried the people, and 20,000 Japanese children marched before the Prince valiantly singing " God Save the King ! "

Manila, North Borneo, Suez, and an aeroplane escort across the desert; Gibraltar once more, and every ship for leagues around sent out messages of welcome. Eddystone was sighted, and Devonport destroyers like black spots on the horizon. Fifty thousand people cheered themselves hoarse at Portsmouth, and surging crowds around Buckingham Palace chanted, " We want our Prince ! We want our Prince ! "

Home engagements had accumulated during the Prince's long absence, and now demands for his services showered upon him from every quarter. Hardly a charity but asked him to preside at its annual dinner ; the legions of the unemployed looked to him for help, and the stricken areas of the coalfields held out supplicating hands. The lot of a Prince of

Wales must have been infinitely easier in the days when tournaments were in vogue.

" One of the idle rich ! " ejaculated a morose individual as the royal car halted in a traffic jam.

" Rich perhaps, but—hang it all—*not* idle ! " came in quick protest from the exhausted occupant who had just fulfilled four public engagements in five hours.

In 1923, he revisited the battlefields in Flanders and motored down Ploegsteert. His thirty-third birthday found him in Johannesburg, and he rode into Bloemfontein heading an escort of a thousand Boers ; the land was at peace at last.

On leaving South Africa he undertook a mission to the Argentine ; people began to think that their Prince was safer at work even though the extent of his duties, which made it necessary for him to give up steeple-chasing, at the same time made flying a useful saving of time.

Perhaps he was in less danger big-game shooting in Africa or photographing wild elephants ; at least it was well that he should have a genuine holiday, and the nation followed telegraphed reports of his activities with eager interest till the King fell ill.

A message flashed through the ether, runners carried written word to the Prince's camp in the jungle, and he turned homeward.

Five nations leagued to speed him on his way, and all Europe held her railway lines clear for the Prince's train ; the navy waited, and now by boat and now by motor he travelled on.

Silent crowds waited at Victoria.

" The King lives ! " Not for the Prince as yet was the burden of the crown.

BIBLIOGRAPHY

BIBLIOGRAPHY

NOTE.—Grateful thanks are due to the many authors whose works are named on subsequent pages. Unless it had been possible to draw upon these, *Kings-in-the-Making* could never have been written.

My sole regret is that it has not been possible to give chapter and verse for the many delightful extracts which have been incorporated in my text. If this book should send new readers to some of the fascinating and erudite works mentioned in the bibliography, perhaps some of the obligation under which the author lies may be counted as repaid.

E. THORNTON COOK.

Accession of a New King, Guide to the Electors on the (1820).
Acland, Life of Sir Henry (J. B. Atlay).
Agincourt, Battle of (Nicolas).
Anjou, Life and Times of Margaret of (M. A. Hookham).
Annual Register, The.
Archæologia (Society of Antiquaries).

Bacchante, Cruise of (Diary of Prince Edward and George of Wales : Ed. by Canon Dalton).
Baker's Chronicle.
Biography, Dictionary of National.
Black Prince, The History of Edward the (G. P. R. James).
Boscobel Tracts, The (J. Hughes).
Buckingham, Life and Times of George Villiers, Duke of (Mrs. A. T. Thompson).

Cambridge, George Duke of (Edgar Sheppard).
Camden's Remains Concerning Britain.
Canada, The King's Visit to (Lieut. T. Bunbury Gooch).
Canada, Westward with the Prince to (Douglas Newton).
Caroline the Illustrious (W. H. Wilkins).
Caroline, Queen (Judge Parry, His Honour).
Cavalier's Note Book, A (Ed. by T. Ellison).
Charles II (Dr. Airy).
Charles II, Diary of the Times of (Henry Sidney).
Charles II and His Court (A. C. A. Brett).

Charles II, Historical and Critical Account of Life of (Dr. William Harris).
Charles II, Personal History of (Grammont : Bohn's Edition).
Charles II, Calendar of State Papers: Domestic (1660).
Charles II, History of His Sacred Majesty King (James Davis).
Charles II in the Channel Isles (S. E. Hoskyns).
Charles II, True Portraiture of (D. Lloyd).
Chronicles, Three Fifteenth Century (Camden Society).
Civil War Tracts (F. Maseres).
Consort, Life of the Prince (Sir Theodore Martin).
Corbet, Poems by Richard.
Correspondence of Sarah Spencer, Lady Lyttelton.
Cornwall and York to Australia, Visit of the Duke and Duchess of (1901).
Cornwall and York through Canada, Tour of the Duke and Duchess of (1901–3).
Court and Society (Duke of Manchester).
Court Life Below Stairs (Molloy).
Cowper, Diary of Lady.
Creevey Papers, The.
Croyland, Chronicles of.

D'Arblay, Diary and Letters of Madame.
Debates, Parliamentary (Hansard).
Delany, Autobiography of Mrs., With Reminiscences of King George.
Dictionary, New English.
Diplomatist, Recollections of a (Sir Horace Rumbold).
Diplomatist's Wife, Letters of a (Madame Waddington).
Doddington, Diary of George Bubb.
Dukes of York, The (Graham Brooks).

East, A Diary in the (Sir W. H. Russell).
Edward I (Tout).
Edward I and II, Introduction to Chronicle of the Reigns of (Rolls Series).
Edward III, The History of (Joshua Barnes (1688)).
Edward III, The History of the Life and Times of (William Longman).
Edward VII (Sir Sidney Lee).
Edward VII and His Court, King (Sir Lionel Cust).
Edward VII as a Sportsman (Alfred E. T. Watson).
Edward VII, The Coronation of (J. E. C. Bodley).
Edward VII, The Golden Book of King.
Edward the VII, The Influence of King (Viscount Esher).
Edward VII, The Private Life of King.
Edward VII, The Tragedy of (Dr. W. H. Edwards).

Edward Prince of Wales (Ivy Sanders).
Elizabeth to Anne, Court and Society from (Duke of Manchester).
Ellis' Original Letters. 2nd Series, Vol. IV.
Empire, The Web of (Sir D. M. Y. Pope Wallace).
Encyclopædia Britannica, The.
England, Chronicle of (Stowe).
England, Constitutional History of (Stubbs).
England, History of (Burnet).
England, History of (Longman).
England, The History of (George M. Trevelyan).
England, The History of (John Lingard).
England, The History of (Lord Macaulay).
England, History of (J. H. Wylie).
England, History of (Lecky).
England, History of (Kennet).
England, History of, Vol. III (Froude, A. J.).
England, Political History of (Sir Charles Oman).
England Under the House of Hanover (Thomas Wright).
English Affairs, Memorials of (Whitelock).
Evelyn's Diary and Correspondence.

Fitzgerald, Memoirs of Mrs. (Langden).
Frederick, Letters of the Empress (Sir H. Ponsonby).
Froissart (Lord Berners' Edition).

Garter, Order of the (Ashmole).
Gaunt, John of (S. Armitage-Smith).
Gentleman of Europe, The First (Lewis Melville).
Gentleman's Magazine. Various Numbers.
George II, Historical Sketch of (Mrs. Oliphant).
George II, Memoirs of the Reign of (Horace Walpole).
George II, Memoirs of the Reign of (Lord Hervey).
George III, Annals of (W. Green).
George III as Man and Monarch (Beckles Willson).
George III, Journal of the Reign of (Horace Walpole).
George III, Memoirs of the Reign of (Horace Walpole : Ed. by
    Sir D. Le Marchant).
George III, Memoirs of King (J. Heneage Jesse).
George III, Annals of the Reign of (1760–1815) (L. Aikin).
George III, His Court and Family (Anon. : Published 1824).
George III and Regency of George IV, Court and Annals of (Duke
    of Buckingham).
George IV, The Court of England Under (Lady C. S. M. Bury).
George IV (Shane Leslie).
George IV, Life of (Percy Fitzgerald).
George IV, Diary of Times of (Lady C. S. M. Bury).

George IV, Memoirs of the Life and Reign of (Dr. Lardner's Cabinet Library).
George IV, Personal History of (Rev. G. Croly).
Georges, Four (Thackeray).
George V, King (Sir George Arthur).
George V, The King to His People. Speeches and Messages of His Majesty King.
George V, In His Own Words (F. A. Mackenzie).
George, Duke of Cambridge (E. Sheppard).
Grenville Papers (Ed. by W. J. Smith).
Greville Memoirs.

Half-a-Crown-Lost (J. Bull).
Hall's Chronicle.
Hardwicke, Life of.
Harleian MSS. No. 6391, British Museum.
Henry IV (Wylie).
Henry V when Prince of Wales. A Character of (A. Luders).
Henry V (Rev. A. J. Church).
Henry V, History of (G. M. Towle).
Henry V, History of the Reign of (Goodwin).
Henry V, Life of (Ed. by C. L. Kingsford).
Henry VII, Life of (Bacon).
Henry VII (Lord Herbert of Cherbury).
Henry VII, Memorials of (Ed. by James Gairdner).
Henry VII, Privy Purse Expenses of (Nicolas).
Henry VII and Henry VIII, Times of (Rutland Papers).
Henry VIII, The Youth of (F. A. Mumby).
Henry VIII (A. F. Pollard).
Henry VIII, Chronicles of (E. Hall).
Henry VIII, Life of (Tytler).
Henry VIII, Life and Reign of (Lord Herbert of Cherbury).
Henry VIII, Memoirs of the Court of (Mrs. A. T. Thomson).
Henry VIII, Wives of (M. A. S. Hume).
Henry and Chief Justice Gascoigne, Story of Prince (F. Solly Flood).
Henry the Prince, His Majesty's Instructions to his dearest Sonne (Roxburghe Club).
Hervey, Letters of Lady.
Hervey's Memoirs, Lord.
Highlands, Leaves from the Journal of Our Life in the (Queen Victoria).
Historical Essay, 1902, Owen's College (J. Tait).
Historic Scenes (A. Strickland).
History, Cambridge Modern.
History of England in Eighteenth Century (Lecky).
History, Parliamentary.

Holinshed, Chronicles of.
Honour, Titles of (Selden).
Hook, Correspondence of Colonel.
Household, Collection of Ordinances for the (Society of Antiquaries).
Households, Royal (Society of Antiquaries).

Jacobite Times, London in (Dr. Doran).
James, Court of (Goodman : Ed. Brewer).
James, Progresses of King (John Nichols).
James, Secret History of the Court of King (Wilson).
James I, Secret History of the Court of (Osborne).
James II, Life of (Rev. J. S. Clarke).
Journal of the Cambrian Archæological Association.
Journal of a Visit (Mrs. William Grey).

Kelly, The Life of Michael (S. M. Ellis).
Kings of England, The (Clive Bigham).
Kings of England, Lives of the Bachelor (A. Strickland).
King in Exile, The (Eva Scott).
King, The Boyhood of a Great (A. M. Broadley).
Kings and Queens of England, Genealogical History of (Sandford).
King and Queen, Our (W. H. Wilkins).
King Emperor's Activities in War Time, The (Ed. E. E. Long).
King Maker, Warwick the (Sir C. Oman).
Knighthood, History of the Orders of (Nicolas).

Lake's Diary, Doctor (Camden Society).
Lancaster and York (Sir James Ramsay).
Leland's Collectanea.
London in the Fifteenth Century, The Historical Collections of a Citizen of (Camden Society).
London Magazine.
Ludlow, Memoirs of Edward.
Lyttelton, Correspondence of Sarah Spencer, Lady.

Malmesbury's Diaries and Correspondence, Earl of.
Marchmont Papers.
Marlborough House and Its Occupants (Arthur H. Beaven).
Marlborough Despatches (Ed. Murray).
Mary, The Biography of Queen (Charlotte Cavendish).
Memoir, A (Sir H. W. Acland).
Memoirs of J. G. N. Nicholls.
Memoirs of the Whig Party (Lord Holland).
Minister, Memoirs of an Ex-Cabinet (Lord Malmesbury).
Monarchs, Collection of English (Bishop Kennett).
Monarchy Revived (Egglesfield).

Monmouth, Henry of (J. Endell Tyler).
Monmouth, Henry of (F. Solly Flood).
Monmouth, Memoirs of Robert Carey, Earl of.
Montague, Letters and Works of Lady Mary Wortley.
Mutton Found, The Lost.

Navy, History of the Royal (Nicolas).
Nevill, Reminiscences of Lady Dorothy (Ralph Neville).
Nichols's Recollections.

Ophir, Round the Empire with the (1902) (William Maxwell).

Palaces in and Near London, Ancient Royal (T. R. Way and F. Chapman).
Parliamentary History.   Various Volumes.
Parliamentary History for the Years 1708 and 1736.
Paston Letters, The.
Peerage, The Historic (Courthorpe : The Somerset Herald).
Perdita, Memoirs of (Mary Robinson).
Philippa of Hainault and Her Times (B. C. Hardy).
Pless, Daisy Princess of (" Myself ").
Pretenders, Memoirs of the (J. Heneage Jesse).
Prince, The Love of Wales to Their Soveraigne (Daniel Powel).
Prince, The Black (R. P. Dunn-Pattison).
Prince in India, With the (Sir J. Fayrer).
Prince in the East, With the (Sir H. Russell).
Prince, Through India with the (G. F. Abbott (1906)).
Prince, Down Under with the (Everard Cotes).
Prince, Our (Edward Legge).
Princesses of England, Lives of the (Miss Strickland).
Prussia and Hanover, Account of the Courts of (Toland).

Quarterly Review, The.
Queens, History of Two (W. H. Dixon).
Queens of England, Her Majesty : The Romance of the (E. Thornton Cook).
Queens of England, Hanoverian (Dr. Doran).
Queen's Wish, The (J. Watson).

Rebellion, History of the Great (Edward, Earl of Clarendon).
Regalis, Liber (Roxburgh Club).
Register, The Annual (1761 and 1775).
Restoration, Mystery and Method of His Majesty's Happy (Dr. Price : Maseres' Civil War Tracts, 1815).
Richard the Redeless (Langlands : Ed. by Prof. W. W. Skeat).
Richard II (Wallon).
Richard II, Annales (Eng. Hist. Society : Ed. by Sir E. M. Thompson).

Richard II, England Under (De O'Leary).
Richard II, Life of (Eng. Hist. Society : Ed. by Hearne).
Richard III (Caroline C. Halstead).
Richard III, Historic Doubts of Life and Reign of (Horace Walpole).
Richard III, History of (Buck).
Richard III, History of (Sir Thomas More).
Richard III, Life and Reign of (Dr. James Gairdner).
Richard III, Memoirs of King (J. Heneage Jesse).
Richmond, Life of Margaret Beaufort, Countess of (Halstead).
Rose, Diary and Correspondence of the Rt. Hon. George (Ed. by Rev. L. V. Harcourt).
Royal Tour, With the (1902) (E. F. Knight).
Royal Visit to India, A (Hon. John W. Fortescue).

Sailor's Life, A (Hon. Sir Henry Keppel).
Saville Correspondence (Ed. by W. D. Cooper for Camden Society).
Scotland, History of (Tytler).
Scotland, Their Majesties of (E. Thornton Cook).
Scotland, Memoirs of the Affairs of (David Moyses : Bannatyne Club).
Shakespeare.
Sidney, Diary and Correspondence of Henry (Ed. by R. W. Blencowie).
Somers' Historical Tracts (Revised by Sir Walter Scott).
Stanley, Life and Correspondence of Dean (Ed. by R. E. Prothero).
Stanley, Letters of Lady Augusta.
State Papers (Clarendon).
State Papers (Thurlow).
State Papers, Calendar of (Ed. by Mrs. M. A. Everett Green).
State Papers, Domestic (Mrs. Everett Green).
State Trials (Howell).
Stockmar, Life of Baron (By his son : Tr. by Max Müller).
Stowe's Annales.
Stowe's Chronicle.
Stuarts, Memoirs of the Court of England in the Time of the (J. Heneage Jesse).

" Times," The.
Tudors, The Early (C. E. Moberly).

Usk, Chronicle of Adam of.

Wales, Life of Henry Prince of (Thomas Birch).
Wales, An Account of the Baptism, Life, Death and Funeral of the Most Incomparable Prince Frederick Henry of (Sir Charles Cornwallis).

Wales, On Baptism of his eldest son, Message from the Late King (George I) to the Prince of (1717) (Broadsheet, 1737).

Wales, Authentic Copy of Pitt's letter to the Prince of.

Wales, An Admonitory Letter to the Prince of (George IV) (" A ").

Wales, An Application to Parliament for Discharge of Debts, Letter to the Prince of.

Wales, Speeches and Addresses of the Prince of (Ed. by James Macaulay).

Wales, Lives of the Princes of (Dr. Doran).

Wales, T.R.H. The Prince and Princess of (By the Author of His Most Gracious Majesty, King Edward VII).

Wales in Canada and the U.S.A., The Prince of (N. A. Woods).

Wales, The Biography of the Prince of (W. and L. Townsend).

Wales, Edward Prince of (Ivy Sanders).

Wales, Letter to the Prince of (W. A. Miles).

Walpole Reminiscences (Lord Orford) (H. Walpole).

Walpole's Letters (Ed. by Cunningham).

Walpole's Last Journals (Ed. by Dr. Doran).

Walpole, Life of (W. Coxe).

Walpoliana.

Wardrobes, etc., of Duke of Richmond, Inventory of and of the Wardrobe of Katharine of Aragon at Baynard's Castle (Ed. by Nichols).

Whig Party, Memoirs of the (Lord Holland).

White Rose, Chronicles of the (Society of Antiquaries).

Whitelock's Memoirs.

Wraxall, Memoirs of Sir Nathaniel William.

INDEX